NOTE CHANGE OF ADDRESS!

Dear F.D.'s, I have a head start on myself f...
both in being a day early and in having a t... ...ation,
curious to see how much one can say on one o... ...draft. I'm
Today is our first full day in our new ... ...have full
command of all those everyday, insignificant ...
times, but nonetheless make one feel much mo... ...nuisance a...
and I had the entire flat scrubbed out from ... ...Wednesday Colum...
drawers with over 72' of shelf paper and disinfected ...ny bottom, had lined t...
but did the monumental task of waxing our three acres of floor and then polis...
ing it with the flat side of a halved, dried coconut whose tiny, stiff dried
fibers are more effective (and much less expensive--like nothing) than any br...
or electric buffer you've ever seen! So there sat our glistening, expectant
quarters, and here sat unequipped more-than-anxious-to-receive-our-shipment
P & G. We were given until Friday to get out of th... ...ts, arrival of
air shipment or no. Friday our t... ...you've never
seen two sadder cartons. ...d that they
must have come via Timbu... ...is in North
...avah not alwa...
...Bennington
...ea shipment.

over and paid the ... ...can
...w we are the proud owners of ... To be
...id's largest and most pre- ... ...the nec-
...thes hamper. Heaven knows what ... ...dealings
...meant for. And what's even more ... ...ted, but
...ut the whole thing is that ... ...bound to
...y ones, that is) don't accumulate ... ...haggling
...re as they did in our home ... ...etorts
...he shirt is barely off one's back ... ...ho is
...eward snatches it up, hand ... ...tion
...the tub, has it on the line, ...learn
...your drawer just as you are ... ...n item;
...t on a fresh one. Had I known ... ...it is
...brought only one of everything! ... ..."cus-
...word about buying things, since ... ...ting
...be my subject of the day. Yes- ... ...the
...us and I went down into the native ... ...bargain...
...some baskets. I have ventured ... ...ve to
...ve market once prior to this, ...unhes-
...o look at things and see what's ... ...d Stol-
...ned then that I would be foolish ... ...ous
...anything unless I wanted to be ... ...wouldn't
...dition to accomplishing the im- 2
...g understood. Columbus, for- ... ...an.
...ks both Ibo and Yoruba (the ...
...st passably). so we would arrive ... ...2.
...he baskets of some old lady ... ...good-
...o places that I never would have ... ...going
...been able to find). I would ... ...r in
...ones I would be interested in ...
...ould start to bargain in Yoruba. ...
...s we would be surrounded by ...
...silent faces staring up at us ...
...fear) which inevitably would ... ...d
...e, the mice the pied piper, to ... ...or
...y are darling things, most naked, ...
...kypine braids projecting out ...
...ead, always barefoot--very few ...
...here wear shoes, no matter how ...
...and curious. It takes a while, ...
...to being an oddity, one of a ...
...minority; and certainly in the ...
...there it is a solo performance. ...
...te people rarely if ever go there ...
...'ll try to give you a description ...
...rtant, smell, of the native market. ...
to all, C + P ...

first fold here

← To open cut here

LICE...
Y...

NIGERIA 6d

Mr. and Mrs. John M. Tyler

Knob Hill

Glastonbury, CONNECTICUT

U.S.A.

← Second fold here →

Sender's name and address : Clark

Federal Ministry of Economic Develop...

Lagos, Nigeria

please send this on the family
rounds (JET - TANTE - AUNT SYBIL)

Letters from Nigeria

A young American observes a newly independent country 1961–62

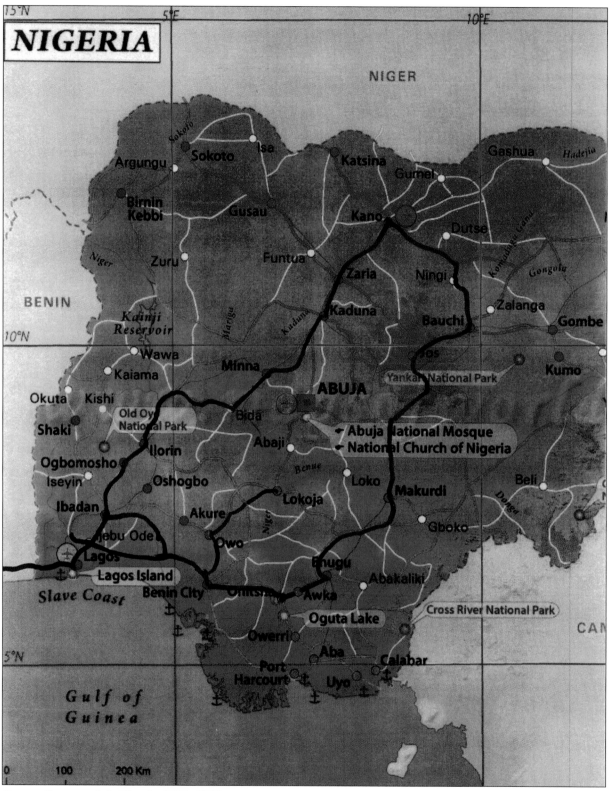

Routes of our travels in Nigeria, 1961–1962

Letters from Nigeria

A young American observes a newly
independent country 1961–62

Gretel Clark

Peter E. Randall Publisher
Portsmouth, New Hampshire

ISBN13: 978-1-942155-13-3

Library of Congress Control Number: 2016930665

Published by
Peter E. Randall Publisher
Portsmouth, NH 03801
www.perpublisher.com

Distributed by
The University Press of New England
www.upne.com

Book design: Grace Peirce

Dust jacket image caption: Conversation just outside our compound with the mosquito patrol.
Note that two are barefoot.

For Columbus Opara
In thanks for his gentle way of connecting
us to his colorful country

Acknowledgments

My thanks to Annette Janes, who made me believe my letters would have an audience, and sustained me through the year it took to transcribe them.

Special thanks also go to my sister, Janell Tyler Fiarman, whose patient support and critical reading helped make this book possible. (With the exception of spelling and punctuation corrections, the letters are word for word as they were written in 1961 and 1962.)

Finally, given the time and effort, my partner in this long ago adventure must be acknowledged. The photos, most of which were captured by Peter, lay in dusty slide boxes under our front hallway stairs, having accompanied us in our dozen moves since these letters were written. With our publisher's help, they are now an important part of this work. We have tried to place them near their context in my letters. In some cases, however, where a space was available after the end of a letter, we slipped in a few that we just couldn't leave behind. I think my readers will agree, the images capture the beauty of Nigeria, its people, their clothes, houses, churches and communities as they were half a century ago.

Introduction

When the offer came to go to Nigeria, Peter and I were finishing our first semester of graduate studies at the University of Michigan. There was no doubt in our minds about going: We would drop everything— our lease, our cats, our graduate work—and fly off to a part of the world neither we nor anyone else around us knew much about. Nigeria—in fact, all of Africa—was indeed a deep, dark continent to the consciousness of most Americans in 1960.

Perhaps I knew a little more than many, having grown up in a house-hold with a mother who worked at the Women's Service Bureau of the Auerbach Foundation in Hartford, Connecticut, and delighted in bringing home visitors from exotic places for dinner or the weekend. She would cook a special meal of the region from the United Nations Cookbook and spread out a giant map of the world to have our guest celebrate with us his or her country. There was always an aura of excitement to learn about a place different from ours. Some of these visitors, in fact, became long-term friends of our family. Their issues and problems came to feel like our issues and problems.

By the time I went off to college, even though I had lived most of my childhood on a 140-acre farm in Connecticut, I knew that I wanted to learn more about the world my mother had shared with me and my sib-lings. At Vassar College, I majored in political science with a goal of going into the Foreign Service. Toward the end of my senior year, however, I became engaged, and traveled to the West Coast. My fiancé, Peter Clark, was serving the second year of the three and a half years required of young reserve officers in military service.

While waiting the six months until he could furlough back east for the wedding, I found a job in San Francisco with the World Affairs Council of Northern California, and I was immediately thrown back into hosting vis-itors from the underdeveloped world (as it was called then). Their stories of hardship and comparative disadvantage reinforced my wish to do some-thing to help raise these countries' standards of living. I assumed that they would not become pawns in what was then seen as a contest between com-munist and "free world" powers.

Meanwhile, Peter, serving as a Naval Intelligence Officer on an air-craft carrier off the coast of China, reached a similar conclusion. He was training pilots to bomb industries and airfields with conventional and nuclear bombs, but his heart told him that this was no way to settle national differences or to promote peace in the world.

One day this thought screamed out to him. There was an alert aboard his aircraft carrier, and Peter had to brief all the pilots and crews of the A3Ds (heavy attack jets) in his squadron to drop bombs on coastal air bases of mainland China. The planes were launched, and Peter was sure they would not return, because they did not have enough fuel to return to the carrier. For these one-way missions, Peter had prepared the crews to ditch their planes, parachute into China, and walk out to Burma. The mission, however, was called back. It turned out to be just an attack exercise.

When Peter returned to Connecticut on leave to marry me, he told my father about his disillusionment. He was angry about the three years of his young life that he had had to spend in obligatory service to his country, in a role that was antithetical to how he would hope to make it safer and more peaceful. (Military service for men of a certain age was mandatory until 1973.) My dad suggested that Peter call our Connecticut representative in the 86th Congress, Chester Bowles, and suggest our idea to him: creating an alternative to military service whereby young Americans could volunteer in something like a "peace army" to serve as technical assistants in the Third World and help make their lives better.

At the end of the summer of 1959, when Peter's tour of duty concluded, we headed for San Francisco for interviews at the American Friends Service Committee (AFSC). We planned to start out by working on an AFSC overseas project. The director talked about our apprenticing on an Indian reservation in Northern California for a year, and then, should we "work out," going to Hong Kong, where we would serve another two years. But when he looked at our résumés, he said, "If you want to make a difference in the lives of people in the underdeveloped world, you should go back to school, get graduate degrees in appropriate areas, and then take your skills overseas. You want to work on the national level."

We decided then that Peter would go back to school and get a graduate degree in economics and I would get one in comparative education. The challenge for Peter, however, was to be accepted into a graduate school of economics when he hadn't taken a single undergraduate course in that subject. He had majored in art and architecture as an undergraduate at Williams College, planning to study architecture after fulfilling his military service requirements.

In late October, he called Williams and found out that the college would take him back as a special student, allowing him to enroll in all levels of economics courses simultaneously, thus enabling him to apply to graduate schools of economics in the spring. (Williams had just initiated a new Center for Economic Development and was willing to support our dreams.)

Completing his studies in the spring of 1960, and poor as a church mouse, Peter won an NDEA (National Defense Education Act) fellowship to the University of Michigan. There he began studies with Wolfgang Stolper (a professor of international trade and development economics). I set to work on a master's degree in comparative education. There, Peter and I became involved with a group of graduate students interested in forming some kind of national service that could be an alternative to military service. Could we create a "peace army" whose activities would be dedicated to working *with* other cultures, not against them?

This was the year that John Kennedy arrived on the Ann Arbor campus during his presidential campaign against Richard Nixon. We had a chance to talk to him about our project. Not long after he became president, he established the Peace Corps. It was an idea whose time had come.

Meanwhile, Peter and I, having interrupted our graduate studies after only one semester, were in Nigeria with Wolfgang Stolper (who was on leave from Michigan) on our own personal technical-assistance adventure when one of the first Peace Corps delegations arrived in Lagos. The letters that follow will describe how the Peace Corps was received and the problems they encountered. The letters will also give the reader something of an inside story of what Nigeria's first year of independence from 60 years of colonial rule was like: a view from inside the National Economic Planning Office that was writing Nigeria's first development plan; and the view of a 24-year-old "student" living in a Third World culture in transition.

Keeping in mind my age at the time, and the fact that the letters were meant to be seen only by family members, I hope that critical comments about some British and American and Nigerian civil servants, visitors, wives or husbands do not offend. I hope they will be read in the context of the time and with a grain of salt.

For the most part, the letters were typed on both sides of single-sheet blue air letters. A carbon copy was made of each letter—one sent to my mother, the other sent to my mother-in-law. The long-suffering "mothers" then retyped each letter and sent copies to members of our extended family. Years later, while cleaning out the drawers and attics of our deceased relatives, packets of those saved letters surfaced. I started transcribing them years ago, during long New England winter days when I could not be out in my gardens. To enliven the text, I have included images from our slides of those sun-filled days of life in Nigeria.

— Letter One —

January 4, 1961

Dear Granny,

Here, at last, we have our present complete! Merry Christmas. . . .

You see, the day we left Ann Arbor for West Hartford and the holidays, Gretel and I were asked to go to Nigeria. We were taken completely by surprise. The Ford Foundation is sending a team of three economists to Nigeria for a year and a half to assist them in planning their next five-year economic development plan. The Ford Foundation sees this as a training mission, and I was asked to go along as the junior economist to help train and encourage young Nigerians. By the time we finish our job, they should be ready to take full responsibility to perpetuate the work we have started!

Well, I do have misgivings about stopping my graduate study at this point, but I feel that this is a very important mission and one I would wait a long time again before being asked to participate in such a project. We will plan to return to Ann Arbor in September 1962 for another two years of study, so that I may complete my PhD.

Now, we have not signed the contract yet, for while the Ford Foundation is ready to send us, the matter still must be cleared by the Nigerian government. We have been expecting to get final confirmation any day now. If all is approved, we will leave this country in the first or second week of February.

This will be our first trip to Africa, and we are very excited. Each day we try to envisage what life in the tropics will be like. As a matter of coincidence, Gretel has been working on a paper for one of her classes concerning the education system and the problem of social change in Nigeria. She will be able to write her thesis for her master's degree while she is there. We hope, also, that she will be able to work for some time on education problems or community development at the village level. Then if all goes well, we'll probably get started on our family while we are there. But, you know we have been fortunate not to start before this; otherwise, we would never have been asked to take this job.

Well, back to Christmas. Our present to you this year will be one that continues all year long. Here is the start. We propose, since we will be traveling around the world and starting a new life in Africa, to send you each week or two verbal or physical "snapshots" of us, our surroundings and adventures. This way, you, who have inspired us and encouraged us to work abroad in these underdeveloped lands, will be able to see us there, and the work we are doing. We had to scratch around a bit for our starting

Gretel's Vassar College graduation photo, 1958

Peter's USN Officer Candidate School photo, 1956

photos: one of Gretel as a senior at Vassar and one of me while still in the Navy.

Well, there you have it. We will probably be sending the next photo from Lagos, Nigeria, our new home!

We will let you know what the final decision is. We await the mail each day with bated breath! We hope the Nigerian government is as anxious to have us as we are anxious to go!

Love to you from us both,
Peter & Gretel

Leaving Peter's Clark family home after a major New England snow storm for train to New York in January 1961

The snow storm prevented our families from taking us to the Ford Foundation in New York (our sponsor). Peter took this photo at the Berlin, CT, train station. His parents on left ("Aunt Jan" and "Uncle Archer in the letters)[1] and Gretel between her parents.

— Letter Two —

February 9, 1961
Thursday noon

Hi!

We are waiting for the plane to Rome, so I am taking the first rest to date to report. The flight over was fine. Much vibration and nearly no sleep, but we recovered during the day and a half in London.

We love the city: saw many of the sightseeing-ish things and visited the Snaggs [Clark cousins]. 'Twas the highlight of our stay. Bill did not arrive till we were just leaving (we went for tea yesterday p.m.), but Eleanor was there and Elizabeth, who just finished school and will be working soon (18?), and Peter, who is studying Law. Tom, the oldest, is working with the railroad and stopped in just long enough to change his coat, say "hello," and be off again.

They are such nice people. [Cousin] Peter is very imposing and personable, Elizabeth so "proper," although I'm sure it's mostly the accent that throws us for a loop, and Eleanor very loquacious, warm, and charming. We sat down to tea as though to eat a meal, with small sandwiches, bread, cake, and cookies. Their apartment, like an oblong slot, is six stories high, with two or three rooms on each landing. It had the usual British heating system—mostly none—and Victorian style was prevalent. They send all sorts of greetings to the family, especially Aunt Pat and Granny. They are planning a trip to Rome, so we asked them to convey impressions and advice to the Sullivans [Clark American cousins] re their impending jaunt.

We hope to see Hans [Gretel's brother] in Rome. We still don't know, though, because we couldn't reach him. We'll call Federico [Italian student who lived with Gretel's family when in the United States] in any case. It is so much more fun to see people.

Did you have any trouble getting home with all that snow? Where did you eat? We're so glad you all came down to see us off to West Africa, even if it was an inconvenience for you—as it must have been. And thank you for the book and cummerbund, and all the many last-minute things you did for us.

Love,

G

— Letter Three —

February 12, 1961
Monday noon

Dear F. D. [fam damily],

WE'RE HERE! AT LAST!! It feels good to slow down a bit after our mad two days in Rome with [brother][2] Hans and Federico. They really gave us a tour of tours, of very large Rome on our very small feet.

We arrived in Rome Thursday evening and went straight to bed. Next morning our phone rang, and there was Hans!—down in the lobby, having taken a night train from Milan. He arrived at 7:00 and waited 'til 8:30 so we could sleep. He came up and waited while we dressed and washed—and then ensued two fabulous days of seeing ancient Rome, St. Peter's, the Vatican, the Pantheon, the Forum, many cathedrals, etc., etc. Each day, we met Federico after work (1:00 p.m.) in the building where he works on the ground floor of the Villa Borghese. You are right, Sandro, Federico is a peach. Your letter to him arrived a day and a half after we did. One thing is for sure, Rome would have been very dull (comparatively speaking) had there not been Hans and Federico.

Yoruba Market woman in Lagos

We took the midnight plane from Rome, Saturday, to arrive on Sunday a.m. in Nigeria.

Lyle Hansen [American economist "seconded" by the Ford Foundation to the Nigerian Ministry of Economic Development] was there to meet us and bring us back to the VIP Flats where we are staying till we move into our apartment, which is over on the lagoon. These are really some quarters! Four very large rooms and a kitchen, very well furnished and supplied with a "boy" who cooks, cleans, washes and irons all our clothes, polishes our shoes the moment they fall from our feet, makes our bed, even if you nap on it, has your netting fixed over your bed in the evening, and does absolutely everything for you but breathe! It takes a little adjusting to, but I think we'll manage.

So what about Nigeria? Guess I'd better reserve any lengthy observations until a later date when they can be substantiated, but here are a few first impressions and reactions.

Office workers at a bus stop

WE LOVE IT. No use beating around the bush. I have that feeling we had on arriving in Williamstown, that we are really going to like it here. The people seem to be a happy, casual lot, industrious and proud—an important quality. They are also curious, a virtue that stands out in contrast to the Italians on the street with their blatant stares.

Our eyes are full of the wonderful new sights, of these barefoot people dressed in hundreds of different costumes, robes, pajamas, headdresses; such a variety of colors, patterns, and textures fill the street and countryside! Everywhere you look there are people on bikes, women carrying enormous baskets of all sizes, shapes, and colors on their heads, and children on the women's backs, slung onto them with cloth, as though they were part of the dress, with only the child's head peeking out.

Patrice Lumumba, Congo's first Prime Minister, was assassinated as we arrived here, and we were told not to leave our VIP Flat for fear of reprisals against the "European oppressor" (foreign whites), who were surely behind his death. Yesterday afternoon, we went with the Hansens and their four children in their motorboat through savanna swamps, down channels that wind through the lush growth, past small native dwellings to a sandy beach that is a strip separating lagoon or swamp from the

New Victoria Island legislator's housing in distance on left beyond Ogogoro Village

ocean. There we spent the afternoon lolling in the sun, waterskiing, and, in general, trying to get used to the idea that this is West Africa, not some resort beach in Florida. Just heavenly! You'll be surprised to know, too, that after being in the sun three to four hours, I have only a minor tan compared to what I would have had if we had been in Florida. But then, maybe that's 'cause it is the winter sun here.

It is hot, however; or, more accurately, muggy. Fortunately, we are arriving in the "cool" season. Nonetheless, the air conditioning in the bedroom feels very good. One just does not hurry. Nothing is taken faster than a slow meander.

Today we spent the morning getting our Nigerian driver's licenses . . . standing in a cement room, one of many that are a part of a long, low building with dirt sidewalks and numerous Nigerians waiting to have various forms filled out and OK'd. It is a very slow process, since everything is done by hand. Several Nigerians offered to stand in line for us, but we wouldn't hear of it.

There is so much more to tell, but my hand is getting very tired and sticking to the paper, so I'll close. Just wanted you to know all is well, and that we are very happy with our new home and country.

Love,

G and P

P.S. Don't s'pose this is the best thing to report right now, since we don't know what it is, but something has hit Peter's tummy that prevents it from holding anything—since noon. Probably just a temporary thing, but it sure has knocked him out.

There is a funny side to it—our cook/steward goes on preparing the meals even though I've told him just tea and toast for Peter. He fixes enough for two, anyway; dresses in white, even puts on shoes for the meals; and I sit down alone to eat for two, when I have trouble eating for one, as you know. I can't just say "NO" when he's gone to all that trouble. Well, tonight, what should he serve me but LIVER!! The one food Peter would love to have, and which I won't even fix for him, because I can't bear the smell of it. So I gulped and ate for one and a half, trying valiantly to remember your words, Aunt Jan[1]: that one must "clear one's plate." Am I a martyr!

View of our sail loft home on second floor of building on right. The Lagos Island Yacht Club is on the point.

— Letter Four —

February 19, 1961
Written on Sunday, typed on Tuesday

Dear F. D.'s,

Here goes for the first installment.

Your letters have been wonderful. Guess the farther one is from home, the more precious is mail from there. Mom, you should get "air letters" or you will go broke.

Today marks our first week, but we still feel very much the novice Africans. I think once our things arrive and we are in our apartment, we'll feel more settled. Tomorrow morning I shall spend with our "boy" (whom we hired Friday), cleaning and scrubbing out the place to prepare for our move—probably in the middle of the week. Hope the air shipment arrives by then.

One view from our living room looking toward the sea and the Bight of Benin

Did I tell you about the apartment? It is the one on the Yacht Club point with a magnificent view of the harbor. In effect, we are inhabiting half of the second floor (there's another apartment on the other side) of the Yacht Club's sail loft—which is on the "ground floor" as the British

and Nigerians call it. So that puts us on the "first floor" according to them. The building itself is none too glamorous . . . an old wooden structure. But the rooms are large: the bedroom the size of a small ballroom, and living–dining areas comprise a long rectangular room with windows bordering the entire outside wall. Aargh, another mammoth drapery problem! The furniture isn't bad.

But the kitchen!! It is downstairs, and since it is meant for the servant only—it looks like an extension of his quarters, or "compound," as it is called. Abominable cement cell-blocks. So, too, the kitchen is a cement cell-block dungeon, but it's graced with light when the door and window onto the back compound court are open. There is a small icebox and a three-burner, tiny antique electric stove, a sink with wooden drain, a storage chest, pantry, and wire cage that hangs from the ceiling. This is not for monkeys or parrots, though I imagine it could be used for such, but rather a storage bin for all foods, flour, and condiments that don't otherwise go into the refrigerator, to keep them from the cockroaches and lizards that abound in this country.

Ah, yes, the lizards. Never have I seen such a variety or such abundance! They are everywhere on the ground and trees, on the buildings and in them. We have one in our flat—a sort of transparent green one that we are told we are lucky to have because he eats bugs.

And, I must admit, I prefer him to the darker and bigger ones that

Our living quarters on left front of this building, overlooking the harbor

Common lizard we call a "Gila monster"

have bright orange heads and tails. They look like miniature dinosaurs. There are others, a bright green that must be a small Gila monster of some sort, and still others that resemble frogs in shape of head and legs but have long slender bodies with even longer tails. Most anywhere one walks outdoors, there are dragon-lizards scampering away (thank God). We're over our initial squeamishness and think of them as you do bugs or squirrels . . . just as long as they don't get too friendly. The birds, trees, and plant life are so exotic and different. I shall speak of them another day. So much for African nature!

Our cook-steward (the "boy" mentioned earlier) is one Columbus Opara. He is Ibo, from the Eastern Region, 30 and married with three children. His oldest, a girl of seven, is living with his mother-in-law back home. The Ibos, we are told, make the best and most industrious servants. He looks about 20, is clean, and speaks English reasonably well. He drives a hard bargain for hire. We are starting him at £11 per month ($30), which is about a pound more than most expatriates pay their servants, but then most people also have two or three "boys" to tend to them and their house, making the workload lighter.

I feel rather uncomfortable about having help, and I don't like the idea of "servant" and "master," as the differentiation is made here. Peter is always referred to as "Master" and I am "Madam." Horrible. I won't begin to describe the way the British treat them. The Ugly American is nothing compared with the Atrocious Englishman! I am advised by all, however, that I would be foolish not to have a cook/steward—first, because of the added shopping and cooking problems, to say nothing of the hand washing for everything done in the bathtub (the only place where there is hot water). Second, the fact that once I start working and writing my thesis, the workload would be too great, since one is able to do at least one-third less work in this climate than what we are used to doing in the States.

I don't know about the first arguments, but the latter may be true. I find that a nap a day is a must for us to survive until evening, and I fall asleep the moment I lie down—something I've never been able to do before; and then I could go to sleep again after being up for just a few hours. "Noon hour" here is from two to four, or 12:30 to 2:30, when absolutely everything closes up in town, in government, and in the business offices. Then, I imagine, people do sleep.

It is really hard getting used to the business hours. Peter works from eight to two and then comes home for the day (and lunch!). When things start to get rushed, he will probably return to the office at three or four for a few more hours. Everyone works on Saturday morning until noon. Then everyone goes home for the weekend, even the storekeepers; if not home, they go to the races, the beach, the polo club, or what have you.

Friday evening, the Hansens gave a cocktail party for the whole Ministry, inviting the British administrators and the Nigerian junior and civil-servant economists to meet the American Clarks and Professor Stolper. The British, to say the least, were a bit uneasy, since few of them had ever been to a "mixed" party. They are clearly uneasy around the Nigerians, even though most of them have been here for five to seven years. On the whole, I would say that the British civil servants one finds out here are rather second-rate, the

Columbus just outside the kitchen

Columbus with his two boys and neighbor children

didn't-quite-make-it-to-the-big-leagues (India or East African Colonial service). They are, nonetheless, much more able administrators and technicians than the Nigerians; but they ought to be. They've had several centuries' more experience! The Nigerians, on the other hand, are delightful, eager, jovial novices. We've taken to them from the start. They are a refreshing contrast to the formal, stiff British.

As we suspected, we Americans find ourselves in an awkward position between the British and Nigerian protagonists. The Ford Foundation team, it appears, will be most effective the less they are associated with the British in the mind of the Nigerian. Nonetheless, without the British, the government would be in chaos. There simply are not enough capable, trained Nigerians to fill the positions now filled by the expatriates; but you can be sure that the government is Nigerianizing the civil service from top to bottom as rapidly as possible. The exodus of Europeans from here is amazing. Some ministries are already completely Nigerianized, and all the top ministers are native. The problem with the Ministry of Economic Development is that the minister, Jaja Wachuku, has been spending most of his time in the Congo working as head of the Conciliation Commission, and it looks like he is on his way to becoming Minister of Foreign Affairs.

Speaking of the Congo, you have probably heard of the reaction here in Lagos to Lumumba's death. The demonstrations were supposed to be peaceful, but things got a bit out of hand when a few people started stoning the American Embassy—which is not far from our home-to-be. There is an additional problem in that the police here are notorious for their nasty tempers.

"... reaction to Lumumba's death."

The force is Nigerian, but the captain is British, and a bulldog. I think they overprotected the American Embassy. Their actions (at least according to many Nigerian reports) precipitated and incited the demonstrators to riot. There is little doubt, on the other hand, that there were "Red" [Communist-inspired] elements seeing to it that the least provocation could be turned into an explosive situation. They were quite successful, too. Tear gas didn't end the rioting that extended into the evening. All Europeans were ordered off the streets, as their cars were being smashed and occupants hauled out and molested. Windows of the American Embassy and the European department stores were smashed. Oddly enough, nothing happened to the Belgian Embassy, the destination of the demonstrators, where they were going to lay their mock coffin.

They never got there, fortunately, since it is on the fourth floor of the building in which the Ford Foundation occupies the "ground floor."

Now the controversy here is over whether to take the Nigerian troops out of the Congo. Thinking is so simpleminded about these issues. The Nigerian conceives of the "UNO," as they call the United Nations, as a separate, autonomous state that has its own inherent powers that it has failed to use. Others see it as nothing more than an imperialist-run institution. And American endorsement of Lumumba's expulsion from the premiership will never be forgiven. Fortunately, there are a few small voices in this din of confused, emotion-packed, racism/nationalism that point out that Nigeria, too, is a member of UNO, along with many other African nations, and withdrawing from the Congo would leave a vacuum only to be filled with worse elements than are now there.

Just a few more comments and then I guess I'll have to save my "must tells" for the next letter. Learning about life and customs here is a dual job, since one must learn of both Nigerian and Nigerian/English ways. The currency, for example, is, or was, part of the British West African sterling system and thus was and still is in divisions of pounds (£), shillings (or "bobs"), guineas, pennies, ha'-pennies, crowns, etc., the only difference being that the money is now Nigerian currency. The old currency is still in circulation, which further confuses me and necessitates being able to identify both quickly. Such archaic divisions of money! Let's hope that the move to change it to a decimal system is successful.

And the driving . . . . We were given a tiny, bright yellow English Ford with right-hand drive and then told to stay on the left side of the road. Now, just you try to remember those instructions after you've gone around a "roundabout." One <u>does</u> remember quickly, however, when meeting the oncoming vehicle, which we were sure was on the wrong side.

Our Ford Taurus in front of Lyle Hanson's house

Driving, itself, is a mad adventure. One fears most the other fellows on the road. I'm sure that the prerequisite for passing a driver's test is the ability to blast with exceptional frequency and clarity the "claxon," especially in the busiest part of town, and at all cyclists who line the roads, and to be able to pass with skill the car ahead of you—doing so only when there is an oncoming car close at hand; taking your half of the road in the middle and being sure at all times that you give the impression of being able to fall asleep any moment, or else that you are rushing your pregnant wife to the hospital.

Finally, there are those hundred obvious objects that immediately become unknown to those who speak the English of London—such as a flashlight that I wished to buy but found I couldn't, because they only sold "torches."

[Hand written]

Uncle Archer, would you send this to Florida and then Granny. We would also appreciate your sending this to Nan and George. Then McBrides to Formans and then 71 Waterside Lane if you really wish to read my silly African gibberish. This will solve the subscription problem to the "Clark weekly," since the cost of individual copies is prohibitive from this distance.

This is really a 24-hour educational experience. Wish my descriptive capacities were more lucid. I should let PBC [Peter] do this, but then you'd never hear from us.

Much love to you all,

G and P

[This was hand written at the bottom of a copy of the above letter by Aunt Jan to Granny.]

Dear Mother,

Archer had this photo-stated at the office, but could only get two copies made. So would you please send this on to Auntie? . . .

— Letter Five —

February 25, 1961

[from Peter]

We are nearly all settled now! Yesterday a shipment arrived by air from the U.S., which will allow us to move into our new house today. Up until now, we have been living in the VIP Flats in Ikoyi (where most of the government people live) and have had everything provided for us. Of the things that came yesterday, five pieces of our pottery were broken, which upset Gretel, so she now fears greatly for the rest of the goods coming by sea. I attribute the damage solely to poor packing but feel the sea freight won't be as mistreated as the air freight.

We really like the country and pace of life! I grant you, we have not been out of Lagos any distance, but the jungle (bush) crowds right up to the city limits. I am overwhelmed at the modernity and construction that I see throughout the city. Perhaps I am not being very critical, but in the last few years this city has changed its face. The surrounding towns remind me very much of driving through any rundown southern Negro[3] community in the U.S.: tin roofs, shanties, filth, and lots and lots of humanity taking life easy. And in Lagos there are the worst sorts of slums, etc., but things are changing very rapidly and new standards are being set.

The cost of living here is fantastic (easily twice that of the U.S.). Gretel is learning to bargain and shop. We have a very keen cook-steward, named Columbus, whom I trust implicitly to look after Gretel.

How is the car sale going? We have a wee little Ford Prefect in which I can hardly get under the steering wheel, but it bounces right along and fits Gretel to a tee. We have adapted without accident to the left side of the road.

I like my work thus far. The first week was spent briefing myself on Nigeria, reading reports, notes taken by Wolf [Stolper] and Lyle [Hansen]—the two other American economists supplied by the Ford Foundation—during the past months, etc. Now I am analyzing a coal-reduction scheme for the production of ammonia sulfate fertilizer, and tar products and chemicals (not feasible!), and making a detailed budgetary study of the Federal, the three Regions[4], and Local accounts for the past 10 years in hopes of detecting trends in revenue sources and expenditures. The accounts are a complete mess! Months of work just to get them straight!

We like it here! Hot, though!

Love,

Pete

Top: Nigerian Ministry of Justice building in Lagos
Bottom: The building boom that came with independence

Top: Typical British civil servant house; Bottom: Lugard House (early colonial dwelling)

These pictures illustrate a planning dilemma: no zoning means businesses and residences are side by side.

Bakery shop

Dry Cleaning

Barber shop

— Letter Six —

February 25, 1961
Saturday

Dear F.D.'s,

I have a head start on myself for this week's communication, it being both a day early and having a typewriter for the first draft. I'm curious to see how much one can say in one air letter.

Today is our first full day in our new home. How good it is to have full command of all those everyday, insignificant things that may seem a nuisance at times but nonetheless make one feel much more at home. By Wednesday, Columbus and I had the entire flat scrubbed out, from top to filthy bottom, had lined the drawers with over 72 feet of shelf paper, and disinfected where necessary. Columbus did the monumental task of waxing our three acres of floor and then polishing it with the flat side of a halved, dried coconut shell, whose tiny, stiff, dried fibers are more effective (and much less expensive—like zero) than any brush or buffer you've ever seen! So there sat our glistening, expectant quarters, and here we sat empty handed, more than anxious to receive our shipment.

Polishing floors with coconut shells cut in half

We were given until Friday to get out of the VIP Flats, arrival of air shipment or no. Friday our travel-weary things did arrive. And you've never seen two sadder cartons. After unpacking them, we are convinced that they must have come via Timbuktu after being dragged across the Sahara by a camel caravan, not always escaping the feet of said animals. Five of our ten pieces of Bennington and Heathware pottery were broken. We await in mortal terror our sea shipment.

This week, Peter and I began our tutelage and practice of African bargaining techniques. It is an art and not to be taken too lightly. To be an effective practitioner in this art is first of all an absolute necessity, and second a social amenity. Our initial dealings were with the Hausa [one of Nigeria's tribes][3] traders from the North. They would not only be insulted, but also disappointed, if you should pay the first price quoted—which is bound to be at least three times what the traders expect you to pay.

Bargaining and haggling over a price, no matter how heartrending the pleas, insulting the retorts, or menacing the threats, is all part of the game. To the American who is accustomed to paying the quoted price without question in a transaction that usually takes a matter of minutes, it is rather disconcerting to learn that here one expects to spend several days negotiating over an item—and certainly not less than 15 minutes or two hours, depending on what it is you are buying.

Even more disconcerting is the technique of the "customer" quoting his "top price" and then working down, instead of starting from the bottom and working up. If you make the mistake of quoting the lowest price you would pay, then you not only defeat the purpose of bargaining but also insult the trader, because he thinks that he will have to haggle down from there with you, which really would be robbery, of which he unhesitatingly accuses you before he dismisses you. On Thursday, Peter, Stolper, and I went to see some Hausa traders. When considering an enormous egg-shaped hamper, we were quoted the price of 3 pounds ($8.40). I said I would not pay more than 2 pounds. Hausa registers surprise and horror. "Ah, no! Two and 10 the Madam must pay."

"Two pounds," sez I.

"Ahhhh, I am a poor man. My brother is sick and dying. I often suffer the pangs of hunger. Since I am desperate today, I will sell this priceless thing for 2 and 2."

My reply: "One pound 15, I think, should be my top price."

"Aa, aa. Good-bye, Madam. Good-bye."

This is my cue to turn and make as though I am going to leave, which I do. Ten paces accomplished, he then pursues me, hamper in tow.

"Madam, Madam, you do not wish to leave this behind. Madam, top price. Top price." (I'm still not quite sure what he means by that.)

"One pound, one pound, and I take it," I say.

Well, to cut a very long process short,—for there are many more stories to be heard, joshing, and perhaps a few insults—I had him down to 17 shillings and was working for 14 ($2) when Peter came over and paid the man a pound (20 shillings).

Now we are the proud owners of perhaps the world's largest and most preposterous clothes hamper. Heaven knows what it is really meant for.

Yoruba markets are managed by women, predominately in blue. They are a powerful economic force.

What's even more ludicrous about the whole thing is that clothes (dirty ones, that is) don't accumulate over a week here as they did in our home in the U.S. A shirt is barely off one's back before steward (Columbus) snatches it up, hand scrubs it in the tub, has it on the line, ironed, and in your drawer just as you are turning to put on a fresh one. Had I known, we could have brought only one of everything!

One more word about buying things: This seems to be my subject of the day.

Yesterday Columbus and I went down into the native market to buy some baskets. I have ventured only once into the native market prior to this, just to look at things and see what's what. I learned then that I would be foolish to try to buy anything unless I wanted to be "taken," in addition to accomplishing the impossible---being understood. Columbus fortunately speaks both Ibo and Yoruba (the latter at least passably).

We would walk up to the baskets of some old lady, Columbus having taken me to places I would never have known about or been able to find. I would point out the ones I was interested in and then he would start to bargain in Yoruba. Within minutes, we would be surrounded by several dozen silent faces staring up at us (mostly at me, I fear) who inevitably would follow us—like the mice of the Pied Piper—to the car. They are darling things, most naked, many with porcupine braids projecting out all over the head, always barefoot (very few of the people here wear shoes, no matter how well dressed), and curious. It takes a while to get used to being an oddity, one of a very clear minority, and certainly in the native market—where it is a solo performance. Evidently white people rarely go there, if ever.

Next letter I'll try to give you a description and, more important, the smells and sounds of the native market.

Love,

G and P

— Letter Seven —

Ministry of Economic Development, Lagos, Nigeria
March 10, 1961
Saturday

Dear Gang,

And I guess it really is getting to be a gang, from the forwarding list Aunt Jan quoted! Wonderful. Hope the content herein justifies it. Certainly the experiences we are having, the entirely new life we have been introduced to, the profound emotional impact of actually becoming involved in a visible part of the world struggle—as we have so many years longed to do—should provide material for volumes.

My delayed communication this week is (1) because I have been writing a "paper" to my comparative education seminar back at the University of Michigan on "How Nigeria is seeking to solve her educational problems and to build a strong system of education" and "Considerations of the potential role for the comparative educator and the educational specialist." And (2) I just completed a rather sizable editing and partial rewriting job of a 30-page report to the Ford Foundation on "Teacher Training in Nigeria" by Dr. Judson T. Shaplin, Associate Dean of the Graduate School of Education at Harvard.[5] He was here for seven weeks in December and January and, to my unpracticed eye, did an impressive job of evaluation. On the basis of this, he made recommendations as to where the Foundation support would be most effective.

Since the Foundation wishes to publish it, they asked me if I would edit it from a conversational (first person singular), frank, and in some instances brutally blunt report to an impersonal, accurate, but softened document for British and Nigerian educators' eyes. Touchy business. I have learned a great deal in the process. It has been an exciting introduction to the very up-to-date inner workings and developments of this part of the education system, along with all the juicy political maneuvering, and British-American clashes over projects in certain regions. Much of it, I fear, will have to remain confidential. This may be an excellent beginning for a thesis topic.

Have I told you the news from Michigan about my graduate studies? As you know, I was admitted last fall to the School of Graduate Studies as an unclassified student on a provisional basis because I had had absolutely NO previous course work in education—the minimum prerequisite being 15 hours of work in the field. Now, on the basis of the 12 hours of work I did there last semester (4 A–'s and 2 B+'s), the committee on graduate studies has agreed to waive the entire 15 hours prerequisite qualification and credit the 12 hours I have done toward my master's degree. My present scholastic standing also allows me to write my thesis while here, leaving only 12 more hours of formal studies to be done when we return.

This past week, we have been to two cocktail parties and a dinner party. The first cocktail party was a reception for Mr. Johnson (who replaced us in our VIP Flat), the United Nations TAB (Technical Assistance Board) Advisor to Nigeria and Ghana. It was given by the Acting Minister of Economic Development (since the minister, Jaja Wachuku, is now at the UN blasting Mr. [Kwame] Nkrumah—bless his brave soul). It was interesting to note the number of British "expatriates" there who hold administrative positions in the Ministry. They far outnumber the Nigerians, despite

" . . . the push for 'Nigerianization . . ."

the strong push for "Nigerianization" in all the ministries. (I'll give more detail about this ministry later, as this is the group with which PBC must work, and from which he is trying to glean any and all possible information—which, from the way Peter talks, he usually ends up researching and drawing up himself). The British civil servant in West Africa comes from a professional pool that sends its most qualified career people to East Africa (the more desirable destination). But imagine what it will be like when they leave—which, for most of them will be in the next year or so—and they will be replaced largely by even less qualified Nigerians!

The Ministry of Education is a good example of the rapidity with which efforts to Nigerianize are taking place. By the end of the month, nine out of 12 of the advisors and administrators will have left their posts, which will most likely remain vacant for some time for lack of qualified Nigerians to fill their places. It is unfortunate that appreciation for the value of the work done by the expatriates in the administration and elsewhere should come only after they have gone and the country must suffer and retrace a few steps while people are given hasty, inadequate training and recruited in order to fill the vacuum. Any Englishman will tell you that things have gone downhill since independence, when the Nigerians started to take over. "You should have been here 10 years ago," they say nostalgically. Of course, we must remind ourselves that these colonial officials were the masters, and they lived in great style, much more so than now. It is much more expensive now to have many servants and keep up a big estate. Certainly not all the British here carry the air of the former "colonial master." But it is hard for the bright-eyed, love-the-natives Americans to keep from wincing when we see the aloof, condescending attitude of many British toward the natives—even the well-educated ones.

At any rate, we never cease to be amazed by the rapidity with which the entire country is changing (despite what our British friends tell us). The tremendous leaps in economic growth and activity, unbelievable strides in educational expansion, the contagious spread of political awareness, and "national" articulation on the street, in the shops, and in the newspapers are constant reminders of the recent "birth" of this nation. One cannot help but be struck by the childlike nature of all this development—its lack of sophistication, naive approach, and penchant for simple-minded reasoning. Yet these are steps expected of all "children" who will develop into mature, responsible individuals.

Wonderful ad in the paper this morning:

WANTED IMMEDIATELY: LITERATE FEMALE BREAD WRAPPERS.

The robust nature of political arguments that rage daily in the papers among the coalition government parties (NCNC—National Council of Nigerian Citizens, representing the East; NPC—Northern People's Congress, the North; and the Western Region's loyal opposition, AG—Action Group) are good indications of a healthy, viable democracy that will grow, not weaken, on their lively expressions of differences. It ensures that no one person, such as Nkrumah in Ghana, could rise to dominate and eventually dictate the scene.

On the other hand, perhaps this "healthy opposition" exists because the really popular, charismatic leader is not in fact the head man, Abubakar Tafawa Balewa. That person is the Governor-General, second in power, Nnamdi Azikiwe ("Zik"). Without a doubt, Zik commands an impressive following of hypnotized admirers who insist he can do no wrong—even when he is exposed for grossly illegal dealings with the Bank of Nigeria. Several Nigerians have told me that if Zik had been Prime Minister, the Congo crisis would have been settled long ago, etc., etc. His followers

Dr. Nnamdi Azikiwe

also have great frustration at the thought of future elections when they will always be faced with the NCNC party of the North, which commands a following twice the size of the total population of both southern regions. This is because the North's large Islamic population, even though tribally diverse, is linked by religion (Islam) rather than shared political goals and values.

Incidentally, we saw Dr. Azikiwe at the second cocktail party. This was U.S. Ambassador Joseph Palmer's reception for "Soapy" Williams [U.S. Assistant Secretary of State for African Affairs; former Governor of Michigan] and his entourage. It was held at the ambassador's home, in Ikoyi. Often thought of as an extension of Lagos, Ikoyi is actually a separate island, separated from Lagos by a small river. Between the "city" of Lagos and the residential area of Ikoyi is a mile and a half of desert.

Then comes Ikoyi, with luxurious bungalows and flats (including the one we stayed in) and greenery. However, that lush plant growth is not everywhere, especially in the residential developments where Wolf (Stolper to you) and Lyle (Hansen) and his family live.

Ikoyi was once a European reserve, but now some Africans in "European posts" have been given houses there. They all have the usual servants' compounds out back. While the stewards are cooking steak and kidney pies for their "Masters" and "Madams," the stewards' wives out back pound cassava root, boil yams over tiny kerosene lamps, defecate on the ground, and keep their usually naked children out of trouble: two worlds living side by side, speaking their separate languages, eating their different foods, and dressing in their different ways. Only the cook-steward has a foot in each culture, but he lacks the education and skills needed to move from his low status.

What I had started to tell you about was the reception for Williams. Yes, the Palmers' house is in Ikoyi—a large, well-manicured, spacious home. As usual, there was a native band playing on part of the lawn, many "boys" dressed in crisp white uniforms serving all kinds of things to eat and drink, and many guests, mostly white. (Generally "white" is synonymous with "European." Columbus is always saying to us, "You Europeans . . . .") Both the Williamses and the Palmers are nice-looking, cordial couples. We also met some of the other U.S. Embassy people, a few businessmen, not all Americans, who have been here anywhere from 10 to 30 years!

Grace pounding cassava to make fufu, a glutinous African staple

Marguerite Higgins (*N.Y. Herald Tribune*) was there. She just happened to be passing through with some other newspeople, trying to drum up interest in the 1962 World's Fair to be held in New York City. I found out the following night at a dinner party—from the man who is head of the Rockefeller Foundation projects here—that she had had dinner at his home the night before, prior to the reception. She struck him as a power-mad woman who had to hoard the limelight all the time. (Sounds like he doesn't like strong women.) Talking about the Williamses' tour of Africa: At the same dinner party with newsmen and USIA men who were traveling with them, my impression was confirmed that their reception here by the Africans, despite anything you may have been reading in the papers, has been warm and enthusiastic. The Africans were impressed with both the visitors' stamina (most of them have had dysentery and other such troubles) and their charm. The Nigerian reporters have not made the faux pas *Time* magazine and other news sources have made in their reporting. Much of the trouble has been in misreporting and misquoting.

While speaking of political figures . . . it has been interesting to note the African attitude to our new American president. A feeling of expectancy about the new administration is pervasive. But I must say, it looks like President Kennedy's honeymoon with Africa is over, and has been ever since he chose to support the Lléo regime. [Joseph Lléo was declared Prime Minister of Congo after communist Prime Minister Lumumba's assassination, assisted, it is thought, by the CIA.] For weeks now, we have been able to read of practically nothing else in the papers (and this is no exaggeration) except "Congo," "Saint Lumumba," and the need to withdraw the Nigerian troops from the UN forces in the Congo.

Did I tell you that we have been studying Yoruba? It is an exceedingly difficult language, since it is tonal. Depending on the pitch of the voice, a word can mean three to five or six different things! A tone-deaf individual could never learn it.

We have been looking very seriously at boats this week, since all the sailboats in Lagos Harbor sit right in our front yard, or to the side of it (anchored in the water). Highest in the running is the Shearwater Catamaran, fastest sailboat in the world: twin-hulled and rather expensive. Peter has already crewed in a race in a Cat, naturally, with the best sailor in the entire club. They won the race, first in a fleet of 20.

Love,

G and P

— Letter Eight —

[from Peter] Dear Folks,

We have word that our goods will arrive by ship in the next week or so, and then we will be right at home. We will also have an air-conditioning unit installed in the next week.

Meanwhile, the water is our means of finding refuge from the heat and humidity. We also sail and swim. Lyle, Gretel, and I are developing an interest in exploring underwater. I bought masks and flippers for us. Now the pressure is on to buy a sailboat. I crewed the other day on the winning boat at the yacht club. There are several classes of boats, ranging from a small, 14-foot dinghy up to a local version of the Lightning. The prices range from $350 to $1,100. The problem with small boats here is that the tides cause 5-knot currents, or more, in the harbor, and stronger ones in the narrow entrance channel to Lagos Harbor. The smaller boats are forced to go with the tidal currents. Therefore, if one wishes to sail out to the beach against the flood tide, one needs a larger boat with a large sail area.

The class I am currently most interested in is the Catamaran, because they are fast and light and will cover large distances in a light breeze. I expect that I would have to pay about $700–750 for one in good condition. They race twice a week here, and the Cats have ten in their class. The Tarpons (Lightnings of

Testing a catamaran

Peter and Policeman

Lagos—minus royalties) are also a large class—say, 15—and have keen competition. I expect that we would be able to sell the boat after a year and several months with a loss of $50 max, and probably a slight profit, if we take good care of it. All the boats are taken out of the water after use and stored in sheds. The worm rot is very bad, so they are washed down with fresh water. We have decided to make sailing our one big relaxation. Therefore, I would like to have the money from the sale of the car sent out here. We'll convert the capital I had tied up in the car into our boat, since all my driving fees, car, and expenses are provided here by the Ford foundation.

Gretel and I will be taking our first trip into the country this next week. I have an opportunity to go to Enugu, capital of the Eastern Region, which will take us through some 600 to 800 miles of jungle, villages, etc.

This last week, I have been digging around for information at the Federal Office of Statistics. It is amazing—the contrast with what I would expect to find at home—three or four senior people, none very competent, collecting information in very unorthodox manners, without knowing what to do with it once they have it. It is truly pathetic and exasperating when we need lots of data for projections into the future. Trade statistics

are at least four years behind what I have to collect (a historical society, I'd say). Well, I'm learning to make do with the very roughest of info.

Poling along the marina

     Love to all,
        Pete

[N.B. When Peter returned to the United States, he helped Wolfgang Stolper write a book called *Planning Without Facts: Lessons in Resource Allocation from Nigeria's Development* (Cambridge: Harvard University Press, 1966).]

— Letter Nine —

March 25, 1961

Well, let's see how this works out. I'm perched on the edge of the wharf that is in front of our house, legs straddling the third borrowed typewriter. Lack of a typewriter for the past week explains (though may not be accepted as an adequate excuse for) my silence when there is so very much to tell, so many new, exciting things to share with you with the passing of each day. But I refuse to do it by hand. You suffer as much from those (written) communications as I do. Not too long now, and the sea freight should bring our typewriter.

One sad bit of news to relate: Night before last, we were robbed. We don't know whether the thief came in through the windows, which we leave open so we can sleep at night—it's so hot—or whether he came in through the front door. I forgot to bolt it (although it was locked) after visiting next door before I went to bed. Gone: my watch, wallet, and change

Rigging our new cat's full batten's sail

purse containing about £3 in cash and the uncashed $15 check Tante gave to us, plus my $2.79 Flintkote stock dividend. I'll write to Tante and tell her to cancel it. Meanwhile, we are grateful that no more was taken. We have learned a lesson, after many warnings from Columbus, to be much more cautious about everything. Thieving is evidently a prosperous business in Lagos.

One exciting bit of news: Yesterday we bought a boat—a Catamaran, fastest sailboat here.

We (with the help of a loan from the bank) bought it from the number-one skipper in the club, who lives right here on the Yacht Club grounds with us. He (Roy Fluellan), along with four to six other Yacht Club members, is retiring and going back to England—for good. Cost: £290. The Catamaran, in case you haven't seen it, is a double-hulled boat, and thus has two rudders. I skippered it in the race on Wednesday with Roy (then still the owner) crewing. Thanks to him, though

there were 40 or more yachts racing, I won! (Or, rather, we won.) There is another race this afternoon, as on every Saturday, and a special one this Sunday. The Fluellans will race it today for the last time. Then, well, we'll let you know how we do. We have the racing rules just about memorized. Still have to learn the nature of the tides and the location of every shoal and buoy.

I just looked up and saw a large school of fish swimming right by me, leaping and diving in and out of the water as though members of a corps de ballet. People can actually sit right where I am and catch barracuda. Just a few weeks ago, a native fisherman saw one leap out of the water not far from his canoe. He immediately chased and successfully harpooned it. Estimates were in the vicinity of 100 pounds!

These native canoes, incidentally, are the most graceful craft I have ever seen. They are rough-hewn from one log and tapered at both ends, lying very low in the water. The paddle is the means of propulsion, and each one is a different size and shape. In shallow water, a long pole is used, à la Venice. If you have a map of Lagos, you will see that we are situated on Magazine Point, the very tip of Lagos Island, facing the mouth of the harbor, which is about a mile and a half away. Right next to us is the home of the British High Commissioner (who has a monkey that is right now swinging around in the trees just a few feet from me). To our left is Five Cowry Creek (whence came the cowry shells that were not too long ago the form of currency used here). The bridge that crosses Five Cowry Creek from Lagos to Victoria Island is to the left and rear of our house, Victoria Island coming toward us at about a 120-degree angle.

The reason I'm relating all this to you is that this creek and the harbor area right out in front of us is full of fisher-people every morning. They come in their canoes, after a night of fishing, to the fish market located at the mouth of Five Cowry Creek (a point about 100 yards down from our window on the shore of Victoria Island). There they are met by scores of Yoruba women dressed in their typical blue wraparound skirts and bubas (their counterpart of the male's agbada), with babies strapped on their backs and sometime baskets on their heads. They buy the fish from the fisherpeople and plop the fish in enormous calabash bowls that they then carry on their heads to the native market. There these "middle women" sell the fresh fish at a handsome profit.

The women, especially of the Yoruba tribes, are the main traders and entrepreneurs in Lagos, with the exception of the Hausa traders from the North. The Hausa women, being Muslim, are rarely if ever seen, because they go into purdah after marriage. Anyway, the noise of the chattering and haggling coming from the fish market across the creek accompanies our breakfast instead of Bob Steele [WTIC in Hartford]. We watch them right from our table.

Roof over yacht club "hard" as seen from our living room windows

It's great being on the second floor. The ship channel has traffic passing in and out of the harbor and lies directly in front of our windows.

It took us more than a week to get over the conviction that each boat coming into the harbor—and they are positively monstrous ships, carrying all types of cargo and passengers—was going to come right into our living room. But no, they turn and pass by, less than 50 yards from our window.

Lagos harbor fisherman, the Mail Boat and floating dry dock beyond

It's really exciting to see ships from all over the world. We are fast becoming experts on national flags and nautical-flag signals. The first U.S. ship we have seen came by two days ago.

Never thought we'd be so excited to see Old Glory! It's hard to believe that only a few years ago (two or three) there was little or no traffic coming into Lagos Harbor. Now, nearly every day there are from four to six ships waiting outside the harbor for berthing space in Apapa in order to come into the harbor. Right now, I can count at least two dozen ships at the Apapa docks, across from Lagos, and about as many anchored directly in front of the marina in the main part of town. The shoreline of Lagos bends out from us, so we can see the whole city of Lagos from here.

It is horrifying to see the native canoes come barreling down Badagry Creek, loaded precariously with bamboo poles like an overstacked hay wagon, with their square, burlap sails out running before the wind and the tide, and swish right across into the center of the harbor.

Twice, now, in the past year they have arrived at that point just as one of these mountainous freighters or tankers is entering this part of the harbor. Both of them, unable to stop, meet, the sea vessel passing through and over the native canoe, mangling it and its cargo as though they were a matchbox and two ants.

Next Day

Well, it is now Sunday afternoon, and, speaking of Badagry Creek, we raced in the long race up the creek from 10 a.m. to 3 p.m. today; we were first across the starting line, first most of the way up the creek to windward. Two other Cats caught up to us on the downward leg and we were racing, nip and tuck, on the last stretch, pulling out ahead as we were just about to round the last island, when we ran aground on a sunken dock, tearing off both rudders and ripping a hole in the rear of the starboard hull, which immediately filled with water. We limped home with the aid of a passing Chris-Craft. Pretty good for our first day out, wouldn't you say? Fortunately we have insurance, but that does nothing toward mending our broken spirits.

Let me tell you of our trip to Enugu, capital of the Eastern Region, about 500 miles from Lagos. We accompanied Chiedo Obinetchi, an Ibo from the Eastern Region, who is one of the Nigerians working with Peter in the Ministry of Economic Development. Chiedo was making this trip to speak to someone in the Eastern Regional Government about his continued work in the Federal Government, whence he was "seconded" (loaned) from a position in the Eastern Region. When we heard about his trip, we asked if we might go along.

By the time we left, it had become a business trip for Peter, too, since there were a number of people on the way and in Enugu who could answer questions the Planning Commission wished to ask. For example, we stopped a little over halfway at the West African Institute for Oil Palm Research (WAIFOR)[6] for some information and a night's rest. There we found a very large plantation with thousands of acres of oil-palm groves employing several thousand workers and research staff. It is a day's drive from any real civilization in rich, hilly green country near Benin.

We had an introduction to the Acting Director of the Institute, and as we drove past the homes of staff members, each one looking like a small manor house, it was hard to believe our eyes after having traveled for a day through nothing but "bush" country, past dwellings and villages of mud houses, and subsistence-level farmers, some growing cocoa and oil palms. With a few exceptions, most of the WAIFOR staff are British colonial civil servants; and of course all of the workers are Nigerian.

Research has been going on at WAIFOR for over a decade for the four British West African colonies to develop a top-grade oil palm: cultivation, harvesting, and processing procedures. If the information they have accumulated to date were ever distributed widely, accepted, adopted, and then practiced by the Nigerian "farmer," he could, within three years, quintuple his harvest! Although Nigeria produces half the world's palm oil, nearly *all* of it is harvested or gathered by natives from *wild* oil palms.

The harvested oil kernels are pounded and then washed from the

West African Institute for Palm Oil Research (WAIFOR). Can you see me at base of the tree?

pericarp of palm kernels that grow in bunches just below where the palm's fronds appear. In a grove on a cultivated palm, the bunches of kernels are only a few feet above the ground and can be harvested from the ground; but on the wild palm, which must fight all the other forest growth and struggle above it for light, this means climbing 40 to 60 feet in the air for the bunches that are, on the whole, rather poor in quality.

The Planning Commission that Peter works with is interested in the possibility of importing hand presses or other types of harvesting equipment to increase palm-oil[5] production; and of cutting down the old, wild palms and encouraging development of scientifically (so to speak) operated groves and plantations, etc. However, the Planning Commission must know all the alternatives, possible benefits, and drawbacks before making suggestions and projections for the Five-Year Plan.

One of the biggest problems, in this case, will be social, since the land tenure system is so complicated it makes plot consolidation almost impossible. Also, the social roles that have grown up around the harvesting of the oil palm—where the man gets the oil and the wife the kernels[7] (remaining after the oil has been squeezed out), which she then sells. Introducing assembly-line procedures would completely disrupt the social and economic fabric of the lives of these people now producing the palm oil.

But let me go back to our departure from Lagos, which was before dawn. The city was already busy with activity, perhaps more energetically than usual, since most of the workers were anticipating the four-day holiday[6] that would start the next day (Thursday to Monday), ending the 30-day fasting period for Muslims [Ramadan[8]]. Although over half of the population of the two southern regions of Nigeria is either Christian or heathen, these Muslim holidays are national holidays, since the majority of Nigeria's population lies in the Muslim North.

So we were a little surprised to find the dark streets already filled with barefoot crowds. We passed a large group of these Lagos Islanders collecting at the ferry wharf, where they would sardine themselves onto a tired ferryboat that belches its burden through the water, across the harbor to Apapa on the mainland. The only people missing from the busy streets were the disabled, the lepers, and the beggars who probably would appear there along with the sun.

As usual, hundreds of Africans on bicycles jammed the sides of the road in one continuous stream as we drove down the Marina and across Carter Bridge to the mainland. Very few people can afford to own cars, so bicycles are the primary mode of transportation throughout civilized areas, second only to foot traffic. Bicycle riders are especially colorful here, since the flowing robes of the agbada, worn by most Yoruba men, give the impression of flight, especially as their enormous sleeves flap wildly in the breeze.

Laundry on river bank

Only a few miles, though, and we were soon in the bush, relieved to

LETTERS FROM NIGERIA

leave Lagos and the busy, hot day that her early activity promised. The lush, deep green of the tropical forested countryside was so refreshing after a month of glaring city life. Although the ground was dry and the streambeds bare, or nearly so, at every water crossing, there were a dozen or more local people bathing, beating and scrubbing clothes, or drawing murky drinking water. Surprisingly, the vegetation appeared lush and very thick, with occasional openings just wide enough for the footpaths that lead to bush villages.

Despite all this greenery, we sensed an air of expectancy that marks the end of this year's dry season and the impending rainy season. The bare spots of ground, worn down by traffic along the side of the road, begged for water, reaching for one's throat with tiny, red-dust fingers. "Not long now 'til the rainy season," we are constantly reminded; "and then you will beg for the sun, just long enough to dry your moldy clothes." We began to have an idea of just how severe this rainy season is, too, as we passed the veritable channels that lead off from the road every few yards all along the way into the bush or to great holes dug in fields. Judging by the size of this drainage system, roads must become rivers when the rains come.

It was really exciting, all those things we saw that first day when an African tropical forest became something more to us than a literary experience. With Chiedo's help, we were soon able to recognize the bamboo-tree "clusters" anywhere in the forest because of their willow-like qualities (hundreds of main stems shooting straight into the air; long, dainty leaves showering down around them like a cluster of maypoles).

We passed cocoa trees, now stripped of their fruit, the harvest season just being over. (Cocoa is Nigeria's largest cash crop, most of it being exported.) Occasional rubber trees appeared in groups, right in among much other bush growth, which, though appearing wild, are tapped. (There's nothing very sophisticated about this agriculture.) And then, growing wild everywhere, are banana, plantain, and avocado trees, pawpaw trees, mango and umbrella trees, ferns the height of a house whose fronds could cover one whole window, and oil palms—the jungle's skyscrapers that splash silhouettes of fireworks around the horizon. Taller still, the silk-cotton's smooth trunk rises from its pyramid base some 130 feet or more, branchless to her roof, a frilly puff-ball cotton topping, loosely held by a wiry frame of branches.

We also learned to recognize the yam and cassava plants, whose "roots" are the major source of Nigerians' food. Many Africans walking along the side of the road carried on their heads a number of yams—long, tube-shaped things, some 6 to 10 inches in diameter. Others carried bowls (made from half a calabash) heaped with the varying shades of white and yellow gurry (a ground, sort of floury form of cassava root), from which they make "fufu," a mashed-potato-like food that they eat nearly every

Palm wine tapper, lower right, about to ascend tree

meal. Lacking utensils, they eat with their fingers. The fufu is pressed into one's palm by the thumb, creating a spoon shape, and this is used to scoop up more liquid foods, such as egusi stew or groundnut stew, staples in the Nigerian's diet.

Tonight, incidentally, we are going to have an African meal. I asked Columbus if he would fix us one, and he said he would not be able to, as he knows only how to prepare Western food! His wife, on the other hand, who prepares all *his* meals, which are strictly African, consented to fix this one for us. We may even drink some palm wine with it, provided it is fresh, since a few days' fermentation is enough to kill a man.

Palm wine tapper

[Written by hand] Columbus just told me that he sent a boy to Ikoyi, where the palm wine will be tapped around 5:00. The palm-wine tappers are fascinating to watch in action. They can ascend the tallest palm tree in a matter of seconds. A tapper does this by taking a large, circular hoop that he usually carries slung over his shoulder, slips it around the tree and himself, and, with his tapping hammer and spike, plus several calabash gourds tied around his waist, he scampers up the tree.

Here, in random fashion, are characteristic sights on the route.

Most of the traffic on the road consisted of lorries, otherwise known as "mammy wagons," into which passengers are packed—on the floor, if there are no benches (I don't know which would be worse) or standing, if there are too many

Lorries with interesting inscriptions

passengers for them to sit. No matter how they are loaded, the rider need not worry about keeping his balance, since he is firmly buttressed by those around him. I shudder when I think of them having to ride this way down the narrow, bumpy road between Lagos and Onitsha, 12 hours nonstop. At Onitsha, one takes a ferry across the Niger River, and then it is another two hours from there to Enugu. Unless you have your own car, these mammy wagons are the only means of transportation between Lagos and Enugu, unless you want to take the train. This requires first traveling two days north to Kano, and then down the other leg of what they call the "wishbone" to Enugu.

We were traveling in a Volkswagen, and even then it has taken us a week for our insides to rearrange themselves to their proper positions. The road, 12 feet wide, is not wide enough for two vehicles to pass each other. Everyone knows this, yet neither Chiedo nor the lorry drivers would give way until, crashing toward each other at a jolting 60 mph, at the very last second one or the other would veer off, the left wheel on the dirt shoulder (remember, we drive on the left side here) and the other tire on the pavement.

I don't think we were ever thoroughly convinced that we would pass the oncoming lorry, no matter how many we encountered. And to top it off, these creaking monsters, splitting at the seams with Africans, all carried inscriptions across the front above the windshield: "Slow and Easy," or "I Believe in God," "The Lord Is My Shepherd," "Charity," "Live and Let Live," "God Knows Best," "May God Be Glorified," "Future Will Tell," "Remember Thy Promise Oh! Lord" (appropriate sentiments, I thought, but could never understand the exclamation mark), and so on and on. Some were written in Yoruba or Ibo, but all to the same effect.

Driving through "towns," if we slowed down, children came running toward the car from all directions, shouting, "*Oyinbo! Oyinbo!*" (white man! white man!), and some of the older ones, "Dash me, dash me" (a "dash" being roughly equivalent to a "tip"). The more explicit would say, "Dash me six pence."

If we didn't slow down, on the other hand, we would have found it rough going to maneuver around the many domestic animals that think they own the road; perhaps "stock" would be a better word for them. This would include chickens (scrawny), house cows (about the size of a small Shetland pony; they can't grow any larger in this part of the country due to the climate and the tsetse fly), pigs, goats everywhere—even in the natives' huts—bearing little or no resemblance to the goat you know, being half as long and high and twice as wide as the American goat. And finally, there is the "pie dog," about the only kind of canine to be found in Nigeria that survives in the climate. They are small, brown, short-haired, good-natured animals. Occasionally we passed a string of horses or a dozen or more humpbacked, long-horned white cattle being brought down from the North by some Fulani herdsman for slaughter.

The Hausa man, incidentally, is easy to spot: first, because he always wears a white Muslim robe; and second, because of his extraordinary height (especially noticeable in the Eastern Region, next to the very short Ibos) and his refined aquiline features: thin lips, bright alert eyes, narrowly shaped and slim body. They look like kings in their robes and by the way they carry themselves. It is believed that their ancestors are of Aryan stock, having come across the desert from Egypt and settled in the Northern Region, in Kano, the southern tip of the Sahara trade routes. These people have been known for their fierce warrior qualities, and, until the beginning of this century, they staged raids continually on the tribes of the southern two regions, carrying off their prisoners as slaves or to be sold into slavery as the trade caravans passed through from the desert.

Slavery, incidentally, has in no way completely ended in this

Hausa men

Coming into Ibadan

part of the world. We have reports of and read frequently in the papers of X number of men being brought into court for having sold, for example, eight girls (as this morning's paper reported) into slavery. Recent surveys in the Eastern Region reveal that several thousand people are "missing." Most likely, some are now slaves, and probably many more were either eaten by their African brothers or sacrificed in the many ways one is offered to appease a certain god or in accordance with the instructions of some Juju man. But I'll tell you more about the Juju men later. We have learned that young girls are taken to Arabia and sold into harems. The men in Peter's office always leave at noon to escort their children home from school in order to prevent them from being kidnapped and sold to slave traders.

The towns of Ibadan (70 miles from here) and Onitsha are two of the largest native towns in West Africa. (Ibadan is the largest in Nigeria, with a population of 700,000.) They are indigenous, as opposed to colonial/Western creations like Lagos. Coming into Ibadan is an exciting experience, since the city is built on seven hills. From any of them, one looks down on a sea of roofs: rusted tin roofs interspersed with palm-thatched roofs that cover the mud-walled structures typical of most African dwellings in Nigeria, all undulating up and down over several square miles of teeming humanity. (The Yoruba people are distinctive from the other Nigerian tribes for their gregarious, social nature, living in towns rather than villages, being urban rather than rural, as are most of the other tribes. For this reason, most of the large towns in Nigeria are found in the Western Region, home of the Yoruba.)

Two views of the Onitsha Market on the bank of Niger River

Onitsha, too, was a sea of activity, housing the largest and very famous native market. One end of the market is bounded by the Niger River, which, we found, could be reached by descending some 200 or more cement steps constructed across about 50 yards of the riverbank. Onitsha is a market town and a transshipment point for Hausa boats that come down the Niger from the Northern Region. These are fisherpeople and traders who tie up their canoes during the day while they sell their goods.

Every square inch of the market area was occupied by men, women, and children selling from their small supplies of goods. There was barely room enough to put our feet on the ground as we wove our way through and by the masses of (mostly) women and their goods, all on the ground. If not on the ground, there

were miles of sheds and stalls where all this trade flourishes.

In much of the bush country, many women don't wear any kind of top covering, though they wrap around their waists yards of material that reaches the ground. Occasionally they raise the wrapping point to just above the breasts, but I think this is more for a change in style than modesty. True, to the wide-eyed American, this is distracting, though not for long.

Top: Note chain gang passing cassava and woman pounding fufu in left foreground.

Bottom: Cherubim and Seraphim

I promise this will be the last page, though I have hardly begun to tell you all that is on my list of important things to report.

Aside from the religious group of Christians (I think) that are called Cherubim and Seraphim (two groups that we passed on the roadside, singing and gyrating in good old holy-roller fashion) on our way home on Sunday, every town we passed through was celebrating the Muslim Eid al-Fitr holiday. In one town, we actually became a part of a long parade of marching Muslims, all men and boys, of course, on their way to the mayor's home to pay him their respects, even though he is not a Muslim himself.

Many wore agbadas, the clothing worn by most Nigerian men, consisting of long pants, full at the knee and tapered a bit at the ankle, a round-necked tunic that is three-quarter length, full sleeves that generally come down to the vicinity of the knees. Then, over this is a large, full robe, sleeveless, though its sides extend down over the shoulders, with, I think, a V-neck, the front and back flaps reaching the ground and connecting either there or halfway up the leg. One would think that with all this material, they would be very hot, but it is very loose and airy, and if one is not "dressing," one can be more casual and wear only one of the two top garments. Most of this material is imported, and some of it is dyed here. The materials are of all colors and patterns. The ones I like best are shades of lighter blue, especially characteristic of the Yoruba people.

I am having a modified version of this outfit made for me out of one of these blues by a tailor who works in a tiny stall down in the native market. He comes here to the house to take the orders and do the fittings. We're also having him make Peter some sleeveless shirts. It's really fun: You just draw a picture of what you want and he produces it for you (I hope). It should be finished by tomorrow. Columbus and I went to the local market and picked out the material on Saturday.

But back to this procession: Each group of men wore its own color of agbada, evidently being from the same family. Those who had been to Mecca were distinguished by their headdresses, made of a white material held onto the head by an octagonal crown of some kind of wooden sticks (a typical Arab headdress, actually). And the few chiefs or headmen were surrounded by various bearers and an umbrella carrier to shade his head. (Umbrellas—or, in this case, I guess, they are parasols—are used by everyone who can afford them as protection from the sun.)

Best of all in the procession were the drummers, with their wonderful tones and rhythms that create a music of their own. The "talking drums" are really exciting to hear. We hear them here occasionally at night, as the sound carries across the water from the native village of Ogogoro. I am looking at it right now, directly facing us on the other side of the harbor. It is hard to get used to these extremes of culture living side by side. Here we can sit in the evening eating our Western food by electric light, perhaps listening to the radio (if we had one), while we can see plainly the fires of a village across the harbor, where the women are pounding cassava and cooking yams over their fires while they listen to their talking drums, which really do talk.

We have been having a little trouble with these people lately, since they have taken to coming across the harbor in their canoes, landing right out here, opposite the house, and then coming into the servants' compound to get water to take back with them. Our stewards and their families aren't very happy about this.

[P.S. to J and A. Clark]

Guess the rest will have to wait, since this is getting beyond the fitting-in-envelope stage. Any luck selling the car yet? We just heard that the Ford Foundation is going to give our Prefect to a recently arrived consultant, and that we will have a larger German Taunus. We don't know what to expect, but are pleased, since Peter's knees suffered in the English Ford.

How is Granny getting on?? Would you pass this on in your edition of this letter to her from us? Tell her that we aren't being slack on providing her with the photographs we promised to fill the book we gave her. It is taking six weeks to develop each batch of photos, since they must be sent to London to be developed. We haven't forgotten her.

Much, much love to you both,

G and P

Living and dining room. Bedroom is through the white doors to the right. Green doors are at top of stairs.

— Letter Ten —

April 3, 1961

Dear F. D.,

Okay, you win. This week it is time to fill you in on some of the details of our daily life, instead of those of the nation. I apologize for not having done this earlier; but I did want to share with you our initial impressions and reactions to this country as a whole, while they are fresh in mind. The new patterns in our everyday life won't change much. But first let me tell you a few news items of the past week.

We have our new (only 300 miles on it) Taunus (German Ford) and it is, without a doubt, one of the best-looking, smoothest-to-drive cars on the road: four gears, legroom for Peter even though it is a small, streamlined vehicle. It is mustard yellow, and, well, we feel very privileged to be able to drive it for the year and a half that we will be here in Nigeria.

Our Catamaran (called *Miss Tibbs*) is all repaired, thanks to the help, materials, and expert advice of half the yacht club and the hard work of PBC. Didn't cost us a penny, so we won't have to claim any insurance. We raced on Saturday and came in 42 seconds after boat number 1. We lost ground on the windward leg because we just couldn't point high enough. We knew there was something wrong with the position of the boom, but of course we couldn't readjust it 'til the race was over and we could ask Roy (former owner) what was wrong. So just wait 'til the next race. There will be one this afternoon if there is enough wind. I will skipper with Roy crewing so that we can learn from him valuable information about the tide flows, channels, breezes, etc. PBC won't race as he has some work to do.

Item number three is that on Saturday I drove out to Yaba to the RSPCA to get two adorable five-week-old kittens: the male is yellowish-orange; the female has black-and-white markings. They're great fun.

There are many other things to tell you about, such as:
- the various dinner parties, formal and informal, that we've been to only in the past week,
- our sail out to Tarkwa Beach (outside of Lagos Harbor on the ocean),
- picnic in the Yacht Club shack out there, and surfboarding in marvelous surf; and, oh yes,
- I expect to get a teaching job shortly through the African-American Institute.
- Peter is doing some special compilations and estimates for Lyle, who received a telegram from Max Millikan [Head of Center for International Studies at MIT], asking for info re Nigeria's

My hair is turning yellow and white

economy. (We think something is brewing in the administration and that through Walt Rostow [in the Kennedy administration] and Millikan, moves are being made toward special aid to Nigeria.)

- We are both either very burned or very tanned, and my hair is turning (bleaching) yellow and white.

But that's enough of that. Let me describe to you an average workday—of which there are six in a week. At 7:00 a.m., Columbus wakes us with a knock on the bedroom door. This he does when he comes up to open our windows (in the living/dining room outside our bedroom) and set the table, and then he goes downstairs to prepare breakfast. Mean-

"Let me describe to you an average work day. . ."

while, we crawl out from inside our mosquito netting (which hangs from the ceiling over our double bed, drifting down from a hoop hung from the ceiling) and emerge from our refrigerated bedchamber to the hot, wet tropical outer world of Lagos.

At 7:30 a.m., we sit down to breakfast: watch the fisherpeople paddle into the fish market across Five Cowry Creek where the Yoruba women come to buy; watch the Japanese, Swiss, Dutch, French, Norwegian, Yugoslavian, British, etc., freighters, trawlers, and oilers come in and out of the harbor; read the three daily national newspapers to which we subscribe; and between ourselves and with Columbus make plans for the day. Peter goes to work at 8:00, and oftentimes I take him there so that I might use the car for marketing. The Ministry, where he works, is only a few blocks from our house.

By 8:30 or 8:45, Columbus has made the bed, draped the mosquito netting above the canopy that hangs over the bed, and washed our clothes, which he scrubs every day in the bathtub and then hangs out on a line in back. He will also have washed the dishes and begun sweeping and dusting—a murderous job in these enormous rooms.

The dusting, however, is becoming less of a chore since the Harmattan has just ended, so we don't have to worry about the daily quarter inch of fine sand particles that build up on our furniture. The sand is blown down across the entire country by the winds coming off the Sahara Desert, which, even in Lagos, colors the air and dims the horizon. You remember my telling of our first glimpse of the Harmattan as we flew out of Kano, in the North, and expecting to survey the country as we flew south across it. Instead, we passed through the blanket of sand and dust particles lying just below cloud level, slicing off our portion of the sky completely from the air and earth below! Since it lifted in the past two weeks, I feel as though I have cleaned a pair of very grimy glasses that I had become used to. Now we can see out beyond the mouth of the harbor, and the color of the water itself is so much bluer.

Back to our "day": If it is a market day (twice a week), Columbus (or both of us) goes down to the native market, where he buys all our fruit, vegetables, potatoes, much of the meat, groundnuts (peanuts), and fish. I get the butter, eggs, powdered milk (which we use only for cooking), canned goods, groundnut oil (which we use for cooking and salads), coffee, and bread. The supermarket, of which there are four in the city, has an extremely cosmopolitan assortment of goods coming from virtually every-where in the world.

I fix my own lunch at 12:00, and Peter eats two sandwiches about that time at the office. Columbus prepares them for him to take to work. Then, when PBC gets home shortly after 2:00 (end of workday), we have heaping bowls of mixed, cut-up fruit that Columbus prepares every day. We bathe in fruit; it is so plentiful and good here! Avocados, pawpaws, and oranges grow right in our backyard. In the afternoon, we sail or study and work. Not much studying to do yet, however, till our books arrive.

Luv,

G

Lagos Island is mostly one to two story buildings.

— Letter Eleven —

April 8, 1961

DEF,

Anthropologists talk about the "extended family system" that is dominant in African cultures, because of the importance of ancestors in the everyday lives of the living. Now that I am aware of the wide circulation these none-too-glorious "chats" (letters) are getting, I am tempted to address you as "Dear Extended Family." So, DEF, here's the latest from WAN, or West Africa Nigeria, an acronym displayed above all license plates and by all proper nationalistic business owners and establishments—those that want business, that is.

At a formal dinner party given by the number-three man in the Canadian Embassy (he has a Catamaran, too), we met the Indian High Commissioner and his wife. Found them delightful; and evidently the feelings were mutual. Yesterday an invitation arrived from Mr. and Mrs. Gurbachan Singh to come to cocktails a week from Wednesday at their home. He is a Sikh.

All invitations, incidentally, are very formal, as is even the supposedly most informal dinner. We were invited to have "left-overs" and "Pot Luck" with a British neighbor the other night and found ourselves eating a five-course meal. Dinner, even when they have no guests, rarely starts before 9:00. Cocktail parties START at 7:30 p.m. We don't dare tell our British friends that we normally have had our dinner before they are even starting on their cocktails; and when we are going out to cocktail parties (usually for the ministry or embassy, etc.), we always have a light supper beforehand. Also, speaking of cocktails, the amount of drinking, formal or informal, that goes on around here in the expatriate circles is appalling, so when out, Peter and I consume our share of Fantas (an orange soda manufactured by Coca-Cola) and ginger ales—which are very gingery.

The rains are increasing now, both in volume and in frequency. It is exciting to watch the storms from our vantage point here, which commands views of such a large chunk of the horizon. The storms gather and travel across the harbor with amazing speed. The rains also release hundreds of "sausage flies" that hatch in the evening and are drawn to the streetlights. Schoolchildren who have no light at home, study by these lights and happily grab the insects by their wings and pop them into their mouths!

With the coming of the rains, my garden boy and I have been very busy. Yes, I forgot to tell you, we have a garden boy named Mike, who comes for slightly more than an hour, three times a week. We pay him £1 a month ($2.80). As of tomorrow, he will wash the car every Sunday and polish it every month and a half for an additional 15 shillings. On that score, one really is forced to keep up with the shininess of the Jones's car. They're fanatic about that around here.

Anyway, Mike and I have been transplanting and fertilizing and sowing all sorts of flowers. (I really had to fight for a decent bargain on the manure from the horse boys down at the Polo Club!) Playing Mother Nature is a most rewarding experience in this climate. I planted some seeds in virtual sand two days ago, and already there are some one-half to one-inch sprouts! I wish you could see the bush/trees lining the long driveway to our house; they have the most exotic red, orange, yellow, or purple lily-shaped flowers you've ever seen. [I didn't know at the time that they were hibiscus, which we had only seen in 3-inch pots at home in New England.]

Last weekend was Easter. I wish you could have seen the mobs that packed the road that leads over the bridge by our house. They were on their way out to Victoria Bar Beach (two miles), to the west of the mouth of the harbor on the ocean. It is a tradition for the people of Lagos to migrate to that beach the Monday after Easter for dancing, swimming, singing, and picnicking.

Occasionally a troupe of masked and costumed creatures playing a marvelous variety of drums and followed by a mob—usually children— would pass over the bridge. At about 4 p.m., the tide of people turned and

Holiday on the beach

Only Westerners (including me) are in bathing suits

there were traffic jams and people jams coming back over the bridge, over Five Cowry Creek, until 10 and 11 at night!

Saturday we saw a strange sight, which might have been part of the festivities. A great clatter and shouting caught our attention as we were coming out of the House of Representatives. There we saw a large band of children, all carrying long sticks, which they were using to beat a stuffed burlap sack. An older individual, who was walking at a brisk pace, was dragging this sack behind him. Even Columbus couldn't tell us what that was all about.

Thursday before Easter marked the opening of the budget session of the Legislature. This was a significant and exciting day, since it was the first session of the legislative body since Nigeria's independence. Peter got me a pass to the balcony of the assembly hall of the new House of Representatives. (He works in the old House of Representatives, next door.) I arrived just as the military regiment and police band, in colorful Hausa uniforms, were presenting arms and doing whatever it is that military groups do to entertain a crowd. There was, indeed, a mammoth one, lining all the streets and hanging from every tree and projection from which there was to hang, in anticipation of seeing Zik [President Azikiwe] pass by on his way to the House of Parliament.

Once inside the assembly hall, a modern version of the British House of Parliament—a rectangular room, seating the Government Party

Top: Nigeria's Parliament Building at time of independence; Bottom: Prime Minister, Abubakar Tafawa Balewa

and the Loyal Opposition facing each other—I looked down from the balcony at the marvelous variety of costumes and colors. Only a few people were in Western dress. Nearly all wore the long robes and tunics of their regions, the Hausa being the easiest to pick out because of their white robes, large head turbans, and veil sashes that wind around their necks. Zik's dramatic entrance was preceded by the Chief Justices. (I always giggle to see Africans wearing those silly British wigs, the symbols of their legal profession.)

Everyone rose. The Speaker of the House gave the invocation, of which two-thirds consisted of a request to grant and bestow wisdom on the gracious Queen. (They must think she's awfully stupid!) And then Prime Minister Abubakar Tafawa Balewa, who was sitting in the first seat of the Parliament benches to the right of

the throne(!), rose and mounted the steps to the throne, where Zik was now seated. He handed Zik a manuscript with the speech that Zik delivered. As I understand it, the speech (a sort of State of the Union message) is written by the Government (Prime Minister Balewa) and delivered to Parliament by the Governor-General, Azikiwe (Her Majesty's Representative; an executive post and relatively powerless, rather like a President + Premier setup. In this case, it is a Governor-General + Prime Minister. In England, it is the Queen + Prime Minister). This may help to explain the anachronism of the throne, from which, as Zik stated at the outset, and which was acknowledged by great applause, the first official speech was being given by a Nigerian Governor-General, marking the official end of colonial government.

In all, it told of the Government's plans for development in every sphere of the new nation's life. But the items that met with the greatest enthusiasm were those pertaining to conscious nationalism, such as nationalization of the airlines, a highly impractical move; full taxation of all expatriates (deserved); and plans to start an official Government press. Its intention is to publish a weekly and monthly periodical in which official Government views will be presented, and efforts will be made to extend an "image" of Nigeria abroad. Here, there were some sounds of disapproval by the Opposition, the Action Group (otherwise known as the AG), the predominant party of the Western Region.

One interesting side note was Zik's costume, or perhaps I should say his lack of one. For the first time, he appeared NOT in Nigerian dress but in the (Western) uniform of the Commander-in-Chief of the armed forces, which he is. Most interesting to note was the reaction of our young Nigerian friends. Needless to say, they, who are very nationalistic, were quite distressed. Another interesting aspect of the whole affair was the nature of the crowds. Evidently, when Nigerians are together as a large group, there is nothing they enjoy more than finding an individual or incident that they can, as a group, cheer or boo or razz. Sometimes they do this by chanting, but whatever they do, they do it together. And, if need be, they invent a hero or character out of some passerby to whom they can call or sing or chant the appropriate things.

Raise the flag! The *Sekondi* (a huge freighter, Elder Dempster Lines) just went by carrying our freight—we hope. I guess tomorrow starts the fight to get our things through customs before it is time for us to leave the country. There is one thing I can say for sure about this African country: Nothing, but NOTHING is done in a hurry around here. I am sure it will be years before even the concept of efficiency could be introduced. Imagine a government operating with only a handful of typewriters, practically no office machinery such as duplicators, etc., just a few phones, and a grossly inadequate postal service that can take a month or more to deliver a letter that is sent and delivered right here in Lagos. Add 100-degree heat and humidity, and you'll have a good idea of what it is like here in Nigeria.

The other day I designed, cut out the pattern (drawn on a news-paper), cut out the white cotton piqué I had bought in town, and, with the hand-propelled sewing machine (a Singer I borrowed from Wendy Fluellan), made myself a scoop-neck, sleeveless blouse that ends at the waist, or a little below. It is held in by an elastic tape, run through the back bottom hem. This successful sewing exploit gave me courage to design an adapted version of the Nigerian man's agbada for my own use. Thus, with the aid of my dubious artistic representation, and more with the aid of Columbus's explanation, plus a yard and a half of turquoise blue cotton that we bought in the native market, we conveyed the idea to the tailor who makes Columbus's uniforms.

The tailor comes to the house for consultations, fittings, etc., but Columbus took me to his shop the day we bought the material. It is a typical stall, along with many others on the mud roads in the native quarters, where there seem to be as many goats and chickens walking around as people. There, in a three-sided enclosure (no door) of about six feet by eight feet, he had a crew of five sub-tailors sewing away on treadle machines. He was very surprised to see me—as was everyone else on the street. But funniest of all, I discovered it has created quite a stir at the Yacht Club.

Evidently it has never occurred to these British women to get the local tailors to make some of their clothes. The outfit consists of three-quarter-length smooth-fitting pants—though not tight—and the very full tunic of the agbada, three-quarter sleeves, also full, round, high neck, bottom ending at the hips and worn outside. All this, he did for one pound. For 7 shillings 6 pence, he turned collars[9] and shortened the sleeves on three of Peter's white shirts. We also had him make PBC a new short-sleeved white shirt. Hum-di-dum . . . I'm busy making couturier plans for the future.

Much love, G

Coming from the cobbler shop.

— Letter Twelve (Part 1) —

April 18, 1961
Tfuesday

Dear Extended Family, and those of the immediate F. D.,

Looks like this is going to be another two-letter communication. I really am trying to practice precision and succinctness, but no matter how well I think I am doing, there is never enough room on these things (blue air letters) to finish what I am relating. As Janell [Gretel's sister] would say, "Eh, bien," let's get on with the matters at hand. I'll start out with small talk and with answers to your questions that have been piling up.

First and mdost important: You must have discovered it already from the extra "d" on the word above, and the unusual spelling in the date at the top of this letter—yes, our sea freight (with typewriter) finally arrived.

> *"Our sea freight finally arrived."*

This machine's keys don't always come out as desired. After much prodding, finagling, and haggling with, first, the Ford Foundation (whose services for their personnel here in Nigeria leave something to be desired—meaning the administrative staff here in Lagos), then the shipping agents, and finally the customs officials, it was delivered Saturday morning. With great apprehension, we opened one carton after another, putting off the china and crystal until last. Finally, screwing up our courage, we opened it—the last box. Miraculously, not a thing was broken or damaged! I say "miraculously," for you have never seen a sloppier packing job.

At last I have our wonderful electric typewriter, even if it does mean that I'll have to reaccustom my fingers to be a bit lighter so those extra letters won't creep in. Ah, and the curtains we made for the apartment in Ann Arbor look lovely on our windows here. We put all 12 of them up in the living room (like our Whidbey Island home, three of the four walls are windows), the only alteration being a hem so they won't drag on the floor. And our Philippine wind chimes are perfect for this place. They are hanging in one of the front windows, where there is always a breeze coming off the water to play on their hollow stalks.

In no time, you can be sure, Peter had the hi-fi set up. The only hitch here (for hi-fi, radio, typewriter, and hair clippers) is that the electric current is so different. We bought a transformer much more inexpensively than we had expected (something like £2 10s). The complication comes in the cycles. For example, the revolutions of the turntable are slower, making the music a whole tone and a half below what it should be. So when we play Bizet's Symphony in C, it is really being played in A. Not only that, the tempo is considerably slowed. We have solved that problem, though, by increasing the size of the disk on the turntable so that the same revolution of the rubber band around this disk now turns it faster.

Today, I shall cut Peter's hair. I know you will be shocked to learn that he has had only a bottom trim from a local barber since we left the U.S. No one has raised an eyebrow, either, because by British standards his hair, now, is the length it should be. I wonder if any of our children will get his curls.

Aunt Jan, you asked who is teaching us Yoruba. Sam Akendi, one of the three Nigerians working with Peter, is our teacher. We started out meeting twice a week, but recently other activities have kept us from being regular. Initial instruction, and pronunciation, however, is really all I need. Already I have been able to have sparse communications with some of the women in the market. Knowing certain greetings—"yes," "no," "thank you," counting and money, departing terms, etc.— and immediately the individual warms to you. It means that at least you are trying to meet him or her partly on his or her terms. There is one part of the market (where the pottery and baskets are made and sold) where I have made a decided hit. Probably 'cause I've bought so much from them. Whenever I go there, they all come out and greet me and shake my hand. Greetings, you know, in Yoruba, can be a lengthy process, including much nodding, smiling, laughter while all the proper things are said. Another reason I think they take an interest in me is that I am so young compared with most of the white women one sees in this part of Africa. The Europeans never came here to settle the way they did in East Africa. And when they do come, it is definitely short term.[10]

You also asked about Columbus's wife and children. Yes, they all live right here in the compound behind our house. The servants' quarters are reasonably large, since the five families who live in this area usually have a minimum of two servants each, even if for only one person (not counting their gardeners and/or drivers). We are an exception in having only one servant. It is more customary to have a cook-steward, a "small boy" who performs most of the "steward"

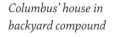

Columbus' house in backyard compound

functions, and a gardener who not only gardens but also washes one's car, polishes and waxes it once a month (which ours does), and cleans the gutters, which, in most cases, are a form of open sewage.

It was pertaining to precisely this point that Columbus and Michael (our gardener) had quite a battle last Friday. Mike hadn't been cleaning the gutter that happens to run directly past the entryway to Columbus' "quarters." On Friday morning, I found Columbus raking out the gutter, and in the conversation that followed, he informed me that this was Mike's job. When Mike arrived for work an hour later, I asked him if he would clean the gutter that day instead of working on the garden. It seems, according to Mike, that this was either the steward's or his wife's job. This rapidly led to insults, then shouts, and within seconds a gathering of all the servants in the entire compound—to support Columbus's argument. Through the mixture of Ibo, Yoruba, Beni, and pidgin English, at full volume, I was aware that this was more a matter of pride than anything else. Both Columbus and Michael are very touchy about their station in

> "...Columbus announced that he was leaving me."

life, in addition to their honesty and stature. Before I knew it, Columbus announced that he was leaving me rather than work with that *@#$!!, and ditto for Michael. Rather abashed by this performance, and shocked at the thought of losing Columbus, I tried to placate them, only to end by escaping the area before they saw my tears. It's all settled now, though, and everyone is back on speaking terms. Peter spoke to Michael, and for an additional 5 shillings a month, he is cleaning the gutter every Monday morning. (It would have been far easier for me to clean it myself, but this business of maintaining one's station, no matter how low, is very important in this part of the world.)

Well, folks, guess I'll have to adjourn to the next air letter.

— Letter Twelve (Part 2) —

Granny asked if we had tropical vegetation like she has in Florida. The answer; Granny, you have probably already read the answer to this in a letter since written. In many ways, the vegetation is very much like what one finds in Florida—such as palms, though the coconut palm is not indigenous, only the oil palm is. There are also pawpaw trees, orange, grapefruit, avocado, and other fruit trees I have spoken of previously. The main difference, I would say, is that, contrary to your statement "I picture your country as barren," this tropical growth, due to the humidity and sunlight, is much denser, bigger, greener, and lusher than anything you could imagine in Florida!

Uncle Ran and Aunt Kay, how was your trip to the Midwest? Wish we had been there to greet you. Speaking of the "Midwest," did you know that last week Nigeria chopped off a chunk of the Western Region and made it into a fourth region called the "Mid-West Region"?

Tante, thank you for the uncanceled stamp. Janell was right. Mother has already sent me back two uncanceled stamps! That should give you some idea of the way the government operates around here. At times I marvel that you get my letters at all. The phone service is equally as incredible. When we were planning to go to Enugu, we wished to call the Institute for Oil Palm Research to let them know we were arriving ahead of time. Though it's only 300 miles away, we had to "put the call in" over a day in advance of the time we wished to speak with them!

Incidentally, because we happen to be in this flat, we are very fortunate to have a phone. Lyle Hansen, with a wife and five children, doesn't have a phone, and probably won't ever get one while out here. Speaking of the phone—well that is an experience to be approached only with great patience and persistence. I find it almost impossible to understand a Nigerian when speaking with one on the phone, though, theoretically we are both speaking English; and I know the Nigerian feels the same way about me.

Still, Tante, I think the answer to your question about the possibility of there being marketable crafts here to export to the U.S. is that there are very few, if any. Most of the work that is done here, whether pottery or other arty crafts (no textiles to speak of), is still so very rough and primitive that it would never sell on a foreign market for anything more than its "primitiveness"—certainly not for being utilitarian in any sense. Some of the sculpture and bush paintings, though primitive, are really quite nice. The Hausa traders also sell attractive leather hassocks (the British call them "poufs") and interesting small bronze figurines. We hope to drive up to Ghana (along the coast through Dahomey and Togo) on a weekend soon to get an elephant lamp or stool that the Ghanaians make out of beautiful blonde wood. [See picture in Letter Twenty-One.] You could send that check directly to us, we can cash it here, and then we'll spend it on just such an art object when we make the trip.

Janell, Jaja Wachuku, who came to your PAC conference, is not the former Minister of Economic Development, he *is* said minister. However, from all we've seen of him lately, he might as well be the *former* minister. You see, Nigeria has no Foreign Minister. That title the Prime Minister (Balewa) retains for his own office. But since it is rather difficult to carry out both functions, Balewa must appoint other top government officials to certain foreign missions. According to all reports, he really has a lot on the ball (you could probably fill us in on that better than we ourselves, by now), and we wish to goodness he would come back home to set his own ministry in order. The Acting Minister Obande is a poor second. I heard him speak in Parliament last week in defense of the Ministry's ongoing projects, including the Ford Foundation advisors. (The ministers must appear before the Parliament for questioning, just as they do in Britain.) It was evident from the lack of respect awarded to him by the Members of Parliament that we would be much better off with Jaja back home.

Yes, some MPs got up in Parliament last week and criticized the Ford Foundation–sponsored economic advisors from the United States. Lyle took it in his stride, but it really upset Wolf. They think it was a "bee" planted in the lackey's bonnets by Pius Okibo, Minister of Economic Development for the Eastern Region. Seems there is some corruption in the government, and with all Lyle's and Wolf's frank and open approach to their research and information—received and given—we think he is afraid that these two American brains are going to uncover something Pius and Co. don't want them to uncover.

> *". . . some MPs got up in Parliament last week and criticized the Ford Foundation sponsored economic advisors from the United States."*

This has been a terrific handicap for the economic advisors, including PBC, due to the jealous secrecy among the three regions (soon to be four) that make up the Federal Government. Now, introduce to this political hotbed some American "experts" whose tools are, of necessity, candid exchange of information and ideas, and eventually someone is bound to accuse them of leaking "secret" information to other regions, and prying into taboo areas. What's more, the virulent nationalism, in the form of Nigerianization of all posts (which I have described earlier), fosters resentment of any foreigner holding a position of influence in the Federal Government. As Peter says, the beginning hasn't really begun.

The real fight will start after the Five-Year Economic Plan is complete (hopefully sometime around August), and it is submitted for Federal Government approval. Two weeks ago, Wolf wrote a preliminary report, which Lyle edited and Peter went over. It was then submitted to the Joint Planning Committee headed by Narayan Prasad, an Indian. Prasad is also Economic Advisor to the Prime Minister and doesn't agree with Wolf's and Lyle's approach to development. So it looks like it is going to be an uphill battle all the way.[11] If you are interested in precisely what the varying "approaches" are, I would be glad to go into that sometime in my simple economic terms.

Clarks, raise the flag! You did a wonderful job selling the car, considering the market et al. Many, many thanks. Also, thank you for sending the $. We are finally in the black again. Hope both of you are feeling better. We had no trouble with the Catamaran. Had it all fixed in four days! Re pictures: We may very well send you the undeveloped film, since it takes six weeks now, sending it to England to be developed. Will write more details later.

— Letter Twelve (Part 3) —

Mom, thank you for the copy of Connecticut Teacher. Your article on E. O.[12] is most interesting, and the introduction very effective. The bed-sheets and Atlantic Monthly have not arrived yet. Will let you know when they come. The CS Monitor wrote us saying that it would be 42 pounds 3 (shillings) and 6 (pence) for the air postage alone, so we decided, "so much for air postage." We're enough addicted that three to four weeks difference doesn't make that much of a difference. (How's that for sentence order?) John Gould's Maine talk is wonderful to the ear out here in the tropics. It's good to have Joseph Harsh back in the house, to say nothing of Stringer, Ripley, Stevens, Frye, Shelton, Ellis, and all the others who have long been CS Monitor "friends." The African coverage and comment is especially interesting. One gets one-sided information reading the newspapers available around here. We also digest every issue of the *New York Times* and the *London Economist*. I also read the *Reporter*, *Foreign Affairs*, and then glance at other periodicals at the American Library here in Lagos. We are probably better read than we were at home on U.S. national affairs, but our appetites are insatiable for news about JFK and his egghead friends—a number of whom are acquaintances of ours (e.g., Kermit Gordon, David Bell, Walt Whitman Rostow[13]—can't top him for a good economist). And textbooks, well, they are positively nonexistent here. I have come to my wits' end trying to find texts in several fields recently. My biggest regret is that we didn't bring more of our library out with us. Do you suppose you could get some books for us?

Uncle Archer, in deference to your request that I incorporate a little more "diary form" in these letters, I shall try to be more subjective. My biggest problem, however, is whenever I start relating something we have done, I am reminded of one million other things, observations, and peculiarities about Nigeria that I want to describe to you. Then comes the end of the paper and I haven't finished my tale. This was particularly true of our trip to Enugu.

Yes, we did get there. We stayed in the only "rest house" in the capital of the Eastern Region! It is a rather dirty town, lacking all the brilliance and wealth of water-rimmed Lagos. But the native dwellings were considerably higher quality than those of any Yoruba town in the Western Region. Peter talked with people in the Ministry of Economic Development but was unable to collect much information from them. We had dinner both nights with different Ford advisors to the regional government. One of the mornings, the advisor, or rather technical expert, from Seattle, Washington, who is drawing up the government civil-service training manual, took me over to the Eastern Region's only training school, where the entire police force and, theoretically, all incoming government administrators, are trained. It is a converted house on a dusty side street. The two-story house

On the road to Nsukka,
Eastern Region

has about a dozen rooms on each floor, if that many, with rough cement floors, walls, and ceilings, folding chairs, and a blackboard in each room. The bell is a handheld table model, and the teaching is in good, old authoritarian, text-oriented, rote-style memorization. (In parts of this country, one is considered "educated" if one is literate.)

From there, we drove out past occasional leper colonies, and then through some beautiful hilly, wooded country to Nsukka, where, last July, the government started building the Eastern Region's University of Nigeria. (Each region aspires to have its own university. The West already has its university in Ibadan, and the North will be starting one soon, probably in Kaduna.) Here, on a wide-open plain, not far from Zik's "country home"—a sumptuous palace—lies the brand new university. It opened, by some miracle, considering the disarray of the building, administrative, and academic plans, last October.

I have probably written to you about the aid ICA [now AID, the Agency for International Development] is giving the university through a contract with Michigan State (our foes from East Lansing). This, in turn, has supplied the university with a bunch of incompetent ugly Americans, who are creating all sorts of havoc by demanding living conditions and privileges that are positively outrageous, considering the circumstances. Many of these individuals, who came out here because nobody wanted them at home, and because ICA offered them so much money, have set themselves up as "advisors," a luxury the university cannot afford when they haven't begun to fill their staff quota, and the teachers they *do* have are so terribly overburdened by numerous and large classes.[14] We had lunch with Phil and Mary Bordinat and their two children (he is head of the English Department on direct hire from Michigan State through the African-American Institute), plus a Mr. Fashola, a Nigerian, who teaches economics. Wolf may ask him to do some research for the [Five-Year] Plan. Just one more note about the university. Essentially it is a political baby, born in the Azikiwe household. This may help to explain its location, so far from any center of civilization, other than "His Eminence's" country home.

Small talk: No luck on a teaching job yet. I'm getting very discouraged. The kittens are growing very fast, and one of them, Dara, still isn't housebroken, much to my disgust. We didn't do so well in Saturday's race. I sailed this time, starting out at the head of the fleet; and then, due to poor maneuvering in the tides (which flood and ebb in and out of this harbor like a raging river), brought us in last! Three other boats, because of the difficult sailing, had already been disqualified.

Sunday we fixed a picnic lunch. We two, plus Roy Fluellan (whose wife, Wendy, is now back in England with their two children, 12 and 13, for their vacation), sailed out to Tarkwa Bay, a cove on the Atlantic. On the other side of the mouth of the "bay" is ocean beach: all accessible only by boat. As before, we surfed on boards in the waves, swam in the cove with our water goggles, flippers, and snorkels, and looked at fish looking at us,

University buildings funded by U.S. ICA (AID)

Michigan State
'advisor' in front of
newly built faculty
housing. Village on hill
in background.

ate our picnic in the Yacht Club shack. A short storm freshened the air, and then we sailed back down the length of the harbor to home.

Roy suggested having tea, true Englishman that he is, on the Yacht Club lawn. An hour later, PBC and I had baked and frosted a gorgeous chocolate-mint cake, thanks to Duncan Hines. I doubt that Columbus would approve, but we were safe, since Sunday is his day off. He, incidentally, is quite a good cook . . . and a cosmopolitan one at that! Having worked for Dutch, Swiss, French, and Americans in addition to British people, he has become a connoisseur of national tastes. I am benefiting by learning how to cook some very interesting dishes. I doubt that I shall bring home any African dishes, though, since their tastes and ours and their foods and ours are a "twain" that shall never meet.

In closing, here is a report typical of the daily stuff in the newspapers: "A hunting bag recovered at Warife, Eastern Nigeria, has been found to contain a human skull and a dismembered right hand."

Lovely, what?

G

— Letter Thirteen —

April 24, 1961
Monday

Well, DEF,

 While you were celebrating "Library Week" last week, with the concurrent intellectual growth implied, we were celebrating "Akogun Week" and the continuation of ignorance and superstition, of which it is evidence. The "Akogun" is a half-naked, raffia-skirt-clad masquerader who paints his face in white and gray to hide his identity and covers his body with whitewash. He is supposed to have supernatural powers inherited from his great-grandfather, Alatish the Great. Alatish, who hailed from Ijebu Igbo but settled down at Abeokuta, was an herbalist and a gunpowder dealer. He is supposed to have been able to cure any kind of illness by reciting certain "inaudible incantations." Now his "great-grandsons" come out during this one week each year to bless supplicating women who are barren or have "sickly" children. To quote a comment in the paper: ". . . the average woman in all these towns seriously believes that once they have been blessed by an Akogun, their period of mystery is over."

 Referring to the newspaper, I have cut out a few short articles that will give you a much more vivid picture of aspects of this part of Africa than I could describe. For example: You may have read, two and one half months ago, about the elections in the Cameroun [currently spelled Cameroon] (eastern border of Nigeria) when the Northern Cameroun chose to form an independent state, which is now the Cameroun Republic. Well, the report is about terrorists from the Cameroun Republic "armed with spears, swords, bows and arrows and led by a chief from the Cameroun Republic . . . ." No words can tell how remote and isolated most areas of the Cameroun are because of the steep-sided 14,000-foot mountains that characterize that country.

 Here's a lovely item: "A palm wine tapper . . . took a cutlass and matcheted his wife," chopping off her two hands because she had sold some gari[15] for 10 shillings 6 pence instead of one pound, "as ordered by him." (The difference is 9s 6d, a little over $1.00.) When her sister came up "in defense, she was equally matcheted. Akpan told the court that he was influenced by the devil."

 A letter to the editor by Sola-Ade Talabi of Lagos says:

> One of the things that has always induced a lasting respect in me for the late Mazi Mbonu Ojike is his uncompromising and infectious spirit of nationalism—boycott the boycottables.

My present concern is the improper use of such titles as "Mr.," "Esquire," "Honourable," "Sir," etc. The most unoriginal and monotonous of this short list is "Mr.," and with my deepest respect to Mbonu Ojike, I am recommending that the word be dropped immediately from our local vocabulary, and if possible, some more homely title like "Mazi" be substituted. The Englishman, perhaps for reasons of traditional conservatism, may love the hackneyed tag like "Esq." and so on being attached to his name, but in the present day Nigeria, it is anachronistic.

There are other reports, such as six men being charged with selling four girls into slavery, of which I have already spoken. Last week there was reporting on more slave trading having been discovered. Some people are running into trouble because of the Yoruba custom "for a man to pledge his own son for money he borrowed from a money lender." In this case, 15 pounds 10 shillings.

So much for the blood and gore. Here is the latest from the waterfront: Placed third in Saturday's race. No race on Wednesday, too calm. Saturday, however, there was enough of a blow to down two masts! We do so enjoy our Cat. Still no teaching position for me. I have obviously come to the most developed part of this undeveloped country. Evidently everyone wants to teach here, and no one wants to teach anywhere else in the country—ironic, 'cause we'd give our eyeteeth to be able to live in the bush and learn what that part of Africa is really like.

"I shall be working full time . . . for the African-American Institute [choosing] . . . applicants . . . for scholarships . . . to American universities."

Meanwhile, however, starting next Monday, I shall be working full time, and possibly overtime, from the way it sounds, with the African-American Institute. Mr. Hill, who is a very intelligent and pleasant American negro and who runs the Institute (which has been open in Lagos since January), will be running a battery of tests in all three regions. This is a part of the narrowing-down procedure for the more than 1,000 applicants competing for the 73 scholarships that are now offered for Nigerian students to study at U.S. universities. (One of these scholarships, Mother, is from the University of Hartford through us. I simply gave all the material to Mr. Hill and he wrote to the President of the U. of H. from there.) When you see him next, do tell him how pleased they are to have another scholarship. Scholarships are like gold out here. My job will be tabulating results and compiling other academic marks and teachers' reports on the individual students. This will last about a month. And THEN I hope something regarding teaching will have materialized.

Aunt Jan asked what we do about drinking water. There are two—no, three—schools of thought. One says: Buy only "purified" water. Another says: Boil all your water and then keep it in the "fridge"—as the British call it. The third says: Aww, just drink it from the tap! We are number three. Were we anywhere but Lagos, however, we would not only have to boil it, but strain it first. As for salads . . . well, we're still on the fence about that. Some people use potassium permanganate in the water in which they wash their lettuce. Others (Ann Hansen, for one) do the above in addition to scrubbing the poor leaves in Tide twice! Other reliable sources insist that potassium permanganate does absolutely nothing. Doctors will argue on both sides of the fence. And we have been told by Roy Fluellan, who is not an alarmist and has lived here for 15 years, that no amount of washing, scrubbing, etc., will do. Unless one can peel or cook the food in some way, it is not safe. (He had amoebic dysentery that almost killed him.) We have eaten lots of lettuce, but after his tale—I still don't think anyone knows—I bought some lettuce seeds and soon we'll have our own and won't have to wonder whether it was fertilized with "night soil." Our milk, which we use only for cooking and the kittens, we "make" out of imported powder. That's amazing, not drinking milk, when we consumed two gallons per week before coming!

I'll write another letter tomorrow.

Love,

G

Mansion, probably that of a cocoa merchant

— Letter Fourteen (Part 1) —

May 2, 1961

DEF,

What has happened to my good intentions? That letter I was going to write "tomorrow" has turned into a week! Ah, well, here it is.

I started a new job yesterday. Since I worked so fast, I am home today, and will go back tomorrow and the rest of the month. I am helping the African-American Institute here in Lagos tabulate and compile the aggregate scores of the 3,000-odd applicants for the 74 American college scholarships. Mr. Hill, the director, is this month administering the tests in all the regions of the country, and we are working like mad to keep up with him so that the results can be announced as soon as possible. It's very tedious, stupid work, but most interesting to see how the organization works.

On Friday, Peter, Lyle, Wolf, and Ebenezer Iwuagwu went to Ibadan for a big confab with the Western Regional Ministry of Economic Development to find out what they are thinking and to try to coordinate their plans with those of the other regions and the Federal Government for the period of 1962 to 1967. They were there Friday night, stayed at the university, and then came home Saturday afternoon, just in time so Peter could race. (Ah, yes, can't miss the all-important sailing events.)

During this time, Columbus and I went down to the local market and bought 120 feet of orangeish-brown vellum material, out of which I made the world's most exquisite bedspread to cover our two beds that are placed together. I made it look more like a bedspread by using yellow bias tape between each of the four, yard-wide panels that run from the head to the foot, making the seam a yellow strip in each case. It looks very nice with the Hausa hamper and the five enormous straw mats that are on the floor around the bed. (Each one is six square feet, but they still look lost in this barn of a room.)

To finish the story of Ibadan, Peter expects to be going up for the day on Thursday, and this time I may accompany him. I'm most curious to see the town and the university. Your comment, Mother, about all the news from Nigeria coming out of Ibadan is most interesting. Certainly intellectually, it is the "center" of the country. And politically, too, it is very important, the Western Region being most "Westernized" of the three (now four) regions, and Ibadan being the center of the Western Region.

Our social life, of late, has included a number of dinner parties, both formal and informal. One was a cocktail party, a political one involving Ministry of Economic Development people. It could have served diplomatic

Top: Ibadan
Bottom: Pot market

Ibadan's active market life

purposes if we wished to use the occasion as such for making contacts, buttonholing someone on an issue, laying the groundwork for future negotiations with certain people (Lyle is number-one maneuverer at these affairs). But for many of the British civil servants, such an event is purely social. They don't think about their work any more than they have to. The new Nigerian officials who are gradually replacing them, however, are reasonably engaged in their work, and thus usually interesting to talk to. But even here, there are many ambitious politicians who are not qualified for their jobs.

Back to the dinners: They have been mostly social affairs with friends, new and old. We had Roy Fluellan (neighbor, sold us the Cat, head of customs) and Eric *"Our social life . . ."* Coleman (also Cat enthusiast and director of aviation) here for a reasonably formal meal, à la British style, in deference to them. We broke down and bought our first bit of imported meat, in this case a roasting chicken from Maryland. It cost more than a dollar a pound. Now you know why we eat mostly local meat, even though it is tough and scrawny. (You should see the chickens Columbus brings home—alive, of course.) No matter how much we would like to have a nice cut of meat occasionally, the price makes it absolutely prohibitive.

The Europeans here are extravagant about their food, insisting on having everything as it is "at home," instead of learning to use local produce. The only real problem, and it isn't necessarily the quality of the meat, is that the only kind of meat one can buy in the local market—and I'm not kidding—is filet steak and stewing steak. If it's pork, it is chops, tenderloins, shoulder, and shanks, never any ribs, roasts, bacon, etc. On general principle, I don't go with Columbus to the meat market. The bloody heads, entrails, flies, pickled and smoked bush creatures, etc., just don't make for ease of mind when eating what you buy. We operate on the principle that what we don't know will make the meat taste a lot better. Needless to say, most of our dishes are stews, meat pies, etc. Soooooo, we had roast chicken that night, and angel food cake (thanks to Betty Crocker), which amazed these cake mix-less Britishers.

Sunday night, Roy came over again and we roasted some hamburger (again, I'm not really sure what that ground meat was) over charcoal, Sunday being Columbus's day off. This was the first time Roy had partaken of such a strange custom and such a strange food. Last night we had the Hansens and the Olmsteads (Chuck Olmstead is one of the MIT Fellows over here for two years, working with the Development Corporation) for a wonderful Dutch meal that Columbus prepares out of rice, dried spices and vegetables, soy sauce, onions, and cubed beef all mixed together. One scoops it up with exciting shrimp crisps that are made by frying small chips to make them expand into light chips (sort of the way popcorn pops out).

He also made a lemon meringue pie that was delicious. Best of all, we got Columbus a magnificent white formal uniform that has large gold buttons, which he wears to serve for these occasions—but always barefoot.

Before a dinner party, we both fuss around preparing things. The nicest part of entertaining with Columbus is that I don't have to spend half of the party in the kitchen once the guests arrive. AND there are no dishes to wash after they all leave. We've also had two dinners out, one being at Wolf's with the Egnatoffs and their young son, Bill. John Egnatoff is Canadian advisor to the Federal Government on technical teacher training. After dinner, Bill played some flute concertos, with Wolf accompanying on the only piano in Nigeria. (It has been tropicalized.) Then we played some duets, I on my recorder.

The agbada I had the tailor make for PBC is perfect nightwear. I also had him make me another pair of three-quarter-length trousers, white with turquoise, crisscrossed ties down the bottom of the sides of the legs, and crisscrosses in front, left and right, over my abdomen like sailor pants. I can wear this with the turquoise top to the other outfit he made. Most successful! Right now I'm making a white sailor blouse from the leftover material of my own design, plus a jumper-dress outfit . . . material from Holland.

On to part two.

Love,

G

— Letter Fourteen (Part 2) —

I swear, if this country has any more holidays, there won't be any days left for working. We have at least one or two a month. The reason is that Nigeria celebrates both Christian and Muslim holidays (the latter of which are plentiful), in addition to celebrating all the British holidays, such as the Queen's Birthday a week ago Friday. The big ceremony (with a representative from the royal family) was to have taken place on the Race Course, which is right in front of the House of Representatives, where Peter works. It was scheduled to take place at 7:30 a.m. with a band, horse guard parade, military marching and colors, gun salutes, and all. They hold it at this hour because if it were much later in the day, the heat would probably prostrate most of the demonstrators and spectators. We were even issued special tickets for the bandstand. But then it rained that night and the Race Course was wet in the morning. Thus, it had to be canceled. Last year, evidently, all the British colonial servants took part in great fancy uniforms with long swords and all the protocol.

Today is the day we—the United States, that is—were to have sent our first man up in space. I wonder if we will. I wish all the publicity could have been canned. Everyone is waiting breathlessly here. Columbus's reaction to [Yuri] Gagarin's jaunt was "before you know it the Russians will have men on the moon, subjugate all the moon people, and charge exorbitant fees to non-Russian tourists, if they let them in at all."

We've been doing our bit of propagandizing right here in Nigeria with this U.S. "cultural" program, which is a crackerjack ice-skating troupe that brings its own ice-making equipment. There have been many pictures in the papers, and the reaction of the average Nigerian to this strange and unbelievable sport is a positive delight. I bought tickets for Columbus and his family, because I knew they couldn't afford them, on the condition that they get themselves to the stadium and back. They went Sunday night, and he couldn't wait till morning to come tell us what amazing things he had seen. The antics and contortions he went through telling us about it, and his repeated exclamations of: "I never dream of such a thing! I never find words to describe such a thing!" had us laughing and exclaiming right along with him. He is sure that they used some kind of propulsive mechanism to give them the speed they had on the ice. The ice, itself, was an object of great wonder. It is two days since, now, and he still talks of it as though he'd been to the moon and back. I find him chuckling and exclaiming to himself as he rehearses each dance and clown act. We are going on Friday.

"Today is the day we—the United States, that is—were to have sent our first man up in space. I wonder if we will."

The weather has been beautiful lately. Aside from two terrifying line squalls that bring with them high-velocity winds and rain—and usually come in the night—we have had sunny weather and a nice breeze for sailing. Guess the rainy season "proper" hasn't started yet. On the whole, it has cooled down considerably to the 80s and even high 70s, with perhaps some letup in humidity. Saturday, however, the breeze took a vacation and the entire fleet, which was sailing a combined race (i.e., not in classes) for a cup, had to struggle even to get over the starting line, since we were close-hauled with a very weak wind and a very strong flood tide against us—enough to make one stand still. The Cats (Catamarans) always suffer in this kind of competition against other classes when there is little wind and most of the legs are either close-hauled or running free. Our fastest point is between a close reach and a beam reach. Then, with a moderate breeze, we can just scream right along, as all the other classes look smaller and smaller in the distance behind us. Now, Mom, we wait anxiously for the arrival of the sailing book you sent us.

Speaking of books arriving, we are sending out birthday presents to you, Daddy, and Aunt Jan. We were feeling very pleased with ourselves for having gotten the presents so far in advance, but when we went to send them out, we discovered that they will still be at least a month late. We have taken heed, and are preparing to do our Christmas shopping so we can get the stuff out in time for it to reach you!

Janell asked about the reaction here to our new president's policies of wooing the underdeveloped and uncommitted at the expense, sometimes, of old allies. Well, there is no doubt about the enthusiasm for Kennedy and his program so far (as opposed to Ike) among informed people here. They are also pleased to see Adlai Stevenson in the UN (despite Jaja's retorts). Kennedy's and Williams's proclamations about "Africa for the Africans," the strong condemnations against South Africa and Portugal, and the vigorous leadership JFK has taken in his stand on negro civil rights and positions in the government and elsewhere have all been widely publicized. I'm sure I could tell you much more about the negroes who now hold office in the U.S. government and what's being done or not done about discriminatory practices in the U.S. than you would ever learn from reading *your* local papers. But, despite the need and requests, there is suspicion about any foreign aid—for fear that it might be a form of colonialism. And this Cuban fiasco has put blot number 1 on Kennedy's name. This is how an editorial in last week's paper put it.

> In the space of one single week, President Kennedy has dealt a mortal blow to the carefully built up image of himself as a realistic and liberal statesman who is aware of the grievous errors of the Eisenhower Administration, and is prepared to right the wrongs already done. People all over the world who had expected a new and vigorous moral leadership from him must be feeling sadly disappointed by America's contribution to last week's events in Cuba.

It is an incredible article, and, although biased, presents facts that the embarrassed American cannot deny. A paragraph in the middle of the article says:

> Well, Mr. President, are you saying that a sovereign government has no right to call for outside help to halt an inspired revolt—which is why America went to Lebanon two years ago and is in Laos today?

And then, at the end:

> "No amount of protestations by President Kennedy and [Secretary of State] Dean Rusk that the U.S. did not intervene in Cuba will convince a shocked world, except perhaps that portion of it populated by British Tories, whose envoy at the U.N., Sir Patrick Dean, upheld America's denial, because "long experience" has shown America never told lies. But Sir Patrick must have such a weak memory, otherwise he should not have forgotten,

so soon, the BIG LIE over the U-2 incident [16] . . . . Not only Fidel Castro should be on his guard, but all nationalist leaders of new independent states, lest they are strangulated by new imperialism headed by America."

Wheeu!!

   Love,

      G

Marina Road coming from center of Lagos toward Victoria Island

— Letter Fifteen —

May 8, 1961
Monday p.m.

DEF,

For the sake of space (concerning sailing), henceforth I shall put our finishing place in the Saturday race and Wednesday race in a corner of the letter. Keep in mind that the Wednesday races are unofficial, with mass starts (40 to 50 coming across the starting line), and the Saturday races are for points, cups, prizes, etc., raced by class. I shall also indicate who was skippering. Here's hoping you can figure it out.

With the coming of the rainy season (not really here yet), we are having frequent fierce, spectacular line squalls with winds that make one wonder that any structures are left standing. Thunder nearly deafens one and lightning takes its toll in lives every time right in this area.) Believe me, everything you may have read about the intensity of tropical storms is absolutely true. I have never seen such long, jagged, crackling, NEAR bolts of lightning, nor ever before been literally jolted and thumped by the volume of such thunderclaps. From our vantage point overlooking the harbor and the city, we watch these gusty, wet, deafening, blinding performances of nature as from a control tower. (Now if only we felt as though we could control it all.) No wonder the native African holds so tenaciously to his deistic beliefs in gods of the Water, Rain, Punishment, etc. Actually, what I had meant to say, instead of all this, was that of late we have had a few days with strong enough winds that when out in our Cat and screaming along on a reach (between a close and a beam reach), we were clocked as going between 18 and 20 knots per hour!

Yesterday, Sunday, we started and ended the day by fishing out in front (i.e., off the Yacht Club lawn), where we have seen people pull in jack fish and even a 200-pound barracuda. PBC had bought me a wonderful little pole, line, and tackle, and Columbus got some prawns in the market (which we often eat instead). Peter has an extra pole of Lyle Hansen's. Total catch: one 54-inch eel on my hook. Urrrk! The reason for the fishing hours was primarily because those were about the times of tide changes. The currents here at other hours are really too strong for one to fish from shore.

Peter's work right now is to compile all the statistics he can collect on the past 10 years of every kind of import to Nigeria. By the end of the week he shall have made projections of the trend for the coming 10 years. He is stalled right at the moment because he has to have his present charts transferred to stencil sheets for duplication. The quality of the secretarial staff being what it is in Nigeria, one cannot expect even the best secretary to follow what to us seem like simple directions. So he is doing much of this mundane work himself, a terrible waste of the government's time, using him for such tasks. My short experience at the African-American Institute has also made me aware of these elementary but basic staffing problems. To give one example: We have two Nigerians on the staff, one of whom received secretarial training in London, and neither of them can file information in alphabetical order.

Speaking of the Institute, we are all working very hard. I come home exhausted from our six-hour day. I'm right in the middle of preparing the profile charts of all those students who passed their Preliminary Scholastic Aptitude Tests (our College Boards) and who will be coming back for interviews. Though it's tedious, I certainly am learning a lot about the backgrounds and qualifications of the students who are applying. Essentially, what I am doing now is reading over their applications, two teacher recommendations, and their principal's report, and then condensing it all into a few words on one sheet. Occasionally I read the autobiographical sketch and the "25 years from now" essays. Most informative! Goodness, the ambition and awareness of national goals of these young people! The final paring-down will be heartbreaking. My wholehearted sympathies are with you, Mother, on your review and selection of the handful of students from the many applicants for the state teacher colleges. There are just too many qualified people who will go unaided.

> *"Goodness, the ambition and awareness of national goals of these young people."*

Right at the moment, Peter is attending his first French class at the Alliance Française. I enquired about it (held in a ramshackle house right behind the House of Representatives) and got the text, which I am pleased is using the oral method, and now he shall be attending from five to six on Monday and Thursday, with me tutoring in between.

Last Tuesday we went to the movies, our first time. After all the terrible stories we had heard about the local cinemas, we had been hesitant; in fact, we were delighted. As with all Lagos cinemas, the building is a four-walled frame under the stars. So if it rains, they get no business. The floor is dirt, and the chairs are regular folding card-table chairs. The films? Well, they are almost inevitably old third- or fourth-rate American Westerns or who-done-its. Or else they are Indian films, which seem to be very popular. This one happened to be *Oliver Twist*. It was magnificent, with Alec Guinness. Peter had seen it but enjoyed it as much the second time.

On Thursday, PBC, Lyle, Wolf, and I went to Ibadan. Their conference with the Ministry of Economic Development planners was very successful, as was mine with Dr. Taylor, head of the Institute of Education at the University of Ibadan. I had written to him a month or two ago, asking about research projects in which they might be engaged, and in which I could participate while preparing for my master's thesis. He had been on leave in the U.K., evidently, and failed to answer me on returning. At any rate, he remembered my letter and was very pleasant. By the time I left his office, I had been informally "hired"—to the extent that all my expenses will be paid and all possible relevant research material and individuals will be put at my disposal—to do a study of the last ten years of teacher education in Nigeria. The last one was done in 1948, and things are really beginning to pop in that area now. Of course, I am delighted and also pleased that I had had a chance to edit Dr. Shaplin's report on just that subject for the Ford Foundation. I have, therefore, already done the initial research as concerns present-day trends.

The university, incidentally, is quite lovely, at least the part I saw. And I'm so pleased to find a library that has more than a few dozen current publications. I expect we shall be using it often. Dr. Taylor got me a special card. Only wish there weren't 90 very dangerous miles between Lagos and Ibadan. It's a treacherous, curvy, bumpy road peopled by treacherous lorry drivers. I think mad French or Italians must have taught the Nigerians their road manners and habits.

Love, G

[Penciled-in on the margin] *Race: Saturday, about 10th (3rd Cat). Late start. P=skipper.*

Scene on the way to Ibadan

— Letter Sixteen —

May 20, 1961
Saturday morning

DEF,

I have been mildly delinquent this last week by not having written until today, but then I don't feel too guilty since there has been no word from that side of the Atlantic for two weeks. I had good intentions of writing. Then, every single night this past week, instead of getting home at 3 p.m., I didn't finish up at the African-American Institute until between 6:00 and 7:30 p.m. This has been one solid week of interviewing, from 8:30 a.m. to 7:30 p.m., the semifinalist candidates for the scholarships. The scholarship winners will receive full tuition from their host universities in the U.S., travel expenses from the Nigerian government, and living expenses from the African-American Institute. Over four years, this amounts to something like a $12,000 investment in every pupil. I must say I am not very impressed with the caliber of the supposed "cream" we were interviewing and who will be receiving all these benefits.

Working with the scholarship board has been a most informative experience. In all, there are about a dozen judges, over half being Nigerian, and rather illustrious Nigerians at that. The two Americans on the scholarship screening board were Rixford Snyder, Director of Admissions at Stanford University, and Helen McCann, Director of Admissions at Barnard. There was a decided difference in the way they voted and the way the Nigerian members of the board voted for the candidates. This was slightly baffling to the Americans, but that is because they completely missed the tribal, regional, and family undercurrents that influenced many of the Nigerian panelists' questions, and, consequently, the way they voted . . . elements that a stranger to this country would have completely missed.

One of the judges, and the only Northerner on the panel, Mallam Issi Wali, is in the Ministry of Foreign Affairs. He was a delegate with Balewa to the Monrovia Conference and was actually Deputy Secretary-General of the conference. In a most interesting conversation with him, I learned of the moderate tone of the meetings, partly thanks to the absence of Nkrumah [President of Ghana] and Sékou Touré [President of Guinea]. He said that they made a conscious effort not to close the door on these men, but he confirmed my suspicion that the strong declaration of noninterference by one African country into the affairs of another was a definite slap at Ghana's boss [Nkrumah].

Peter's French lessons are progressing slowly but surely. I help him out with occasional drilling sessions. He is going through a period of slight frustration working with Lyle and Wolf. Lately they have been using him more as a messenger boy than a research assistant. I think, however, that once he latches onto a thesis topic and starts getting his teeth into it, things will change.

Right now, we spend far too much time with our boat, or simply relaxing, which is somewhat justified in this climate. I have yet to see "cool" weather come. Your talk of spring and blossoms has been our only reminder that these are the months of April and May, instead of it being one long year of July and August. The advantage of this, however, is that our investment in a boat is fully justified, since, instead of sailing two to three months out of the year, we sail all 12 months of the year.

Columbus got the shock of his life the other day when he stepped on our scales. He had expected to weigh about 12 (stones that is, according to the archaic English weight system where a "stone" equals 14 pounds). Instead, he saw something like <u>165</u>! Let's see, then, according to the English, I weigh 7.5 stones and Peter weighs about 12.5 stones. Yes, we've both lost some weight since coming here. Peter has had his bouts with what we think was malaria a month ago (didn't last long) and then some tummy upset day before yesterday.

Here is the latest on the races. A week ago, Wednesday, when all classes compete against each other, I won: first out of 30 or 40 boats, including our handicap. Then on Saturday, Peter, skippering against our class, pulled a spectacular feat after dropping down to 7th or 8th on the first two legs (because we sailed in the wrong part of the tide, something the experienced sailors in this harbor knew about) and then passed everyone in the fleet but the boat in first place, and almost overtook him, too. Thus, we won second place, gaining us a slew of points. Then this last Wednesday, I skippered (against all classes again) and placed 4th. Should have done much better. Having learned from my mistakes, I skippered again this Saturday, and this time we WON a Saturday race—more points. (Points are accumulated over six months from Saturday races. At the end of the period, the boat with the most points wins a cup. This is for consistency.) Next week, PBC will skipper in both Wednesday and Saturday races.

About a month ago, Columbus and I saw an interesting thing. We were out in back of the house talking while he was polishing all our shoes when we heard some drumming and singing that got progressively louder. It was coming from in front of the Yacht Club. We grabbed the binoculars and ran out to the water's edge, where approaching us from the other side of the harbor came a very large native canoe carrying 22 passengers, all dressed in their best clothes. As usual, the children were naked. Their song was more of a chant as the drums throbbed out intricate (at least to me) rhythms. Columbus and one of the boat boys explained to me that these were Ijaws (a tribe that lives on the water in the Eastern Region) who live

Water taxi as seen from our windows

up the creeks directly across from us, and who traditionally make their living from the water by fishing.

What I was watching right in front of us, as it was, for they came right up to within 50 yards of the bank to perform their ceremony—was their annual sacrifice to the gods of the water according to the instructions of their Juju man. The drums stopped and the singing stopped. A man up toward the bow of the boat leaned forward onto one knee, delivered a five-minute "sermon," holding out over the water in each hand what looked like two silver bowls with some food in them. When he was through, he submerged the bowls in the water and brought his hands up empty. The drumming and singing/chanting started again. Everyone picked up their paddles and the colorful craft turned to re-cross the harbor. Columbus, who, like most Nigerians, has a terrible fear of the water, regaled me with many other Ijaws customs. One custom is the practice of throwing four- to five-day-old babies into the water. If the child swims back to safety, he or she is considered a part of the tribe. If not, the baby drowns—rightly so, it is felt, for this means that the child is not truly one of them.

Love,

G

— Letter Seventeen —

May 29, 1961
Monday morning

DEF,

The rains came down in such torrents this morning at breakfast time
we thought the roof (which is none too stable nor waterproof) would come
down with it! All this time, Columbus was scurrying around muttering
about how it always rains like this on Mondays—his day for washing the
bed linen, which is quite true. Peter waded his way out to the car. By 9 a.m.
it had started to clear up and our garden boy was already out busily scrubbing down the gutters.

> *"Muslim holidays . . . the yacht club had a day long race."*

Last week, Thursday and Friday were Muslim holidays (the Muslim "Christmas"), so of course everyone
else took the two days off from work. Thus, on Thursday
the Yacht Club had a daylong race up around Abechi
Island. The start was at 10:30 in front of the club. Peter
skippered and had a beautiful start, being first across the
line and then shooting out ahead of the fleet across the harbor to Badagry
Creek. The morning was spent tacking up the creek about seven miles to
the end of Abechi Island, where a finish line was constructed for us. We
came across the line 41 minutes ahead of the second boat, everyone having
run aground on an average of at least twice. All the Cats were at least 10
minutes ahead of the other classes.

We dropped anchor and went ashore, where we were greeted by three
dozen little naked "pickins" and their nearly as naked elders, who had gathered under a spacious grove of oil palms to watch us land. We spread out
our towels and sat on our centerboards. We then picnicked while the rest
of the fleet came in and crossed the thin stretch of land on which we were
situated. There we amused ourselves for a while in the ocean surf that was
pounding ferociously on the other side of the bar. When time came for us
to clear camp and set sail for the start of the race home, there must have
been at least four dozen black youngsters (if nothing else, they usually
wear a string of beads around the waist, neck, and ankles—to preserve
health, ward off evil spirits, etc., according to beliefs of the various tribes)
descended on the bottles, paper, and debris left by our English compan-
ions like vultures on a dead carcass.

The starting gun found us stalled on the line with a broken tiller bar.
By the time we had performed the needed repairs and were underway,
the rest of the fleet was rounding the island far across the creek. Then,
within 15 minutes we had caught them and passed everyone, including

all the Cats. The wind had shifted enough so that instead of running free we could sail on a reach most of the way down the creek. By the end of an hour and a quarter, the nearest Cat was at least two miles behind us. THEN, unwittingly, we took the wrong creek, and while we fought our way back up it to right our mistake, all the Cats passed us. Nonetheless, we passed them all again, and finished just a minute and a half behind boat number one. Despite all this, we didn't have a chance to win the day's race, since the handicap on the Cats made it impossible, unless there had been a gale wind and we had not had to beat to windward over half the course. (Handicaps are set on triangular courses, not straight upwind and downwind legs.)

Peter had a cold at the beginning of the week, so on Wednesday I skippered with a gentleman crewing for me who had been in a Cat only twice before. We were missing a batten, and the luff of the mainsail was too loose. Nonetheless, I got a good start, was first around the first mark, then no one passed me the rest of the entire race! That night, since Peter was still feeling rather punk, we missed the cocktail party given by Jaja Wachuku for the Ministry of Economic Development to meet the visiting NYU professors. Tuesday, though, we had cocktails with the Middletons. He is a junior officer at the American Embassy. His grandmother has evidently met the Clarks, since she is living in the Hartford area. They are nice, but not very popular out here.

Ebenezer Iwuagwu, who works in the same office with Peter at the Planning Unit (PhD in economics from Wisconsin), left yesterday with a group of officials and businessmen who are taking a whirlwind trip around the world to visit a number of countries in search of aid and investment to develop the economy. Personally, I think it is a waste of money and time; most of them really know very little about economics or about the evolving plans for Nigeria's development. Lyle and Wolf have been "boning Iwuagwu up." You may see notice of the delegation when they arrive in the U.S.

Yesterday we left here at 7 a.m. with Roy and Wendy Fluellan, who are making a trip to Idiroko, a town on the southwestern border of Nigeria, where they lived for a year back in 1948. Roy was Customs Officer for the various stations that lined that part of the border with Dahomey. (They have always had great problems with the smuggling that went on, and still does—in great volume—along the coast.)

The long row of casuarina trees that Roy planted along the police barracks [in Idiroko] is now a stately avenue of green. The house in which they lived, whose mud floors have since been cemented, is crumbled and cracked, eaten away by insects, grown through by tropical plants and inhabited by lizards. I couldn't help but think of your comment, Janell, about the temporality of all things nontropical built in the tropics. Then we drove down the dirt road that connects the villages lining the border. This is all Yorubaland. The only difference between the Yorubas on one side of the border from the other is that on this side their second language is English, and on the other, it is French. As we drove into and through the villages, we were greeted with screams of delight from hundreds of voices that shouted, "*Oyinbo*" (white man) or "*O dab o*" (welcome, hello, good-bye). We snapped hundreds of pictures, everyone crowding to get in them. The little boys for some reason all struck the pose of a menacing boxer.

We passed a stream and stopped to take pictures of the "launderers" below, but we were thoroughly distracted by the mob of naked children who insisted on performing various antics for our cameras. In one village, we came upon a huge mud/cement/wooden duplicate of a European Romanesque cathedral rimmed on each side by the mud and rush huts of the villagers.

We stopped to take a picture, and within half a minute the entire town was lined up in front of us to have a picture taken! I wish there were space here so that I might describe to you the wonderful variety of faces, dress, scar-markings, and headdresses that we saw. Such colorful, friendly, people!

Nigeria had a famous boxer whom boys imitated.

Love,

G

　　　LETTERS FROM NIGERIA

Joyful encounters

*I found this water
carrier enchanting with
her facial make-up and
clothing of beads.*

— Letter Eighteen —

June 6, 1961

DEF,

    Guess I'll be extravagant today and not use air letters, 'cause I have a feeling I shall go well over the space allotted in them.

    <u>Racing news</u>: My week for skippering—beat all the Cats in the Wednesday race and came in second (two seconds after the number-one boat) of the entire fleet, placing us third overall after the handicap time was added on. Saturday, just a race against the other Cats—we placed first. This week, as of Sunday, we turned the boat over, sanded her down, and are in the middle of a new paint job, changing from blue hulls and yellow decks to flame-red hulls and gray decks. We are using the revolutionary polyurethane, semiplastic paint that should last us far longer than our tour here in Nigeria.

    Last night we went to our first formal affair—a dinner party given by Jaja Wachuku and the Ministry of Economic Development for the rest of the ministry, prominent American business people, Nigerian dignitaries from various ministries, and for the team of American experts that has been here for three weeks assessing Nigeria's capacity to receive economic aid. This is still pretty much confidential, but evidently the U.S. pow-

> *"Nigeria to receive economic aid."*

ers-that-be have singled out Nigeria and India for their main concentration of aid for economic development. Peter wore his formal dinner jacket and I my new white-and-black sheath (Christmas present from Mamá). It was fun getting dressed up; the meal was delicious—given at the Federal Palace Hotel. The speeches were the usual "palaver," to use a good African "pidgin English" word.

    We expect to make a trip to Ghana in about three weeks. We have plans to buy another Cat in Accra for £150, tow it back, and resell it here for £250 or more, since we feel the boat market is very good here right now. We'll tell you more about the scheme when plans jell.

    Yes, the U.S. "Freedom Rider" episodes have certainly caused a stir here. I'm sure we get better coverage of such goings-on than you would ever dream of getting there! The fact that some whites participated on behalf of the colored is a very important *new* note. But, oh my, the American whites are more often than not compared with the South African whites! This quote from an article in yesterday's paper should give you an idea of what I mean:

    The following comes from an article scorning "Communist witch-hunters in Nigeria."

"In recent years we have seen the lot of the American Negroes, as second class citizens of a country that boasts leadership of Western Democracies. My advice to fellow Nigerians is that we must stop playing stooge roles for America in this country. The Americans are as bad as the white South Africans. . . ."

Now that Columbus's eldest daughter (7 and a half) has come to live with them, we are making efforts to get her placed in a school here in Lagos. I had to write to the principal of the school in the Eastern Region, where she had been going to school, to get an official transfer certificate for her before the Education Officer here in Lagos would consider her case. Yesterday, the certificate having arrived, I took Columbus and Victoria down to the Education Office, and the officer never showed up. We were told that he will be there tomorrow. After we see him and register Victoria, he will presumably try to place her in a school. Heaven knows how long that will take. Efficiency and speed are not what I would deem Nigerian attributes.

The other night it was very clear. One had the impression that the moon was hanging from a frond of the palm tree outside our window. Peter picked up the binoculars, with which we supervise *all* the activity in the harbor, you can be sure. He was struck by the clarity of the craters that he could see on the moon. After we marveled and oohed and ahhed, PBC ran down to Columbus's compound. (The dinner meal was over, Columbus had washed up the dishes and "closed" for the night.) Peter wanted to get Columbus so he could look, too. Columbus has long been concerned about whether there really were men on the moon. He is afraid the Russians will land there first and take them over, in addition to setting up strict immigration rules for any non-Russian travel to the moon. On looking through the binoculars, though, he exclaimed: "Oh, I guess there be no man there. I see no one moving around. It be all quiet!"

We have been giving him periodic lectures on the universe, the movement of the sun, moon, and earth, what makes night and day, why Nigeria is warmer than England, etc. Our globe is the first "map" he has ever seen. As far as he knew, the earth was flat, certain gods made the night and day to come and go, etc. We haven't spared a point—taking him into the bedroom at night, using a flashlight as the sun, the globe as earth, and a ping-pong ball as the moon. We've probably enjoyed those lessons more than he. I'm sure he doesn't begin to absorb all that we try to explain to him. This becomes evident when he rolls back his eyes and lets out long, high-pitched "Ohhhhhhh's" or "Ahhhhhhhhh's" and nods his head with great amazement and incredulity on his face. "Ahhhhhh, you men who get big learning, get much sense in de head." The usual exclamation is "Izzat so?!" in a very high pitch. (He has a beautiful, low, rich voice and very expressive black eyes.)

While I am on the subject of Columbus. . . . It is extraordinary, some of the conversations that I have with him. Two days ago, I was reading Melville Herskovits's _The Myth of the Negro Past_—specifically, the chapter in which he deals with "the African Cultural Heritage" of the tribal units around the area of West Africa where we now live, and where Columbus grew up. The conversation that ensued was a perfect illustration to me of exactly what I had been reading. Herskovits's points could not have been more effectively driven home!

"Read, read, all Madam do is read!"

"You know what I am reading?" I explained briefly that this book was a study of the black man who was taken from this very part of Africa some 150 to 200 years ago, what their reactions were to slavery, and how much of their African culture had been carried over to the new country, my own, principally.

> "Ah, you get much knowledge from books. We people who no read get knowledge from our fathers and grandfathers. They tell us what we learn tru de mouth. An we nevah foget dat things. What dey tell us we know to be de truth. An we nevah foget. But den de white man come an some of our people learned to read an write and learned dat some of de ways was foolish and bad. Before we used to have big fear to born de twin babies. An if dey born, one or de two get killed. But now we know dat is foolish doing."

I had read at great length of the various practices, depending on the tribe, of killing twin babies. The Yoruba generally kill both and then carve small wooden replicas of the babies (though they look like small grown people) called ibejis (pronounced "abege"), which they then worship. The Ibo tribe that I had read of used to take both of the twins shortly after birth and leave them in the "Evil Forest" to die. Columbus, an Ibo, comes from a tribe whose practice was to kill only one of the babies. I asked him what happened to the babies after the white man came.

> "Oh, at first when de baby was took out to die, de Catolic sisters got dem and kep dem. Soon dey teach us it is bad to kill de pikin. [Reference here is to "pikaninnies" or small children.] Dere was a big man in our village. He work for John Holt and have big money. His wife, she born two pikins and dey get fear. Dey kill one. But de whole village was against it for dey know by den it is a sin to kill de pikin. Now, you know, I tink ever-one have his God. An de big God, he punish dis man an his wife. His wife, she get big tummy trouble an she have it since dat time. She nevah have anoder pikin, and dat be 20 years now. De man,

"Conversations with Columbus are extraordinary."

he get big trouble wid de people of the village. He go to court an lose much money dere. He win de case, but since he is dealin wid so many traders, dey be many peoples close to him. One day dey poison him. An it get tru to his heart. His heart, he always give him trouble. He be sick man an nevah work good again."

Columbus is a good example of the "enlightened" African. "He get knowledge of White man." He is a specimen of the transition stage that Nigerian culture is experiencing and will be for a long time to come. It's a strange marriage, this, between traditional polytheistic systems and the white man's monotheism; between divining systems or magic cults and the revelation or power of God. A second look at the impact of the missionary teachings of Christianity on the African of this part of the continent reveals the fact that the new has not replaced the old but rather has been welded onto it with a few modifications of both.

For example, he knows it was a "foolish ting" to fear having twins. But he notes it is a <u>sin</u> to kill either of them; that, in one way or another, an external force (that of God?) will punish the sinner. His former beliefs concerning what we would call magic and fetishism have been broken down to a certain extent by rational teachings of the white man. On the other hand, the white man's religious teachings, especially those of the Catholic Church, allow him a simple carryover of his fetishisms and magic practices to another set of values and beliefs. Thus, as Herskovits puts it, "though forms of worship may have been adopted, not all of African world view or ritual practices are lost."

> *"The Juju man . . . plays a very important role . . ."*

The interesting, inconsistent combination of conflicting worldviews that can be held by one individual was especially apparent to me when, a few months ago, and on and off since then, Columbus and I have discussed the Juju man, native medicine, and modern medical practices.

The Juju man, by no means extinct, though outlawed in Nigeria, plays a very important role in the lives of the tribes of southern Nigeria. He is a diviner who, through a long period of study, is able to predict the fate of a given person, cast evil spells over others or over entire villages, perform certain healings, protect, etc. By throwing a set number of seeds, herbs, etc., and performing a kind of mumbo-jumbo (that sounds too story-bookish to relate here), a Juju man's divination is based on a complex system of combinations and permutations of items and actions tied up with a whole body of mythology and interpreted in the light of a given situation.

Now, in principle, Columbus agrees with the government (which was British when the law was passed) that outlawed Juju practices, since, as he puts it: "Dere be too many bad Juju men. You nevah know if you get a good one or a bad one." He has told me, however, that should he know of a "good" Juju man, then if, for example, he wanted to know how his family was, from whom he may not have received word for a long time, he would go to that Juju man and ask him how his family is. The Juju man here in Lagos would be able, in his Juju fashion, to tell Columbus how his family is. He might also tell him that a certain member of his family will die before the end of the year. Then, of course, Columbus asks how he can prevent this from happening. The Juju man says that, on payment of a certain fee and the presentation of a certain sacrifice (humans not excluded, depending on the case), he will perform certain rites. Meanwhile, Columbus must buy the Adam's apple of a monkey, certain dried lizards, beads, and what-have-you—that are sold in any number of local market stalls, stocked specifically with Juju merchandise to brew up and eat or sacrifice or hang from a tree or . . . .

Anyway, you get the idea. I don't mean to make this sound too far-fetched, because without a doubt there are certain Juju men who really "get power"—such as the one to whom a European took his wife after she had been hit by a poisoned arrow, which blinded her. No modern hospital could restore her sight. As a last measure, they took her to a Juju man who administered some potion that restored her sight.

There is more, but I shan't burden you with my ramblings. Will save them for next time when my fingers seem to be more accurate.

Our love to all,

G and P

Juju Market

— Letter Nineteen —

June 14, 1961

DEF,

Here goes another splurge of stamps. I know that what I have to babble about this time will go far over an air letter's space for talk. Ahhhh, extravagance!

I'm glad I waited a bit over time to write this, though not sure your feelings are the same, 'cause had I sat down when I originally planned to, I would have put my depressed feelings on paper and not made you any happier. Oh, I was sooo very discouraged about the job situation here.

Absolutely nothing in the teaching field has opened up, despite all my efforts in this overdeveloped city in an underdeveloped wilderness. Not a soul who has a job to offer would dare to advertise in the paper for fear of suffering the inevitable avalanche of applicants (10 out of 10 totally unqualified) who would apply. The only way one gets a job (which, again, for women will rarely be anything but a ghastly, boring, secretary-typist kind of job) is via the grapevine. One must let people, who know people, know that one is twiddling one's thumbs in boredom, fighting that feeling of uselessness (my worst enemy). There is the added complication that I am an expatriate and thus can never become an active part of the community. I must be content with the few interesting Nigerian acquaintances I am lucky enough to have, and the much wider circle of acquaintances (though few they are in this area) of Europeans and occasional Americans who are out here.

'Scuse me, looks like I "unloaded" anyway; and no need to, because my spirits are flying this week!! Saturday afternoon, Tom Wilson, the UNESCO Representative to Nigeria, called three days ago to ask me to start work for him on Monday. To recapitulate, I met him by chance about three weeks ago when interviewing Dr. John Egnatoff, the Canadian advisor to the Federal Government on technical teacher training. They share the same office. Egnatoff, who incidentally gave me a considerable amount of background information on teacher training for my research project, had to leave the room for a moment for something, so Wilson queried me as to what I was doing, my interests, etc. Turns out that my research, my familiarity with the Ashby Report,[17] my paper last semester at Michigan and comparative studies fit in beautifully with the kind of work he is doing.

When Egnatoff returned, I took out a clipping I had snipped from a paper some weeks earlier concerning an educational coordinating body that the Ministry of Education was setting up. I said I was interested in knowing if this body might need some kind of assistant, secretary, what-have-you, just so I could have the opportunity to work with them. Egnatoff asked Wilson about it, and Wilson exclaimed, "Is it a job you are looking for?" He then indicated that he needed an assistant to help him prepare reports. Then, on July first, he would have that person become the assistant secretary to the UN team of experts that is coming out to Nigeria to assess Nigeria's current request to the UN Special Fund for aid to set up advanced teacher-training colleges in each of the four regions (including the Federal Territory). When I left, he said he would call me up to let me know if and when I might start work for him. Well, after two and a half weeks passed, I had as much as given up hope.

What a wonderful job—at least so far! Instead of doing all of someone else's typing, I have someone to do mine! I have been writing requests to be submitted to the UN that are for the most part condensations and quickly assembled facts gleaned from reams of statistical material and facts concerning the projected costs and plans for the colleges of each region. Most interesting has been writing the "background" introductory sections. This necessitates relating the particular project to the region's educational system, and then to that of the Federation, with particular reference to the role it will play in the projected plans for development of the economy. In this case, it would be to train the estimated 43,000 or more high-level workers who will have to be added to the present 23,000-person workforce by 1970. This would enable the economy to continue to develop at the rate that was established in the years just prior to independence. It's unbelievable, but the Ashby Report, and the many evaluations that have followed it, put the required annual output of advanced trained teachers—to teach this manpower force—at 3,000, when right now there are no more than 30 added annually to the Grade 1 teaching force! Not that I'm a pessimist, or anything: but. . . .

I don't mean to talk so much about me; just have to add a few more details. In addition to the help of Wilson's typist, I have the services of his messenger boy, who now greets me at the car when we arrive and carries whatever I have with me and almost myself up to the office. I am working in Ann Melville's office, which is just around the corner from Wilson's. Ann Melville, incidentally, is a delightful older Scots lady with quite a brogue. She has been here in the Colonial Service for over a dozen years, and she also happens to be our next-door neighbor. The office building is the Old Secretariat, located a few blocks down the Marina from us, with the most fantastic architecture. But I won't go into that now.

Most fun is that now both of us, PBC and I, are working for ministries with all the same kinds of technical problems, British quirks of administration, and Nigerian inadequacies and adequacies. Thus, we have the same hours of work: 8 to 2 Monday through Friday and 8 to noon on Saturday.

The weather is COLD and wet. Here it is the 14th of June, and we have had rain every day this month. A few days the sun came out just long enough to dry the accumulation of several days' wash. So Columbus rushed madly to get it on the line for the few hours of precious sun before the rains returned. This sun Columbus calls the "deceive" sun, because it stays out just long enough for you to put out your damp, moldy belongings and open up the windows before it scoots behind a downpouring cloud. At times, pour down it does, so heavily that I wonder if there is much difference between the atmosphere and two fathoms down under the harbor.

"The weather is cold and wet . . . with terrific line squalls . . ."

Several nights, recently, we have been awakened by the most terrific line squalls we have ever experienced! In this case, they bring not only exceedingly heavy torrents of rain but equally heavy blasts of wind, which, last Wednesday, were of hurricane force. The first thought we had when waking about midnight was that something was trying to pound down the entire east wall of the bedroom. When we went out into the living room, whose three sides are all jalousie windows, it was like stepping into a glass cage in the cascade halfway down Niagara Falls. The windows are louvered in this room, and those on the east side might just as well not have been there. The heavy sheets of water, with that fantastic force of wind behind, were spraying right through every closed slat (even though they overlap and are tightly latched), as though someone had a high-power fire hose aimed at the entire side of the house!

Peter slipped on some clothes and ran down to the Yacht Club. There he discovered that four of the Cats, since they are the lightest class of boat in the fleet, had been picked right off their trolleys, and one had been thrown into the water, where it was banging against the concrete hard when he found it. Ours, since we had been painting it, was upside down and safely snuggled in under the shed. PBC and the three night watchmen (whom the Africans call "watch-nights") were unable to pull up the stray Cat. Since the owner has no phone—like most people in this town—Peter drove over to his flat, not far from here. It was Chuck Olmstead, one of the MIT Fellows. He dressed and came down. They recovered his boat and managed to secure all the other Cats before going back to bed. The next morning, when Peter went to work, he found his office window completely covered by the leaves from a mammoth tree that had been blown over in the night.

Aside from this occasional drama, however, the rain has been mild though continual. For the first time, we have been able to wear sweaters. Columbus, of course, bundles up with several layers as though headed for the North Pole. He even occasionally puts on shoes!

Speaking of Columbus, we took him to the movies last night to see

J. Arthur Rank's presentation of *Christopher Columbus*, since we have told him of his namesake at great length. I'm not sure, though, if he really has any concept of place, since he had never seen a globe or a map before he came to live with us.

Racing: Last Wednesday, as mentioned above, our boat was upside down, getting many coats of polyurethane (plastic wonder paint). But since it rained, anyway, there was no race. Saturday was a lovely day. It cleared in time for the race, and the downpour for the day didn't come until just after the last boat crossed the line. This was a very special day and race, since the whole fleet (classes combined) was competing for the coveted Commodore's Cup. Peter skippered for the race, got a fairly good start, and then just shot out in front of the fleet, where we stayed for the entire race, increasing the distance between us and the other boats the entire race. We crossed the finish line approximately six minutes before the next boat, which was an Osprey. Though we were quite excited, our hopes of getting the cup were not very high, since with that particular wind we had a fairly heavy handicap—a 15-minute handicap under the Tarpon ("Lightning" to you). But the first Tarpon to come in was some 16 minutes, and, well, we stood around biting our nails, with all the other Cat owners encouraging us and telling Peter what a magnificent job he had done, and wishing the Officer of the Day and his assistants would hurry up and finish their adjustments for handicap calculations so we would KNOW. As is the case for a prize race, everyone gathers to hear the results and pre-dictions—this time, there were about 50 to 75 people. Yes, you're right, we won! You should see the cup! It is big and shiny and sits on a large round, black stand. This we get to keep for a year. To keep for good, we get a silver beer mug. Quite handsome. Our boat boy said to us as we were leaving that some men had already come around to look at our paint job to see what kind it was, etc.

Two days ago, when we got home from work, we discovered that the electricity was off. Turns out that the electricity man had simply disconnected it. The Ford Foundation, which is supposed to pay our bills, hadn't paid last month's bill. We ate by candlelight that night a delicious supper cooked by Columbus over his own tiny kerosene burner stove. "Dis bush cooking," he announced. "De people in de bush never have worry about ECN [Electric Corp. Nigeria]."

> *". . . we discovered that the electricity was off."*

Our dinner Monday was delicious, courtesy of Jaja Wachuku and the ministry, for the economic aid from the U.S. Jaja was late at a cabinet meeting, but he did come, and we, seated at different ends of the very large banquet room, met some interesting Nigerians. Peter wore his tuxedo, which he swims in, though it was custom-made in January just before we left the U.S. He also wore the cummerbund and matching bowtie you gave him an hour before we flew out of N.Y., Clarks. He looked very nice: tall, brown, and handsome, not that I'm prejudiced.

Saturday we had dinner at the Hansens', a going-away affair for Mrs. Kingsley and her daughter. Donald Kingsley is head administrator of the Ford Foundation here in Nigeria and in Ghana. Semi-dull people. But we were flattered, since Ann Hansen, for this occasion, sent her cook over to learn from our cook a Dutch meal Columbus had prepared one evening when we had the Hansens here for dinner: Nasi Goreng [a traditional Malaysian dish, cooked with scrambled egg, anchovies, dried small fish, and Malaysian spices]. And, speaking of dinners, we are about to leave for the Olmsteads' for dinner, it being nearly 8 p.m., the dinnertime around here. We do, however, refuse to succumb to the ridiculous eating hours of the British when not eating out.

Friday, shortly after noon, we leave for Ghana. We plan to spend that night in Lomé, Togoland, after passing through Dahomey. We will arrive in Accra around noon Saturday and will stay there with a friend two nights. Monday we leave with that friend. (His name is André Margerie. He sails a Cat here at the Yacht Club. He is a Frenchman and sells British products along the West African coast.) We will drive to his hut on the Volta River, where we will spend that night before returning home the next day. While in Accra, we, along with André, expect to close a deal with the man who has a Catamaran there that he is selling to Peter and André for £125. They hope to resell it here in Lagos for somewhere in the vicinity of £300. I have permission from Mr. Wilson to go on the trip (as if I wouldn't go anyway).

Peter's work seems to be going along fine. He had a very fruitful half-day conference with Wolfgang Stolper one day last week when Wolf went over the big study Peter is doing on the balance of payments with special focus on the import and export projections, including the factor of import substitutions and increase in domestic production.

Stephen Awokoya, Federal Advisor to the Ministry of Education, with whom I have had two interviews now for my research, left for Boston yesterday to attend a Ford Foundation–sponsored conference at MIT on education in Africa. Watch for news about the conference in the paper— especially in the *Christian Science Monitor*. If some quirk of fate should take Awokoya to the Hartford area, do go see or hear him. He is a very substantive man.

I had planned to discuss the pros and cons of a visit from any of you-all "chez nous" while we are here, but that will have to wait till we get back from Ghana. Just let me answer some of your many questions.

Aunt Jan, the map you have of Lagos is probably right, and you're reasonably accurate, putting us in the middle of the King George V Memorial Park. This is directly behind us, where the big soccer games are played *every* night from about 5 to 7. We are located right out on Magazine Point, where Five Cowry Creek separates us from Victoria Island. Both families should be receiving detailed maps of the area plus Lagos Island, with all sorts of pencil marks scribbled in.

Mother asked: "What has Columbus been eating that he should be gaining [weight] while you two diminish?" Well, I'll tell you, Mom, he eats gari, fufu, cornstarch porridge—all the many forms of pounded yams and cassava. Grace (his wife) does the pounding with a very large mortar and pestle "out back" in the servants' quarters. Despite the abundance of fruit around here, the Nigerians' main "nourishment" comes from the gari and fufu that seems to accompany everything they eat. Columbus has fixed us some interesting native dishes lately, but I'll have to review the names and methods of preparation with him before I try to relate them to you.

What do I have in my garden? Zinnias, which seem to be the only things that really have flourished, gladiolas, a marigold-like plant, many kinds of ferns and ivies, geraniums, great elephant-leaved things, some plants that have bright red internal coloring, some yellow or white contrasts, two bushes of blushing hibiscus, a fiery red-flowered hedge, a long willowy green hedge down another side of the yard that has small, daffodil-like yellow flowers, many different varieties of red-green-leafed things that I don't like, other bushy things, and, well, you can see my gardener doesn't know the names of many of the things he brings me (from heaven knows where, they just seem to appear!!). But the variety is infinite, and some of the foliage and flowers quite exotic. Then of course there are my attempts at chives, mint, lettuce, radishes—none any too successful. Worst of all, something is very effectively eating up my entire garden. I'm quite sure it is grasshoppers. Don't know where I'll get the proper spray. Nor have these line squalls helped.

> *"What do I have in my garden?"*

Mother, among the scholarship applicants who made the semifinals, there were half a dozen girls. I think four of them will receive scholarships. Results should be announced by the end of this month. We've made our recommendations from here; now we, or rather the Institute and the aspirants, are waiting for the New York office not only to approve but also to find places for the candidates by matching their desired field of study with the school on their list that offers that field.

Aunt Jan asked about Lyle Hansen and Wolfgang Stolper. I will give you some details on them in the next communication. Meanwhile, much love to you all. We eat up your letters.

Gretel

[P.S.] Race: Wed., 2nd, disqualified: over start line too soon. G=skipper.

— Letter Twenty —

June 24, 1961

DEF,

This ungainly sized paper [typed on legal size] is used by all the ministries of the Nigerian Government. The accumulated days that have passed since my last communication to you means there is an addition of many more observations for me to pass on. Thus I shall utilize these monster sheets. Hummm . . . where to start. My notes fill three pages! Guess I'll save reporting on the Ghana trip till after my report on our "business of living."

Weather: Very cool these days. I even occasionally wear a sweater and can wear long sleeves to work in comfort for the first time. It is considerably cooler here than it ever is in Connecticut in the summertime, but slightly (to put it mildly) wetter.

Sailing: Last week I skippered. Wednesday I was first of the fleet across the finish line, but with the class handicap on Catamarans, I came out third of about 25 when the time was added on. Saturday, racing this time only against Cats, I placed first by five minutes. Only four Cats raced,

"Gretel at the helm."

and some of the good competition was not there. Sunday was a beautiful, cool, clear, windy day—perfect for a sail beyond the training moles outside the harbor. We sailed out to Tarkwa Bay, where we met two of the MIT Fellows. They own another Cat, so we sailed out together. It was very exciting, high, high waves and a strong wind . . . a bit scary at first, but I daresay we were much braver about it than they. However, I think we are better sailors. We raced out around the Fairway Buoy that guides ships into the Lagos Harbor and back. We were blinded by the great sheets of spray that came at us as we beat to windward, wondering as we ascended a mountain of water, just what the descent would be like. One time a wave came over the entire deck that didn't break until it reached the stern, and then did so right off the stern deck, leaving very little water with us. At other times, the cockpit (if you can call it that) would be completely inundated. Being raised above the waterline, as the cockpit is, between the two hulls, the boat is self-bailing, and is dry in a matter of seconds. Once back inside the mole, we positively skittered along on the placid waters, hulls flat on a broad reach at approximately 18 knots. Most exhilarating!

Sunday night we had dinner at the Hansens', with Wolf Stolper and Ben Lewis[18] and his wife, who have just arrived for seven weeks, courtesy of the Ford Foundation. He will be consultant to the Ministry of Transport, I think. Lyle and Wolf were hoping to get him out here on short-term work with them, but this is the closest they could get, evidently. Seems the Nigerian Government is getting a bit touchy about having too many American advisors around, and to have three in the same unit was more than they would tolerate.

This is unfortunate for the Economic Planning Unit, since in the past two weeks they (Lyle and Wolf, that is) have been working up to a fever pitch of hysteria over the mass of research, projections, and evaluations yet to be done before the deadline for the Five-Year Plan overtakes them. You may recall that the deadline, when we came out here, was to be August. From what I understand, now, it is being extended until mid-October. Frankly, I will be surprised if it is ready by Christmas! As it is now, they are doing all their own original fieldwork and statistical research, when they should be able to go to the appropriate ministries and the Bureau of Statistics and just pick it up. Those are jobs they were not hired to do and should not have to waste valuable time doing. The only ways they will ever get information vital for planning for the future is to go out and collect it, then tabulate it themselves. It makes for a harried team of men. Peter has been up late every night this week, writing reports and "projecting" developments of various sectors of the economy on the basis of information—which he has had to spend the entire day ferreting out of interviews with various companies, or from unfiled files that he may be lucky enough to come across.

Back to the social life: Saturday night we had dinner at the Thompson's home. They are both probably in their 50s. He is with the British Council, which is dedicated to the propagation of British culture. We met them at a dinner party, given by the Rosenbergs for us two couples. (Lillie Rosenberg, an American Negro, worked with me at the African-American Institute. A delightful girl. Her husband, Sherman, a white Jewish man, is here teaching chemistry at Queens College, a girls' secondary school, brought here by the African-American Institute.) On the other hand, Rachael Thompson teaches English at Queens College. She is undoubtedly the most articulate English woman we have met here. In a thoughtful sense, she is aware of political and historic, etc., problems other than just those narrow, immediate things that touch one's life. She is vivacious. On the whole, I find the British women out here such a dull lot. Their lives are narrow, even though they are exposed to a vast array of nationalities and cultures. They remind me of the "Navy wives" I encountered when living with my Naval Intelligence Officer husband (in another iteration of his and my life) on Whidbey Island in Puget Sound. Ohhh, their unnaturally high, cutting, affected-sounding voices. . . . Anyway, it turns out that Rachael Thompson is not really British, since she was born in Beirut, daughter of a Greek professor at the American University there.

A motley group of young people was at the Thompsons' dinner, including a large number of Americans. One of the Americans was a rather empty girl, though nice, brought out here by the African-American Institute to teach in a Roman Catholic mission school in Yaba. She has never taught in the U.S., having been schooled in a New Jersey teachers' college. Another group was the Blanchard family, he having been sent here by the American Friends Service Committee, to do—I don't think he nor they were ever quite sure what, except to have a Friends representative somewhere in West Africa. We weren't too impressed with him, either. Seems he's trying to "reconcile" Zik's NCNC, the North's NPC, and Awokoya's Action Group to bring the country together: another Nehru, trying to act as arbiter and conciliator. He is also doing work with the Social Welfare Center, though his work in the U.S. was in mass media, i.e., broadcasting. Ah, me, I'm glad we became a bit more practical after leaving our dreams on Whidbey Island in search of a job. But then I doubt that you think we are very far down the ladder from these idealists, what with all our extended exposure to educational theorizing. This is the reaction we get from so many so-called down-to-earth businessmen, school-of-hard-knocks, get-out-and-do-it people whom we meet here.

I can't seem to stay with our experience at the Thompsons', so let me go back to Saturday early afternoon. Peter called me at the office to tell me that Olu Ogunniyi was in town. We had gone to see him at Williams College last December on our way back to the U. of Michigan after

Christmas vacation. He was one of the 23 students (fellows) attending the Ford Foundation–sponsored yearlong seminar on economic development at Williams. Having completed the program (MA), he is back in Nigeria working in the Department of Statistics at Ibadan for the Western Regional Government. (They have much better people than the Federal Government in this field.) He had come down to Lagos to attend a meeting of the Joint Planning Commission and Peter ran into him there. Olu came over to have lunch and talk of Williams and the problems of the regional and Federal Governments. We hope to visit him and his family in Ibadan.

While we're on the subject of visitors, let me tell you about the 108 Crossroads Africa American students "hitting" Lagos last Friday. June 23rd came, the day you had written to me that Vernon Ferwerda[19] and Co. would be arriving in Lagos. I was a bit distressed, since we had never received any word from him confirming

> "... let me tell you about the 108 Crossroads Africa American students ..."

this. I noticed in the paper that day that the Crossroads Africa group was arriving. Then on Monday, one of the Nigerian secretaries in the Ministry of Education came in to tell me of the delightful Sunday luncheon she had had at a friend's house with four of the young Americans—who, it turns out, were in Ferwerda's group. So I knew they were here. Then, on Sunday evening, evidently late, while we were at the Hansens', we had a mysterious visitor, according to Columbus, who waited for us for a long time but wouldn't give Columbus his name. From Columbus's vague description (since, according to Columbus, our visitor was a white man, and that is enough to distinguish him), we gather it was Art Hyde, Williams classmate and fraternity brother of Peter. Your mention of Art's letter to you had us prepared, Aunt Jan. Evidently his group left the next day for Sapele, so we never saw him.

And then Monday arrived, bringing cold rains and a long day of work at the ministry. I came home very tired and undressed to crawl in bed for a nap. Peter never got home until 7:00, having worked late on projections, of which I spoke earlier. At about 4:30, Columbus knocked on the bedroom door to inform me that I had a visitor. Rather disheveled, and still buttoning up, I emerged into the living room to find Vernon Ferwerda in a dripping raincoat clutching the little G. Fox & Co. bag of goodies you sent us, Mother. Thank you! His first remark was, "By golly, you are pretty!! Your mother was right. It was worth coming to Africa for!" Needless to say, I was a bit startled—and wondered what in the world you had told him, Mother. Being an exceedingly loquacious individual, Mr. F. filled the next hour with tales of his recent problems, excitement, political observations, and energized reaction on arriving in West Africa for the first time. As a student of this area, he obviously found it exciting to see his studies and grasp of political/historical Nigeria come to life.

He told of his problems trying to reach Porto Novo, Dahomey. Since there are no direct telephone communications to our neighbor country directly west (only two hours from here), the only way he could reach someone there would be to call, through the signal station in the harbor, a ship out on the ocean that could, in turn, call a French boat that could call Porto Novo. As you may know, his group will be spending several weeks of the summer with a matching group of students from Dahomey constructing a dispensary for a hospital in a small village not far from Porto Novo. I am a bit distressed at the limited French-language fluency of not only the leader but also the entire group (11 students). This will be their only means of communication with their fellow workers. How much easier it would be if they were to be working on a project here in Nigeria.

Later that evening, shortly after Peter got home, we received a troop of visitors: Mimi Winter, Dave someone, Williams class of '59, and Bill, a handsome American negro; all are in Ferwerda's group, full of sparkle, vitality, giggles, and excitement. (For those of you who don't know, Aunt Jan and Uncle Archer had dinner with Mimi and her family not long ago, knowing that she was coming to Nigeria. In fact, they showed her some slides we sent home to be developed, which, incidentally, we would like very much to see ourselves. As she and her group were coming over Five Cowry Creek Bridge from Lagos Island (where they were staying in flats behind the Federal Palace Hotel) to Victoria Island, she recognized our house. This is because we had taken a picture, right from Victoria Island bridge, of the Yacht Club and consequently our home. Mimi saw this in West Hartford. [See photo in Letter Three.] Pretty good memory!

They had been tramping all over Lagos just looking at the very different way of life, talking to anyone who would talk with them—which means just about everyone here in Nigeria. They were enchanted with the friendliness of the Nigerians and their delight at meeting Americans, which is understandable, since there are not many Americans to be seen. Some of the Nigerians were intrigued with Bill. They couldn't understand how he could be black and talk like an American. This was something that amazed Columbus when Lillie Rosenberg came to see me one day. After she left, he exclaimed, "But she talk like you, Madam! How be dat?!" He knew that black people grew up in America, but all the nuances of their reflecting an entirely different culture never occurred to him. I assured him that she was an American just like me. That she grew up the same way I did, so naturally she speaks the same way I do, and that her skin color couldn't affect any of these things.

After much talk with these delightful youngsters who, it appeared, were going to stay all night, I had to tell them that we were due at a dinner party by 9 o'clock. They were clearly starved. When I went to the icebox to get out sandwich material, there wasn't even any bread. There was only a pineapple, which I sliced and gave them in pieces that they ate like half-moons of watermelon, holding onto the rind on their way out. Peter drove them back to the flats. Then we prepared very poorly for what turned out to be a very plush, rather hysterical dinner party at Antoine's, one of Lagos's better restaurants, of which there are only about two or three here.

Our host was André Margerie, fellow Cat owner with whom we stayed in Accra, and who also accompanied us back from Ghana through Togo and Dahomey to Nigeria. He is a delightful, semi-young Frenchman who speaks English with a British accent. He had also invited two other couples, elderly British Yacht Club acquaintances! We knew the men, since we sail with and against them; but I had never really talked with the wives, since they sit on the lawn, as do nearly all the wives, socialize, and sip tea while we are out racing. The meal was delicious and the conversation a bit like a specimen out of the late 19th century—in all the high, poo-bah tones, the "oooh, dahling, should I tell . . . ?" twitter, twitter, ". . . that story about the . . . ." Aargh. André, on the other hand, is a charming soul: interesting and natural. He left the following day on the mail boat (we call them "liners" in the U.S.) for Freetown, where he will have a few weeks' vacation. He is an importer for many British and a few American firms of goods to West Africa with offices in Lagos and Accra.

The exciting thing about André's departure is that on the same boat, but going to the U.K., was His Highness the Governor-General Azikiwe.

The Mail Boat departing with long-time British colonial civil servants

Nigerian bugle corps in farewell salute and British civil servants bidding "good-bye"

And what a spectacle that was! Both Peter and I left work at our respective ministries at noon. Every ship in the entire harbor, which includes several dozen, was gaily decked out with all its signal flags waving from the yard-arms, halyards, and every spar on which a flag could be hoisted. It was a colorful sight. I've never seen big, dingy old freighters look so frivolous. I am sure, too, that traffic was jammed all the way from the Apapa wharves to the Lagos Island Carter Bridge.

It had been a gray morning, but as the ship crossed the harbor to get into the main channel taking it right by the Yacht Club, the sun came out, and the great military cannons, which had been rolled up to the water's edge down the marina a short distance, boomed out a 21-gun salute. The WAY (bon voyage) and RBA (good-bye) signal flags hoisted above the Yacht Club deck danced gaily as Zik, André, and several hundred other waving specks passed by.

The only sad note to this is that many of those "specks" were expatriates who, perhaps teary-eyed, were leaving Nigeria for the last time after 10 to 20 years of Colonial Service. In line with tradition, up went their hats floating out over the sea and down into Lagos Harbor like a shower of salt. Without a doubt, they have helped make this country what it is today—a remarkable transition over only a half-century of administration. Nigeria has much more to be thankful for to the British than to resent for all their empire-building. I am sure, however, that the colonial service officer, finding himself a thing of the past, feels an occasional pang of pain as he is whisked aside in a gesture of ingratitude by an eager young (in the political sense) nationalist who is at last taking the reins of his country in his own hands from "that man who held them too long," in his view. After another few years, however, of trying to run their own house, I am sure that the experienced and perhaps enlightened Nigerians will start to express their appreciation for what has already been done for them.

Race of the Tarpin Class

Flash: This being Wednesday, we just raced (since that last paragraph, written a few hours ago) in the general race. This time, Peter skippering this week with a handicap time of 5 minutes, 10 seconds (very small this week), we still WON. Tune in on Saturday for the next results.

We've been having "African chop" lately, including all sorts of interesting soups. Last night, I swear, Columbus put some kind of hay in the soup. Also had gari (made from pounded cassava) with a mixture of fish, red-hot pepper seeds, chopped up bitter leaf, palm oil, egusi, a dehydrated fruit/seed compound (forgot name), dried and then mashed crayfish, and maybe a few other goodies, too. Columbus always asks us the following morning if we have slept well.

I mentioned in the last letter that I would discuss the "pros and cons of a visit." Evidently some of you mistook me to mean the pros and cons as to whether you should come at all! Far from it! We are most anxious to be able to share some of our experience with our families. Without a doubt, a trip here is certainly worthwhile. The first question is expense—which you must decide. And the second question, if the first one is decided in the affirmative, is what part of the year would be best?

After much questioning of people who have been here year-round, we find almost unanimous agreement that August is the best month, since it is a breathing spell between the rainy season and the Harmattan.[20] Thus, it is dry, cool, and clear, with nice breezes (good for sailing). It will also mean that travel around the country will be easier, since with the rains, as right now, most of the roads are gutted, rutted, and even washed away in places.

This is not a beautiful country. If you want to see beauty in Africa, you must go to East Africa, where the climate is also quite pleasant year-round.

However, Nigeria is intensely interesting—especially to one who has never seen traditional, tribal African life, or a country other than one in the modern-day Western world. Believe me, it will change your entire outlook on both life and the world. You will have an opportunity to witness, superficially though it may be, the growing pangs of a new nation at perhaps its most dynamic period of development and change. One doesn't have to look far to see the catalytic effect of the impact of the West on the cultures of this area. Until very recently, they had remained unchanged for literally hundreds of years! And, too, there are many parts of the country that still remain untouched; a replica of society as it was before Christ . . . some being pre-wheel societies.

Within easy reach are the three regions of the country, fascinating in their diversity. Then there are four countries to the west along the coast—again, different examples of very newly emergent countries. I had hoped to tell you of them in this letter, but that was a trip so full of new things that I hope you will forgive me if I put that off until the next time. You're probably tired of reading this verbiage, anyway.

We look for your letters every day. I haven't been so mail-conscious since I was at Vassar waiting for Peter's letters to come! It is wonderful to hear from family when we are so far away. Distance certainly lends something, if not enchantment, to news from loved ones.

Much, much love to you all,
Gretel

[The following was hand written on the back of Letter #20.]

[P.S.] Aunt Jan, the golf "under par" sounds marvelous. Have you done it again? Yes, Elspeth Rostow is W.W.'s wife; a charming, very intelligent woman. We were impressed when they spent two days with us in Lakeville, Connecticut, where we helped Maude Hadden run the Institute of World Affairs. They also have two young children, though she still manages to teach at MIT part-time, write, and lecture! She and Walt, incidentally, met in Geneva, where they were attending the Institute of World Affairs when the Haddens had it there.

About birthday presents: I would only suggest very light things, since it would cost a fortune to mail anything, even by third-class boat! We'd love to see the pictures we sent undeveloped to you. Could you send them?

Much love to you and Uncle Archer,
G

— Letter Twenty-One —

July 14, 1961

DEF,

    'Scuse the long silence, but to be perfectly honest, I have been so tired in the afternoons after getting home from the ministry that I usually have just enough energy to eat the bowl of fruit Columbus fixes for us each day and then fall in bed to sleep for an hour or two. And THEN, after awakening, if it isn't raining, I somehow inevitably find myself out on the water with Peter to experiment or try out the latest change he has made on the Cat. We now have all new rigging—stainless steel, completed paint job with polyurethane; we've scraped down and revarnished, with the same paint, the mast, tillers, and tiller bar. Now we just have to reshape the centerboards and refinish them, in addition to a dozen other minor changes, such as putting in sliding jib fairleads, a track across the stern so that we can slide the mainsheet rigging in or out depending on our position to the wind and the wind's velocity, perhaps even a boom vang, etc., etc. I guess a boat owner never stops trying to "tune up" his craft.

    It's been like a renaissance, however, with the arrival of *The Science of Sailing*, which you sent us, Mom and Dad. (It arrived here last week.) We have been reading and studying it like the Bible! It is certainly one of the very best such publications we have seen, and has been extremely useful. Every day we have a new problem with which to confront it.

    We have raced many races since I last wrote. I don't think we have lost one since then. We have missed one or two because of bad weather. This Wednesday, Peter won with the addition of a three-minute handicap. Last Saturday, which was the Ladies' Race Cup, there was a very heavy wind. Consequently, although our racing time was not even one hour, my handicap as skipper of a Cat was 25 minutes. Wendy Fluellan in a Tarpon (who gets no handicap) beat me by four seconds. HOWEVER, there is still a question as to which one of us gets the cup, since Roy, who entered her and the boat in the race—failed to write this down in the racing book, a technical rule, though he paid his three-shilling entrance fee. Thus, the Officer of the Day disqualified her. Roy was furious and put in a protest. The Protest Committee, after long deliberation, decided in his favor; and then two members of the Yacht Club Committee protested the Protest Committee's decision. So the whole matter will have to come up before the Sailing Committee, of which Peter is chairman. Slightly awkward situation. That meeting will be held in another few days. I think the only reason for all this fuss is that Roy is famous for his poor sportsmanship, and a number of the old-timers are out to get him this time. I couldn't care less.

We have had some lovely days, cool and breezy. We have also had RAIN. Last week it came down steadily for three and a half days. We had pots and pails placed all over the house to catch the steady stream of drips that come through our "holey" roof. The most comical dripping spot is directly over the toilet seat. True, we don't need a pail under it, but there comes a time when you just have to sit there and get wet. The stream of drips is strong enough now that, out of desperation, we have taken to carrying an umbrella with us when we go to the bathroom.

On Monday, Wolf (Stolper) invited Peter to come to dinner—this is a lunch meal of chicken curry with all the trimmings served at 2:30—with Lyle. (For those of you who are strangers to these names, they are the two economists Peter is working with, the advisors to the Federal Government.) Believe-it-or-not, included at this "dinner" was Barbara Ward![21] Just think, they had her all to themselves for an entire afternoon—till 6:30! I was green with envy. By reports from all three men, my admiration for her is not unfounded. You probably know that her husband is the Minister of Economic Development in Ghana and has been instrumental in the development of the Volta River Dam project. I suspect that her next book will be written for the layman about economic development.

Since I had to use the car that afternoon, Lyle brought Peter home; when they arrived, they were both just bursting. On their way from Ikoyi (a European residential sanctuary, though inhabited by many African ministers now), as they were coming around one of the roundabouts (so typical of British traffic-direction devices), they saw a mob of Africans gathered around its circumference watching a group of American girls and boys in jeans (a Crossroads Africa group) who were cutting the grass there and raking it away. I find it hard to keep my blood pressure down when thinking about this; but really, of all the excellent ways to make absolute FOOLS of themselves, they couldn't have picked a better way. I know they are making an impact, but I am sure that the Crossroads group has no idea of what kind of position they are putting themselves into in the eyes of the African AND European, for that matter.

I learned from a newspaper report that they are working for the PWD (Public Works Department), doing the kind of work that only common laborers do, of which the city has a surplus right now. They plan to plant flowers in the circles, help with the slum clearance, etc. Next time we see them, we are going to take Columbus with us and get him to walk through the crowd and listen to find out what the reactions are, since he speaks both Ibo and Yoruba. Meanwhile, we have nothing against anyone breaking tradition or customary practices, such as girls wearing pants in public and doing the work of men. But imagine the shock of the Nigerian who has never seen a white female in anything but proper dress doing dirty physical labor. In this society, there are plenty of Africans to do the kind of work the Crossroads volunteers are doing; many of these Nigerians are out of jobs. What Nigeria needs is *skilled* laborers. If these kids want to "work with the common people" (which I'm sure few would do at home), they should go to some village in the bush where there is a more equal society. They should not be brought to plant flowers in one of the largest cities of West Africa.

Prisoners being brought to work on public grounds by policeman

Speaking of groups of young Americans, the Experiment in International Living group arrived last week and has gone to Ibadan for a week of orientation. They will return to Lagos, where they will live with their host families for three weeks and then be off for a few weeks to tour Nigeria. I have been in touch with the Nigerian leader. He seems to have things very well in hand and carefully planned out. A refreshing change from the way things are often done around here.

A week ago, Monday, we had dinner with Mr. Winter, Mimi Winter's uncle, who had lunch with Uncle Archer one afternoon in Hartford. Obviously new to the country and unaccustomed to the eating times, he invited us to dinner at the Federal Palace Hotel at 6:00 p.m., whereas the British wouldn't start a dinner engagement until 9:00. That is usually the convening time. I still prefer the former. We invariably shock the British with our early dinner hour—7:30. There was a Yacht Club meeting at 5:00, and we thought it would be through in time. Hah! At 8:30, Peter came staggering up to the house after I had driven over to the hotel to have a ginger ale and make conversation in hopes that the long-winded British would be a bit less so that evening.

It was fun talking to the American visitors, who plied us with questions about everything from the state of the economy, the possibility of foreign business investment, who the important people are to see for information about this and that, to local reactions to picture taking. We were both a bit surprised by how much we *do* know about what makes things tick around here. Our personal acquaintances, just due to the fact that they are white, all hold important positions in a variety of fields. Also, our work in two Federal Government ministries, Economic Development and Education, has put us in contact with many leading Nigerians. I guess the main difference in a country like this is that it is not very difficult to know a large proportion of the top echelon, because the group itself is so small.

The UNESCO Commission on the University of Lagos is arriving by air today. In fact, I am writing this letter in the office, since Tom has gone to the airport to pick them up, and I have no work to do. Actually, only four of the members are arriving: the Frenchman (Chief of Missions, who is Director-General of the French Ministry of Education), the two NYU professors, and Conrad Ivanov (Vice-Rector of the University of Moscow). I will tell you more about them, the three Nigerians who are illustrious individuals, and two other members, once we get underway. Sittings (the Nigerian term for a meeting) will begin next Monday, the 17th. We shall be meeting with the Prime Minister, the Governor-General, many of the key ministers, union leaders (e.g., Teachers Union), association secretaries, etc. I hate to think of the workload once they start deliberations, but until then and for the past week I have had much time to myself. I have been using it to do research in the Education Library and archives for my thesis topic. I have been surprised at the numbers of documents and quantity of reading matter I've been able to unearth. Now I must go through them all and take notes.

The Fourth of July: I can't remember when it has been more significant. Neither Columbus nor any of the boat boys at the Yacht Club knew what "the Fourth of July" meant to an American. So we quickly told them that "this is <u>our</u> day for celebrating independence from the British. What's more, we had to fight for our independence, while the British colonial government <u>gave</u> you your independence!" Response: "You mean you, too, were once a British colony?!" Ah, we and the Nigerians have another link to forge the bond between us.

We were invited out to dinner at the Mitchells', an American Ford Foundation family, along with the others of the American clan, to celebrate the Fourth. When packing in Ann Arbor, I had stuck in a tiny replica American flag, which we took along for the occasion; and Peter had come across some old firecrackers—the light, throw . . . and *bang* type. These we parceled out to the children after the meal. I doubt that any packet of teeny firecrackers ever evoked as much excitement or as much attention as these did on the coast of West Africa: little sparks to commemorate the birth of a nation we have grown to appreciate ten times over since having left it. It would take me twenty more pages to enumerate the many things about our culture that we have come to appreciate, because of their absence from life here in Nigeria. There are so *many* things that one takes for granted as being a natural part of life: cleanliness, health, education, automation, opportunity, safety, comfort, freedom, telephones, electricity, a wide variety of healthy foods. Where we come from in the U.S., there is also a reasonable absence of racial prejudice and a certain acceptance of nonconformity. In most traditional societies, one risks one's position in society, no matter which rung of the ladder one is on, by stepping outside its narrow confines.

GHANA

I guess I've put this off long enough so it will involve only half the amount of paper it would have taken originally, since half of the details have left me. I did make some notes, however, so please bear with me while I try to pull the trip together.

It was just a month ago, on Friday, June 16, that Peter and I were driving out of Lagos in a torrent of rain after having slipped away from work early to have a hot lunch, which was ready at home thanks to Columbus, pack the car, mostly with the food in the icebox that Columbus had prepared, and give our farewells. Great safari!! Well, after all, we were out to drive through four new countries.

Going into French territories was fun, too. Because I speak French, the officials in both Dahomey and Togo did not use English. Besides, I doubt that more than one or two of all those we met, even those on the Nigerian or Ghanaian borders, could speak English. This much I can say for the French colonialists: Their colonized people have been tutored well. I found it much, much easier to understand the French-trained Yoruba than the English-trained Yoruba. It is very significant that, in Africa, English has been reduced to a pidgin form, whereas the French language spoken here is as pure as that in France.

We had to go through six border stations (customs, immigration, police, etc.) each way and had very little trouble. The border station at Dahomey, a typical example, is a series of ramshackle buildings and mud huts surrounded by all kinds of livestock, chickens, etc., and numerous children hawking cigarettes (sold individually), roast corn, stale crackers, prehistoric candies, and so on. All the forms we filled out were solely in French. Interestingly enough, they still had "A.O.F." (Afrique Occidentale Française) on the forms, even though both (former) French territories we passed through had gained their independence within the past year.

There were a number of other changes, the kind one would find traveling from England to France. We switched from driving on the left side of the road to the right side, which is not so easy when you have a car with the steering wheel on the right side of the car.

The towns we passed through and stayed in were almost exact replicas, with an African touch, of provincial towns in the south of France: wide streets with rows of large shade trees on both sides, little boulangeries, patisseries, culture centers, and hundreds and hundreds of little Citroens and Renaults buzzing up and down the spacious streets (mostly mud, of course).

In Cotonou, we stopped to pay £4/10 (how nice to be typing on a British typewriter!) for visas. That's £4/10 (or $12.70 per person) for a resident of Nigeria just to put one's foot on Dahomeyan soil. Moreover, this visa must be renewed every three months! Yes, it's outrageous, but

Dahomey is trying to get even with Nigeria for having refused to allow any French commercial (or noncommercial, come to think of it) traffic cross Nigerian borders. Since most of Dahomey's economic transactions are with France, this caused a considerable hardship for Dahomey. (Nigeria enacted this as a censure against France for having dropped a bomb in the Sahara, with plans to do so again.)

The drive in Togoland is right along the seacoast, through miles (kilometers, that is) and miles of coconut-palm plantations. The palm trees were planted very methodically in neatly spaced rows by the Germans to hold the sea back when they were the colonial masters in this country in the early part of the century. Now they provide a good business for the local people, whose villages are usually situated right on the edge of the beach. They also do ocean fishing from dugout canoes.

Their "houses" are fascinating. They are small, circular structures, not very high, nor more than a few yards in diameter. They are made of dried palm branches and fronds, with a roof of the same material that sits on top of a circular building in the shape and style of a Chinese coolie hat—its brim hanging over the edge. These saucy huts are arranged in circular fashion, usually with a reed fence surrounding the whole compound. In the center, one will most likely find an open

Top: Dahomey and national flag

Bottom: Togo

cooking area and the remnants of some large fish or animal that is festooned with little trinkets that are there to ward off spirits for religious or symbolic reasons.

We arrived in Lomé, the capital of Togo, shortly before 8:00 p.m.; registered at La Benin, a large, modern hotel; and had a wonderful French dinner there. The next morning, I called downstairs and ordered "*du café au lait et des croissants*," which were brought up for breakfast.

Before leaving Togo, since Lomé is right next to the border with Ghana, we took time to sightsee in the city. Again we were delighted with its freshness and space and the impression that it is much cleaner than the Nigerian cities we know. Driving out of town, we passed what used to be the residence (a virtual castle) of the German Governor-General of Togo.

Then [in Ghana], back to English, left-hand driving, wrong-way-round roundabouts, and all the rest. There were many new things that we noticed very soon after entering Ghana, however. The entire trip through Dahomey and Togo, we had been in Yoruba territory. But now we found ourselves in Ashanti territory, where the dress of both the men and the women is different; even the choices of patterns and material were new. The men, as you have seen from Nkrumah's pictures, wear their robes wrapped around their waists like a skirt (*lappa*), and then the long remaining end of the material is drawn up over one shoulder and then

down under an arm. In contrast, think of the pictures you have seen of Azikiwe in his national agbada. The Ashanti men are also much taller than the Yoruba, the Ibo (who are very small), and most of the other southern Nigerian tribesmen. No match, however, for the tall, imposing Hausa of northern Nigeria. One of the most noticeable differences of the Ashanti women from those of southern Nigerian tribes is that they do not plait (twist and braid intricate, tight patterns) their hair. Most of them wear it just cropped short.

Top: Togo

Bottom: Dahomey compound. Note different wrap of textile.

While we were waiting for the ferry to cross the Volta River, we saw our first picture of Nkrumah (propaganda type) on the wall of the tiny ticket office. This face and name we were to see at least one hundred times over before leaving Ghana. Not only are many institutions, training camps, shops, and roads named for him, but, most disturbing (pardon if I show my feelings), his name is found in one of the major roundabouts in Accra. It hangs on an enormous building-size neon flashing sign: KWAME NKRUMAH CIRCLE, each word under the other, flashing on and off in a different color alternately from top to bottom all day and all night long.

Once across the Volta, we found ourselves driving through terrain quite different from any we had seen since arriving in West Africa. It was wide, rolling green grassland with only an occasional tree. What a refreshing change from the very thick bush that characterizes southern Nigeria, Dahomey, and Togo! It looked like land perfect for large-scale farming, but we saw no evidence of it. We also saw many new, brightly colored birds.

Accra: We arrived in the early afternoon and found "Lottie's House," where we stayed the three days we were there with André Margerie, our Cat-sailing friend from the Lagos Yacht Club. André works with a Mr. Lottinger, who was away on vacation. They do a large-scale importing business for many British and some American firms all along the West African coast, and they have offices in Lagos and Accra. The owner being away, we not only had the run of the house and the master bedroom—a lovely modern home with beautiful, spacious gardens and a view—but also the excellent service of his staff, who cooked our meals, made our beds, etc. Just like home . . . in Lagos, that is.

The city? . . . . Well, it is very large, much more so than Lagos, since it is not on an island and thus confined in space. All the same stores are there, but much larger and more of everything. It is like Lagos, only more so. There is a great deal of building and construction going on, many new modern buildings, including a large USSR showroom on the main drag, where Russian products from kitchen cutlery to cars are displayed. André came home one afternoon while we were there and reported a conversation he had had with a man through whom the government was trying to sell Russian-made cars—which no one wants to buy.

Lottie's House is located in a West Hartford–type neighborhood just across from the airport. We were most interested to see the fleet of Russian Ilyushins that they have there. But back to Accra: I would say that the most striking difference we noticed is, in general, a higher standard of living. Because of the gold mining and moreso because of the cocoa plantations, there is a very large population of reasonably well-to-do Ghanaians. There is a large, well-off, native residential section of Accra. The average per capita income in Ghana is higher than that of Portugal or Spain.

'Scuse the change of typewriter. This, briefly, is what we did while in Accra. That evening, André took us out to dinner, along with half a dozen young business acquaintances, to a French eating/dancing type of place. As might be expected, we didn't even start to order our meals until 11:00 p.m. Most interesting were the people, not too much older than we, who were working in various importing businesses, or were in the process of setting up factories of one kind or another, oftentimes the first of their kind in the particular country. All are making a mint for themselves. What I mean to say, in a little less slang, is that business opportunities and possibilities appear, on the whole, to be unlimited. There is no direction for consumption to go, except *up*, for at least the next few decades. For example, look at all the bare feet that heretofore have been unshod. A few decades ago, almost 10 out of 10 Africans had never heard of nor seen a sneaker, much less wanted one. Today, due to the revolution of rising expectations and acquisitiveness in developing cultures, the rate in the growth of demand has risen, and is continuing to do so at geometric rates. Thus I have the impression that, given the introduction of some new product or commodity into these societies—if it takes hold—the demand for it will continue to grow much faster than anyone's ability to expand facilities for increased production.

In my own field of education, I am watching this phenomenon spread like wildfire. In this case, it can be seen in the rising demand for educational facilities and opportunities. Basically, it started out as demand for universal primary education. But no sooner does a portion of the population have a primary education when the pressure for secondary education becomes paramount. From there, you guessed it: Teacher training, higher education with all the fields of specialization, etc. Nigeria hasn't reached the last stage. Right now, it is facilities for secondary education that are needed. You will be amazed to learn that over 50 percent of the young Nigerians holding Certificates of Education that are above the primary level have achieved them by studying on their own, and then taking exams through U.K. correspondence courses. Imagine 50 percent of our American high school students getting their degrees as the result of their own independent application! If only our students could appreciate what it is to NOT be able to take for granted secondary schooling and their passport to a career.

The next day, it rained on and off all day. Therefore, we drove out to the University of Ghana. It is a very impressive-looking institution situated on some hills outside of the city. The architecture is rather baffling. All the buildings are of the exact same material, a red mud-brick with red tile roofs that drape over the eaves in oriental style with white trim. In a way, it reminded me of Stanford University's architecture, with its Southern California, Spanish-mission appearance. Most interesting of all, however,

Top: Gretel and Andre at U. of Ghana

Bottom: View of University from top of campanili tower

was the physical layout. What it amounts to is a long series of quadrangles that are lined up end to end, ascending a hill, on the top of which is a campanile with a tower that commands a view of lovely rolling hills to quite mountainous countryside.

From there, we drove inland to those great mountains that are 30 miles away and serve as a backdrop to the city of Accra. And then up we climbed on a steep, winding road that took us through cool mountain villages with million-dollar views. I am sure that the road would never have been tarred had Nkrumah's "country home" not been there. It is being remodeled to look like the palace of palaces. Our destination was the Botanical Gardens, where, on a high mountaintop, we wandered through plantings of tropical vegetation of all varieties. I nearly froze; it was so cold up there.

An amusing incident occurred just as we were about to leave. Returning to the area where the cars were parked, we saw a large group of Asian men who were posing with clenched teeth and chests thrust out for each other, singly and in groups, as they snapped pictures right and left. We were conjecturing about who they were when one of the guides came down with a guestbook to be signed. We decided that they must be a mission of Chinese economic experts (on communal farming, etc.) or some such thing; perhaps agricultural advisors out on a holiday. As soon as they had driven out of sight, André and Peter rushed over to the guide to ask if they, too, might sign the book—their scheme for finding out who the gentlemen were. They were clever, but the Asians were even more so, because they had signed their names, homes, and occupations all in an Asian script. (Our guess, nonetheless, is probably not too far off, since there is a very large community of Chinese and Russians living in Accra and working in some capacity with the government.)

That evening, we had a spaghetti dinner at the home of Tom and Drew Millington. He is one of the young businessmen whom I referred to as being at dinner the evening before. Tom, a good friend of André's, is the gentleman I have also referred to in an earlier letter—the person from whom we are planning to buy a Catamaran. And buy it we did. Peter and André bought it from Tom, who had been trying to sell it for the past year for £125, including a beautiful, new towing trailer. The boat itself appears to be in excellent condition, has good Terylene sails and a number of extra parts. Peter and André plan to sell it (and not the trailer) here at the Lagos Yacht Club for something in the vicinity of £300 or up! (That is what Cats are selling for in Lagos.) What's more, it is arriving here free of charge, on the Black Star Line, since Tom has connections with them. We may have to pay duty on it, though. Now, if only it would come.

Back to the dinner: The Millingtons' house happened to be on the other side of the Kwame Nkrumah Circle (flash, blink, blink), which is on the other side of town from Lottie's House. Well, when we arrived at the circle, we found that those cars that had dared to brave the circle were almost swimming around it, while some unlucky souls had already stalled. The water from the day's rain was flooding through that main artery of town like a river. Forty-five minutes later, when we finally managed to get to the other side of the circle—by a very circuitous route on Accra's pitted, rutted mud roads, we had to park the car about 100 yards away, take off our shoes, roll up pants, hold up skirts, and slosh our way down the last bit of road. Most interesting is the fact that the Millingtons happen to live next door to the Leader of the Opposition. You may know that all of the parliamentary members of

". . . all of the Parliamentary members of the opposition party are at present in jail"

Ashanti stool from Ghana

the opposition party are at present in jail; and although their leader isn't with them, he might as well be. (Nkrumah doesn't dare put him in jail, since he was so instrumental in working for Ghana's independence.) Yes, Nkrumah has effectively cut him off from easy access, since the government has erected barriers to the main entry to his house. Thus, the only way to get there is over a long, unrepaired mud road that, whenever it rains, is automatically flooded out.

The spaghetti wasn't bad.

The next day we went shopping, looking for Ashanti stools, but we only found a miniature. We did come home with a nice small native boat which now sits on our mantel—a bronze miniature work. We also went to the "harbor" to watch the fantastic way the boats are unloaded. Accra is not blessed with a nice, protected harbor as is Lagos. Thus, freighters must anchor in the open seas one-half to a mile out and wait for fleets of small native canoes, paddled (with forked paddles) by a dozen or more men who chant their way out to the freighters and back. They must carry in everything, from all the imported foodstuffs to automobiles. (They say that there are as many cars on the bottom of the ocean at that place as are produced over a week at General Motors.) The paddlers must wait for the perfect wave, which they then mount and paddle like mad to get their canoes up through the surf. It was an incredible sight to see these athletic men dragging the loaded canoes high up on the sandy beach, fully loaded with their valuable cargo.

It rained all that day.

The drive home, with André this time, was in beautiful weather. We had hoped to be able to spend the last night (which we spent in Accra) in Andre's hut on the Volta, 70 miles from Accra. But due to all the rain, he was afraid that the hut would be floating. On the way back, we waited long enough at the ferry for me to buy some earthenware pots in which the women do much of their cooking. They also carry them filled with water on their heads. (I purchased them both, large ones, for one shilling, or fifteen cents.). We also walked along and peered in the many pots that were brewing various forms of "palm oil chop," as it is called; one was a goat stew, and of course there were the women pounding yams with a pestle in a giant wooden mortar to make fufu with which to eat the different types of "chop." (Fufu, to repeat an earlier description, has the consistency of not-too-wet

Cream of Wheat. It is scooped up into one's hand and pressed into the shape of a spoon against the fingers. Fufu thus becomes an efficient "spoon" for getting the stew from bowl to mouth. Eventually it, too, is eaten.)

There were "shops" there, too, where everything from peppermint balls (imported from the U.K.) and old clocks to shoes were sold, in two-by-four-foot stalls. In some of these, I noticed pictures of Patrice Lumumba on the wall, the way you would see a picture of Christ in the home or shop of a poor Puerto Rican. You could certainly say that, in the eyes of the African, young Patrice (one of the very few educated Congolese leaders) has been canonized.

Top: Dahomey fishing village

Bottom: Dahomey

Before leaving Dahomey, we stopped outside a fishing village to take some pictures of the many canoes on the water and the nets that were stretched out to dry, making an interesting pattern against the sky.

While Peter was snapping here and there, André and I, sitting in the car, were surrounded by about two dozen woolly headed youngsters. "*Donnez-moi un gâteau, monsieur. Donnez-moi une cigarette.*" André, being French, embarked on a delightful conversation with these youngsters, to whom he must have distributed a pack and a half of cigarettes—to be given only to their older brothers and fathers, of course. Their French was impeccable! We asked them questions about the village and their school and where they had learned all their French. It would have been a one- or two-room structure with its French *père*. Would that the French taught in the U.S. schools could equal this. André said that they used better grammatical forms than a French child in France would!

The only thing that I saw, which I would just as soon forget, but which I cannot since we see it all the time here in Lagos, are the bathroom habits of the Africans everywhere you go. In the city or the bush, on a main street or a back track, they behave the same—with complete disregard for modesty or decency, men and women alike relieve themselves. These habits are encouraged in the city, too, because open sewage is available everywhere. Thus, all one has to do is walk to the edge of the road and . . . Nursing mothers, whether they are sedentary or walking along at a brisk clip down the road, the feeding process goes right on.

The trip was thoroughly enjoyable. As a result, I think our perspective on Nigeria is quite altered. Certainly our political perspective has changed. I'll talk about this in a later letter. It is good to be back in free Nigeria after passing through four capital cities in one day, back to our Columbus. He's wonderful to come home to. He was standing out in front waiting for us, having opened the house, dusted, and then closed the house every day. He greeted us as though we were his parents—though he is clearly older than we—returned from a three-month trip. And good to be back to our kittens.

So here it is now, Sunday evening. Yesterday we won another cup— the Catamaran trophy. Peter helmed.

Two members of the UNESCO Commission have arrived, the Russian (who looks like a peasant farmer and doesn't speak English) and an unexpected Italian. Before our sign-language patience runs out, we hope that Conrad Ivanov's interpreter arrives. The others should have arrived today. Tomorrow deliberations begin.

Lyle came over this morning and asked if I would like to come to their house tomorrow at 1:30 to have lunch with Barbara Ward! Guess what I said.

Much love to all,

G

— Letter Twenty-Two —

July 28, 1961

DEF,

It is much more difficult now for me to sit down at a typewriter when I get home from work after sitting at a typewriter all day. But being the martyr that I am—here's the latest from West Africa.

The weather now is positively GEE-OR-GOUS!! I think that as of this week we can pronounce the rainy season over—or reasonably well over, so that we don't have to suffer solid weeks of rain for another 10 months. We can welcome in the gusty, windy, cool months of August and September. It's really winter around here. We actually wear long sleeves to work. Occasionally I even find a sweater necessary.

The sailing, as you might imagine, is positively out of this world. (Won last Saturday's race. Now we are doing some repair work on the hulls—to make them more watertight, for this Saturday's race. Thus didn't race on Wednesday.)

Peter at the helm

[Penned in later] *Won the race this Saturday, but no competition. PBC=skipper.*

Word has gotten round that we have bought another Cat in Accra. Now if only the dern, blasted *&&@#$%&*^%! thing would get here. The comment has been: "So now you're going to settle who does the skippering once and for all—a boat for each of you." Actually, they are not far wrong, since either Peter or I will be skippering it in all the races until it is sold. We're in no hurry to sell it and are quite sure we can get a good price. The only complication will be in having to buy one of the few old clunkers in the club in order to get berthing rights, then chopping up the clunker for kindling wood. Right now, the sheds are up to capacity with 98 boats berthed—right here in our front yard, so to speak.

Grace, Columbus's wife, is due to have her fourth child sometime within the next week or so, and Columbus is sooo excited, you would think it was his first. A month and a half ago,

I told him that I would like to get something for Grace, and we discussed what might be most useful and lasting and what she would really need. We decided on a bed for the baby. (I had already decided before the discussion.) Without one, Columbus would have to sleep with two of the children while Grace slept with the baby. Last Saturday, Columbus and I went down to a little shop on the edge of the local market where we knew there were some carpenters. There we negotiated for a bed that is being made to specifications. It will be ready this Saturday. All their work is done in mahogany. (Mahogany, along with teak, is one of the more common furniture woods around here.) It will be 3 feet 3 inches long and 2 feet wide—big enough to last the child until it is five or six. It will have high slats and the proper posts for mosquito netting. It will cost £4. On Tuesday, Columbus went to see a mattress maker, who two days later delivered a mattress that will fit. It is stuffed with cotton, I think. The choice was between cotton and grass. That will cost £1/10. I told him that he must buy a rubber or plastic cover and linen for it. All this has been done without Grace's knowing. (I've given strict orders for secrecy, and Columbus plays along with great glee.) As you must know, I am doing this more for Columbus than for Grace.

Speaking of playing Santa Claus, last week when Columbus announced at breakfast that he would need some more money for the market (he shops for us in the local market—"bargains" is really the word—for fruit, meat, and vegetables every Tuesday and Friday morning), Peter produced an extra 7 shillings for him to spend on a chicken for his family. The last time we had chicken, a lovely stuffed roast fowl he had cooked, we asked him how often his family ate chicken. Many stewards, even here in the city, keep chickens—which are forever getting into my flower bed. Most Africans, no matter what rank, seem to have goats and chickens as a natural part of the household. Columbus said that usually at Christmastime he splurges: 7 shillings on a chicken for his family. This rather horrified us, and reminded us again how rarely he or his family ever get to eat real meat other than the dried crayfish that they mix in with their stews, or the bits of cheap stew meat that appear in the egusi soup. Well, that afternoon, Columbus insisted on bringing me out to see the chicken he had tied up in the spare room (which they should use for cooking, but they store things in it while Grace cooks outside over an open fire). The next day, with great flourish, the chicken was killed and dressed. For the following two days, we were showered with profuse thanks from him, his wife, and children—as if we had given them a year's supply of chicken meat, which it *was*, come to think of it!

This last week I went on a sewing jag. I've been down to the local market's textile area, where the variety and volume of materials and patterns are just amazing. The variety of prices quoted for the same kind of material is also amazing. I was looking for some American khaki similar to shorts that the tailor made for Peter. For that same material, same color even, I was asked everything from 6 pence to 4 pounds 6 pence. There were hundreds and hundreds of women who don't even have stalls, have just a few inches to sit on with their wares along the roadside. One pathway was so crowded there was barely enough room to pass between the piles of material. The market women buy from Lebanese or Syrian wholesalers, who in turn get their textiles from Holland, Japan, Red China, Great Britain, Germany, Switzerland, and Egypt. "American khaki," incidentally, is made in Japan. I found this out later: big letters stamped on the material.

The (UNESCO) Advisory Commission at the University of Lagos, for whom I am the secretary right now, has been working very hard. They hold sessions all morning and many afternoons with representatives of the ministries, organizations, and professional societies, such as engineering, law, etc., who have all been asked to prepare briefs relating to their particular field. For example, the Ministry of Health needs courses in medicine, the Ministry of Labour (as the British and Nigerians spell it) courses in business, commerce, and economics. Overall, the Commission was looking for advice on the kinds of courses the "professionals" think should be offered, and seeking general programme (British spelling) recommendations.

"creating the University of Lagos"

'Scuse, I'll continue this on another air letter. [There was no more space.]

Last week the UNESCO Commission spent a few days interviewing in Ibadan, capital of the Western Region. Tomorrow they leave for a few more days of interviews at the new University of Nsukka in Enugu, capital of the Eastern Region. I, sniff, won't get to accompany them. They expect to be through their preliminary draft by the 19th of August, at which time the entire Commission (nine men, counting the Russian interpreter) will fly to Paris. There they will write the final paper and hand it to the director of UNESCO, who, in turn, will hand it to the Nigerian government. This, I am told, is to prevent leakage.

I don't have a very high opinion of the Americans on the Commission. They were chosen as sort of a desperation move by Jaja Wachuku[22] who made the blunder of inviting an NYU team to come to Nigeria to work on the proposed University of Lagos without ever even telling the Minister of Education (Aja Nwachukwu) that they were coming until they had arrived.

Jaja has now been reappointed, by the way, as Minister of Foreign Affairs. The Ministry of Economic Development will never miss him, I can assure you. His heart was never in development planning or economics. The Frenchman, Capelle, who is Chef de Mission, is very capable and well qualified. The Italian, who arrived unannounced from Paris, was sent back last week, equally as quietly. The two Nigerians are excellent men. It is a shame, however, that no one directly involved in education in Nigeria was appointed. The Vice-Rector of Moscow University has been somewhat of a problem, since everything must be interpreted for him and from him. This, to say nothing of his political affiliations, has isolated him from the others. He also spends valuable time telling the others how much better the Russian system of education is. When the Commission had a press conference for reporters from the national papers, the question was asked: "Would there be any aid coming from Russia?" since much money was coming from UNESCO, ICA, and some from Great Britain. Ivanov's reply was: "Russia, as a member of the UN, would be giving money through that organization in the UNESCO contribution." Then he went into a five-minute rapid-speak of memorized figures of the numbers of Nigerians and Africans who were already in the Friendship University, the University of Moscow, etc. Capelle had a hard time cutting Ivanov off before Ivanov was sure the reporters had his information.

"The Russian member has been somewhat of a problem."

I get to hear some of their sessions but spend most of the time typing up and duplicating their "minutes," briefs that are to be presented, doing correspondence, contacting ministries and organizations to be sure they are coming to meet with the Commission at a certain time, and seeing that they get their briefs in, etc. I enjoy it. In the process, I have met a number of people whom I have been trying to contact for my thesis research. So this, also, has been helpful.

Two items in the news have particularly interested us. One is [Abubakar Tafawa] Balewa's current visit to the United States and his talks with President Kennedy. We, of course, beamed with pride at mention of the Five-Year Plan. (Little does the public know that the American president is praising the work of Americans, not necessarily Nigerians, when praising Nigeria's Five-Year Plan.) Wolf obviously did a number-one sales job on Rivkin[23] (head of the four-man USAID economic mission that was here two months ago). Peter says the mission team met with Wolf and Lyle officially almost every day that they were in the Lagos area. And then Wolf, who is a personal friend of Rivkin and has worked with him on projects at MIT, had daily private sessions with him at the Federal Palace Hotel. (Wolfgang Stolper, by the way, I am convinced, is more pro-Nigeria than the most nationalistic Nigerians . . . and mostly on the basis of sound economic judgment. His conversation with Barbara Ward at lunch the other day was just amazing; but I will get to that later.)

Speaking of the two economists with whom PBC works, Wolf has just gotten over a long bout of "the fever," as it is called out here—"malaria" to you. He is at present in Addis Ababa at an international conference for economists particularly interested in Africa. Lyle, on the other hand, has been doing a considerable amount of gallivanting around this country, collecting data and seeing projects. (Wish he'd send Peter on a few of these "tours." Poor Peter gets so tired of collecting statistics, making projection charts, and so on, without the excitement of making the overall evaluation judgments and recommendations.)[24]

The second news item that particularly interested us is Kennedy's call-up of reserves over the "Berlin crisis."[25] We heaved a sigh of relief when we heard that bit of news over the BBC morning broadcast the other day, thanking our lucky stars we were in good old, unstrategic West Africa—far away from reservist activity. We're still curious to know how extensive this "call-up" has been. Meanwhile, Peter chortles with satisfaction that he is here and not in Ann Arbor going to monthly Navy Reserves "Weekend Warrior" meetings at Grosse Isle.

Well, I take back most of what I said about the Crossroads Africa youngsters. They are staying in the dorm at King's College, where I work with the Commission, so I have met a number of them. In fact, four of them came over this morning (it is now Sunday) and I took two of them out in our Cat. André took the two others in his Cat. They are good-looking, intelligent, wholesome young Americans. From what they have told me, they have been begging the Department of Social Welfare, which has planned all of their activities, not to send them out on these ridiculous projects. (Remember the Crossroads cleaning crew I wrote about?) The following is a quote from the first page of a letter typed on a stencil sheet that I gave to one of the boys who was writing home en masse. He failed to throw away the carbon, so my prying eyes read it over. I think you'll be interested to hear his reaction at being located in Lagos for the summer. To start in the middle of a paragraph, it reads as follows:

> . . . This arrangement made our Crossroads project unique and served as quite an initial disappointment to many of us, for one of the objectives of Crossroads had been to put the American student in an African village where he could live and work with the people on their level, and, in doing so, learn to know and understand them, their life and their ambitions. Living in Lagos, the most modern city in West Africa, certainly did not offer this to us at all.

And so on. So . . . my views have changed somewhat. Now I think the Department of Social Welfare should be hanged for how they are posting the Crossroads Africa students.

Love, G

[A hand note written on the margin of the letter says:]

P.S. The book you sent on sailing took the usual time to get here—a little over two months.

— Letter Twenty-Three —

[N.B. The following two letters were sent specifically to my mother, thus were never copied and disseminated to the DEF. They are more personal in tone.]

July 30, 1961

Mom,

This is a "Come to Africa" letter. In fact, it is a "You're crazy if you don't come!" communication.

You mentioned that you were thinking about coming (or the possibility of coming) the last week of November and the first two in December. To begin with, the last thing YOU would need worry about re coming is weather. I know that it's the old $ that concerns you most: but that I cannot argue with. You only live once, and I don't think that can really keep one from doing what he or she would like to do, especially when it is as exciting and as broadening as coming to a place such as we are living in right now.

But back to the weather: The really hot weather doesn't come until the months of January, February, March, and even then it is no worse than the Connecticut River Valley in the summertime, just more continuous. If my memory is correct, you LIKE that kind of weather. Well, November–December will be very pleasant—just perfect for your tastes. It would be much too cold for you right now. This is definitely not summer weather in our sense of the term.

Here's a good argument: Think of all the postage you'd save by bringing over the belated b'day presents and early Christmas presents and taking back ours for you. Really, sending anything other than by mail boat is prohibitive in price, despite the time it takes. If you had sent that sailing book by air, it would have cost you over double the price of the book. Well, multiply that many times for packages from our end at Christmastime. Yikes!

Which reminds me: Grandma's postage money is used up almost as fast as it arrives. She is very sweet to send it. . . .

I had to laugh today when it occurred to me, after the young people from Crossroads Africa left, that while you are busy entertaining foreign visitors to the U.S., we are busy entertaining foreign visitors to Nigeria—except they are usually fellow Americans, but nonetheless, "foreign visitors." From the tales they have told about their illnesses, tummy troubles, liver infections, etc., I am grateful that we have been as healthy as we have. I have had absolutely no trouble at all, just overwhelming fatigue in the hot season.

Guess I got a little off of the main subject. The thought and feeling is still there. I know you would love our cats, our Cat, our view, our Columbus, and our new, very exciting country, to say nothing of its colorful people.

DO COME!

Love,

G

Almost biblical this woman winnowing her grain on bank of the Niger River.

— Letter Twenty-Four —

[This letter was designed to shock my family with the super-casual announcement that I knew would surprise them: a grandchild due in four months. This air letter, which she never copied, is the only one in my mother's stack of saved air letters that was marked with a big red star.]

August 9, 1961

Dear Mom,

The news of your proposed trip to visit us in December has been THE event of the week! Our only regret is that you won't be able to stay longer. It is a long way to come for such a short time. But then I guess we should be glad that you can come at all.

. . . Yes, we have an extra bed, even an extra room (very small) that is . . . . [text omitted]

We have been making a list of all the things you should see and do while you are here. I will probably stop working that month, since I expect to have a baby by mid-January,[26] so I will be free to take you around. What great fun it will be.

You really should see Ghana and the intervening French territories while you are here. We could do this by car. You should also see the Northern Region—a world quite different from the southern regions of Nigeria. This has been one of our "musts," too, which we have been hoping to do before January and the relative confinement that will come after the birth day. . . .

There is another "must" that has been plaguing me as our time here gets shorter and shorter, and it is something that your visit would make so much easier. I should have all the basic research done for my thesis, now, before January. Much must be done in Ibadan, seeing people, visiting teacher-training colleges in and around that area, and doing a certain amount of research in the library at the University College, Ibadan. (My topic, you may recall, is on the trends and developments in teacher training in the Western Region of Nigeria over the past decade or so.) Since I have been working, this trip has been out of the question; and before then I didn't go because Peter couldn't accompany me. With you here, we could drive up for a few days, stay in the Ford Flats at UCI [University College, Ibadan], and from there drive out to a number of surrounding villages to visit the educational institutions, and to see the people I must interview. This ought to give you a new perspective on education. It would not only allow me to fulfill my purpose, but give you a much better opportunity to see what is typical of Nigeria than what we could show you in Lagos. Peter just said that we should send you a slew of books, which you could read

Top: Washer women walking by the Ministry of Economic Development
Bottom: Majestic, tall woman in front of Lagos laundry shed

Lagos laundry drying field

before coming, that would put you miles ahead of the average visitor to Nigeria. We'll get them together.

Of course, details on clothing, etc., will be forthcoming. The only thing that I would advise you to look into right now, and the sooner the better, is passport and visas. These things can take much time. We were able to have ours taken care of in a month's time (a record) only because the Ford Foundation got the government to give us special privileges. If you start now, you might have it taken care of in time.

Another little detail, which determines whether you get into a country or not, is *shots*. Find out what you need and where you will have to go to get them. If I remember correctly, the Winter girl from Hartford had to go to New York City to get her yellow fever shots. (Seems to me at least New Haven should have them!) Annoying details, but necessary and requiring much time to administer.

You must come light, too, so we can load you down with Christmas presents.

Oh, goody, goody, we can hardly wait! I am sure you will never regret this adventure.

> Much love,
> Gretel

— Letter Twenty-Five —

August 10, 1961

DEF,

This will be a short one, I think. I am in the midst of curtain-making for our bedroom. I'm trying to cover the six very long windows in our bedroom, four of which are double doors—a lot of curtain! (I've already designed and made a blouse with the remainder.)

The Commission is off in Kaduna and Zaria in the Northern Region, and, after typing and stenciling steadily for four days, I have been able to catch up with the work they have been piling on my desk. Preliminary drafts are being prepared for the creation of a curriculum for the University of Lagos (to be). Between trying to make sense out of the Russian interpreter's terrible English, the Frenchman's impossible writing, one of the American's inexcusable grammar and sentence structure . . . AND the different ways of spelling practiced by the English–New Zealand contingent and the American–Canadian members, plus my *own* versions, of course, well, it has been a bit trying.

Just to give you an example of the way the British write their English, I am going to make this paragraph a specimen of their Programme Writing. *It is hard labour, changing the whole colour of things when one must use such old Fashioned spelling, and capitalising (never use a Z) of every other Noun, whilst being an American and in the centre of this jolly mess, I say: "Enough of these Archaic Methodes!"*

THE NATIONAL ECONOMIC (Five Year) PLAN, which literally is *the* plan being evolved in the country right now, is beginning to take shape, but only as the result of long hours of hard labor (how nice not to have to use a "u" in that word) by Wolf, Lyle, and PBC. Peter has been seeing many heads of this corporation or that branch of government, to collect data and statistics and make projections. There is much legwork involved to draw up a plan of this sort, with none of the "facts" clear in the available material one would expect the government to have. But then, we have to keep telling ourselves that is why we are here—because Nigeria is an underdeveloped country lacking the expected statistics. The joke among expatriates is to throw up one's hands and wail, "WAWA"—West Africa Wins Again!

The other day, who should walk by my office but Art Hyde! . . . Peter's old Williams College buddy. I'm sure he was more surprised to see me than I him, 'cause I knew that he was somewhere here in Nigeria. Since then, we have entertained him for lunch, a sail, and lots of talk, getting caught up on all the doings in Williamstown and what his Crossroads group has been doing here this summer. He came back the next afternoon, which was yesterday, and crewed for me in the race, this being his second time in a Catamaran, and knowing next to nothing about sailing. We won the race over 21 other boats, despite a handicap of five minutes and five seconds! He did very well. Then he stayed for supper.

Art's Crossroads Africa group has been building an auditorium for a boys' club in Sapele. I think they may have finished their project. They leave for Ghana on Saturday and then return at the end of the month. Sapele is a good day's drive from here, not far from Benin in the Western Region. The youngsters have been living and eating very simply. But I must say Art was pretty excited to see the meat, vegetables, and salad that we served him. The crew has been doing something constructive for a community, and, most important, having contact with young people of their own age. Four of them are students from University College, Ibadan, who joined the group for the summer. This interaction, incidentally, is the central purpose of Crossroads Africa, not necessarily that of building projects for a community.

There has been the usual rash of cocktail parties of late. In the past two weeks, we have been invited to three different cocktail parties for the UNESCO Commission: one to meet the members of the World Bank Mission who are doing a survey of Nigeria, another given by the Japanese Consulate to meet a Japanese economic expert who is here on a trade mission, and another, a purely social affair—a going-away party for a girl who had been here for two years working for Shell BP. Of the other parties, we attended about half.

Most interesting was a buffet dinner given by Justice G. B. A. Coker and his wife. Justice Coker is an outstanding Nigerian. He is a member of the Lagos State High Court and also on the UNESCO Commission. They live in a mansion over on the mainland. Never, never in my life have I seen such a "spread"!! There must have been 250 people there, most of whom were prominent Nigerians. This was a refreshing change from the British and expatriate crowd we see so often at social affairs, and they were all dressed to the teeth. The house is large, and their patio and gardens even larger. They had used their dining room and one of their living rooms with enormous tables to lay out the most incredible feast you can imagine. There were whole cooked fish the size of our dining-room table alone: about five of them. There were whole cooked chickens, stuffed and surrounded by all sorts of rice and vegetable and salad dishes. But most spectacular were the two baby lambs that had been roasted and laid out whole: feet, neck, and all, with stuffing in their middles right on the table. To get the meat, one simply took a great sword and sliced off a chunk from its side!! There were also innumerable other interesting meat dishes, homemade potato chips (since nothing like that would keep long enough to be sold commercially), sausage rolls, etc., etc. Another two tables were covered with desserts: giant-size, elaborately decorated cakes, plus large pineapples stuffed with fruit. We ate with some Nigerian lawyers. I will relate part of our conversation in the next letter.

    Luv,

       G

Handsome formal dress of Lagos office workers. Woman's dress is made from traditional textiles

— Letter Twenty-Six —

August 21, 1961
Lokoja, Nigeria

Dear Mom,

Here goes without a machine. I know it will be as hard on you as it is on me, but my typewriter is inaccessible, being 370 miles away. Peter and I left Lagos yesterday with less than 24 hours' notice to accompany Lyle, two of his sons, and his "small boy." You will see on your map that Lokoja is a town (15,000 pop.) located right at the fork where the Niger and Benue Rivers converge on their way to the sea. Peter and Lyle are here to talk with the Inland Waterways people, but I'll talk about that in the DEF letter later in the week, when we are home and I have an efficient typewriter.

This will be further "palaver" about your projected trip. [Then follows a complete air letter of advice as to: what clothes to bring: everything sleeveless, open-necked, open shoes if possible. Nothing tight, 'cause one is wet with perspiration most of the time, making sleeves, necks, belts, etc., unbearable. <u>The importance of taking malaria pills even before arriving</u>; possible activities; <u>what to study</u>: "It's easy to study Ghanaian and Nigerian political development, since they illustrate each other so well by contrast." And the letter ends with: "I wish you were on this trip with us now. You'd love it. I see things around me pretending I am you seeing it all for the first time. This part of the country is quite beautiful and the villages and people fascinating."]

Love,

G

House boats at Lokoja on the Niger trade for months on each voyage down river.

— Letter Twenty-Seven —

August 27, 1961

Dear Mom,

Goodness, gracious! One would think I had dropped a bomb on Knob Hill [where my parents were living in Glastonbury, CT.] I must admit, I'm terribly pleased to hear that you are as excited as we are, despite our efforts to be calm and casual about it. Only one or two people here in Lagos know, though I am over halfway through my pregnancy. You wouldn't know either, except that, after much thought, it seemed better that you know in view of your projected trip. This letter will probably get there before the one I wrote to you from Lokoja, since the mail from there must all come down the river by boat before it is flown out of Nigeria. So I may repeat myself a little in answer to your questions.

I feel fine. In fact, haven't felt better nor had more energy since coming to Nigeria. The first few months of pregnancy, I must admit, were a bit trying, but not bad. The only thing I dread is the last two months that will be in the hot weather. Do I have a good obstetrician? Well . . . I doubt there really is such an animal in this part of the continent. After much consideration, however, I have chosen a Dr. Wood, a general practitioner from the U.K. who has been here for over a decade and is known for his good service and clean clinic (as compared with what else is available here in West Africa). He is a very casual character. I went to see him at the end of my third month, and, well, I know more from the books that Jean Plews (a friend of mine in Ann Arbor who had a baby just before we left) gave to me, knowing of our plans, than I will ever learn from the doctor. The books are good guides as to what I should eat, how much weight I should gain and how fast, etc., etc. I figure that by the time of delivery, I shall weigh what I weighed just prior to my wedding. Then, when the time comes, I shall go to the clinic and have the baby—natural childbirth, as most babies are born out here. I feel exceedingly relaxed, confident, and, above all, grateful that our parenthood could be exactly as we planned it!! I know we shall make good parents, too. (Just think of all the training we've had with Fliege, Mouche, Sacha, Kam, Seri, Obi, and Dara.) [All recent and current pets.] Waiting until we really wanted a child makes it so much more exciting. And my, are we impatient!

Things for a layette? I plan to buy another plastic dishpan, just like the one we use in the kitchen, which will be its bed and bath. That, I hope, will be the extent of the furniture. I don't want anything but the bare essentials, since we will be here only a few months after it is born, and I have the impression that most people (Western people, that is) get themselves much too bogged down with baby equipment. Other necessities should not be difficult to find in the large department stores here in Lagos. I will say, though, that a Namaw-made [referring to Grandmother] blanket-wrapper, such as I have seen her manufacturing before, would probably come in very handy. . . .

What about maternity clothes? Well, so far my regular clothes have been fine. The store offerings are enough to make even a peasant woman shudder, and patterns (Simplicity, Butterick) are as scarce as obstetricians. Consequently, I am designing and making all of my maternity clothes with the aid of two basic patterns I have been fortunate to get. The possibilities for variations are unlimited. I am becoming quite the seamstress, and have learned a lot by having to make some of my own patterns. I bought an issue of *Vogue,* and among the usual extremes of their ultra fashions, I found some that could easily be made for maternity wear—waistless, etc. So one day, picture in hand and Grace's (Columbus's wife) hand-operated Singer sewing machine on the table, I made me a very smart, cactus-green,

Gretel's home made maternity dress

chic, linen sack-style tunic (three-quarter length to midthigh) that I wear over a skirt (rust/yellow-colored), which I made ultra pencil style. Most effective, and smart to wear, pregnant or not. People comment every time I wear it: "Where did you find such a smart dress in Lagos!!?" I never let them know its origin or purpose.

Yes, I can get milk. Initially I tried drinking dried Carnation skim milk in addition to half a dozen other whole-milk brands that are dried. They all tasted dreadful. So now I am drinking SAMCO milk (Swedish-African Milk Co.), which is dried milk imported by this company and then reconstituted and sold in cartons as whole, fresh milk. Quite good, but very expensive. That, however, is the one foodstuff that I am rather consistent about, in addition to the large bowl of fresh fruit that Columbus prepares for us every day. In an

attempt to eat enough meat and protein, our food bill has almost doubled, making savings nearly impossible. The cost of food, even though we buy most of it in the local market, comes to more than twice our food budget in the United States. The extra allowance that Ford gives us to help meet these expenses doesn't begin to make up the difference.

No, I don't think you should have to be here when the baby comes or after. I have Columbus to do all the work for me and take care of Peter when I am at the clinic. Besides, you should be coming to Africa to see *Africa*, which would be rather difficult during or after delivery. As I mentioned in the other letter, the best time for you to come would be as soon as possible before *it* comes. The sooner that is, the more mobility and freedom I shall have—like Sept., Oct., Nov.-ish. And DO come for four weeks. That would be wonderful.

Much, much love,

Gretel

Awka, a town we passed through on our way to the East, is famous for its carved doors.

— Letter Twenty-Eight —

August 31, 1961

Dear Extended Family,

Long time no write to. It's true, the longer I wait, the longer the list becomes of events to relate, the more formidable the task appears, and thus the more difficult it is to sit me down and begin. Well, here goes.

I've already had one interruption. Discussing dinner for tonight, I discovered that, in addition to the nice leg of lamb Columbus bought in the local market the other day, we are to have boiled English-style cabbage, which, frankly, I'm tired of. In fact, this whole boiled approach of the English to their food leaves me and the food in an uninteresting, wet and soggy state. So, armed with my bible, *The Joy of Cooking*,[27] I'm attempting to rectify the situation. The cabbage will be parboiled and then disguised with grated cheese, chopped nuts, and a cream sauce. I usually plan on preparing a dish twice with Columbus before he can do it alone. We have a nice cooking relationship, however, since for every recipe I teach him, he is able to teach me one, too. Also, at last I am learning, under his tutelage, to make good gravies and sauces and soups.

Back to the business at hand. Since my last DEF communication, the UNESCO Commission, for which I was working, has left. That was a week ago Saturday. Then last week we were away in Lokoja.[28] This week PBC has been working from 8:00 a.m. to 8:00 p.m., and sometimes later than that. Meanwhile, I have taken up my thesis "investigations" in earnest.

Now for the details.

Saturday, August 19, the UNESCO Advisory Commission on the University of Lagos left Ikeja Airport after a rather intensive month and a half of investigations, followed by preliminary writing here in Nigeria. By that time, I, too, was heaving a sigh of relief. The work I had been doing for them was always interesting. It was just the volume and pace that got me down. No matter how interesting the material was, after a while I became tired of being a duplicating machine and impatient to start writing my own thesis instead of reproducing someone else's investigations, notes, and hypotheses. The only satisfaction came from using my brain on such momentous matters as correcting spelling (yes, me!), punctuation, grammar, and sentence structure. (Shocking, some of these "professors.")

The Commission had been juggling with a variety of questions, such as: the advisability of inaugurating part-time studies (evening courses) toward a degree, correspondence courses from a Nigerian-based institution instead of from the U.K., establishing a nonresidential "city college" that is actually built around a more commercial/professional line of studies, and so on.

All of these matters mark a real break from the classical British-academic model of higher education that has had sole monopoly on formal post-secondary education in West Africa. To most observers, these changes will appear to be a lesser version of the education they had so far. This is because the new, more practically oriented curriculum and method of obtaining it, as the university may offer it, will be suspect in the eyes of educated Nigerians. They will have no regard for its great practicality and ability to meet the pressing needs of the Nigerian economy. This is a cardinal aspect of the education here in Nigeria that always depresses me: the adoption of Britain's most snobbish attitudes toward education (i.e., one isn't worth anything unless one has gone to certain schools, has a certain kind of accent, has studied certain types of courses, etc.). This includes the often impractical, expensive way of providing physical plant and faculty, with plush accommodations for each student—who is never expected to do any physical labor, such as making one's bed or cleaning out one's room—and a faculty that enjoys the most incredible array of special privileges, allowances, and benefits. All of this stands out in stark relief, set in an underdeveloped country that is least able to afford such attitudes and practices.

> *"The UNESCO Commission on the [creation] of a U. of Lagos has been juggling with a variety of questions . . . marking a real break from the classical British model of higher education."*

These are some of the problems the Commission has had to face, and is trying to alleviate by setting up an institution designed to meet the country's immediate needs in business, law, commerce, medicine, engineering, and education. Lack of such education is becoming more and more serious here due to the current institutional patterns and practices one finds in higher education in Nigeria.

Plans are to have the University of Lagos open in October of 1962. If so, this will make it the third university in Nigeria (with a population of 40 million people). The first and only one up until last fall was University College at Ibadan. Then last October, the university at Nsukka in the Eastern Region was opened rather hastily. Before long, the Northern Region hopes to have one of its own universities established in Zaria—though how and why I will never know, when one considers that there are only 10 boys from the entire Northern Region, population of 20 million, in secondary school; and that school is in Lagos!!! Fewer than half of these boys will be qualified to go on to higher education. Where does the Northern Region expect their students to come from? Certainly no southerner (being non-Muslim) would go north seeking higher education.

Meanwhile, additional moves are being made toward establishing a second university in the Western Region at Ife, the supposed center of Yoruba culture, since the university at Ibadan is under the jurisdiction of the Federal Government. I am concerned about the feasibility of such institutions when the quality and quantity of good secondary schools is hardly high enough to feed the existing institutions of higher education. The Federal and regional governments seem more than willing to spend their limited capital on impressing the public, promoting news about "establishment of a new university." The government's resources should be spent on training teachers to provide to secondary schools. Then their graduates will eventually justify the building of additional universities.

The UNESCO Commission members were in Paris all last week haggling over the final version of their proposals. Nerves and tempers were slightly frayed by the time they left Lagos, because of their heavy schedule, social engagements, and the occasional need to iron out differences of opinion while in session. For example, the Russian delegate insisted that his wording be used in his joint draft (with the Englishman) on curriculum and faculty for engineering studies. He insisted that it include such expressions (in translation) as "the intelligentsia" when referring to the "educated."

The Saturday they left, I picked Peter up at noon, feeling, I think, as bedraggled as the entire Commission combined. I was covered with mimeograph ink (the British call it a "cyclostyler") and relieved that I had been able to finish all the briefs and drafts that had been left to me. I didn't want to have to return in the afternoon. Our Saturday afternoons are fairly well taken up preparing for and sailing the Saturday race.

When I picked up PBC at the House of Representatives, Lyle Hansen was first to come out. He announced that we were leaving with him for Lokoja at 7:30 the next morning. His two elder sons and his "small boy" would also be going. Traveling by car to Lokoja is a day's trip northeast of Lagos. The town is located right at the confluence of the great Niger and Benue Rivers, which divide Nigeria roughly into her three regions.

The purpose of the trip to Lokoja was to see the Inland Waterways Department people about river transport of all kinds, their present problems and projects, and the ramifications of the possible construction

Road north of Ife headed to Lokoja

LETTERS FROM NIGERIA

of the much-talked-about Niger Dam. All of these developments, of course, have to be evaluated by the planners of the next Five-Year Plan for recommendations and monetary allocations, etc. Had they gone a week earlier, I wouldn't have accompanied them. Not more than half an hour out of a job (I wasn't prepared for it to be curtailed quite so immediately after the Commission's departure), I was embarking on a new adventure.

Adventure it was! The drive, as usual, was through lush, green, tropical bush of very dense undergrowth. Then at times, as we got farther north into refreshing, open forest stands and were entering into the Middle Belt. (This is a region marking the pagan nether-nether land separating the Muslim North, proper, from the somewhat Christian southern regions.)

We emerged onto open savanna tracts ringed by bulbous mountains that appeared to have been dropped there by mistake. Here the people appeared to be much poorer; the clothes, on those who were wearing them, were rags, although they appear to be strong and well fed. Because the soil is poorer (laterite), a subsistence-level family is outside the cash economy of export crops and lacking a commercial crop to sell.

We passed many hunters with their Dane guns slung over their shoulders. These guns are homemade, out of an old pipe and some wood. We also passed a number of weighing scales along the roadside. These are for weighing the akara seeds or beans grown in this area. They are dried

Trip stop in the Middle Belt among "bulbous mountains that appeared to have been dropped there by mistake."

Top: Ibadan, city of seven hills
Bottom: Street in Ibadan

in the sun and later ground up and used to make a variety of fried and palm-oil combinations. My favorite is the akara ball, sold everywhere on the streets. It is prepared by mixing the ground beans with onions and salt and chopped peppers and then fried in groundnut oil.

A new cocoa season has begun, there being four harvests a year. We saw a great deal of cocoa seeds laid out on mats to dry in the sun. It was most satisfying to see the growing pods on the short cocoa trees. Cocoa trees, incidentally, grow in the forest understory, as the middle layer of foliage. They are a key element for the growth of Nigeria's wealth, since this is the main high-value export. It will continue to be so as long as Nigeria remains one of the only three large producers of cocoa for the world market, along with Ghana and Brazil. It is estimated that the average farmer earns for himself £325 per acre of cocoa a year. A handsome income.

Our first stop was in Ibadan, on one of the city's hilltops. There we relaxed for a few moments and looked out across the sea of rusty, sheet-metal roofs that cover the thousands of mud houses in this, West Africa's largest city of 600,000. It is really quite a spectacle, from our vantage point, of African dwellings: a wondrous study in many brownish hues, and trading activity made more dramatic by its setting there on "the seven hills."

Only the gregarious Yoruba people could have created this city. To one whose eye is used to the modern, brightly colored, multistoried structures of Western cities, the drab brown, one-storied city of Ibadan is an unusual sight.

Artisan demonstrating the "lost wax process"

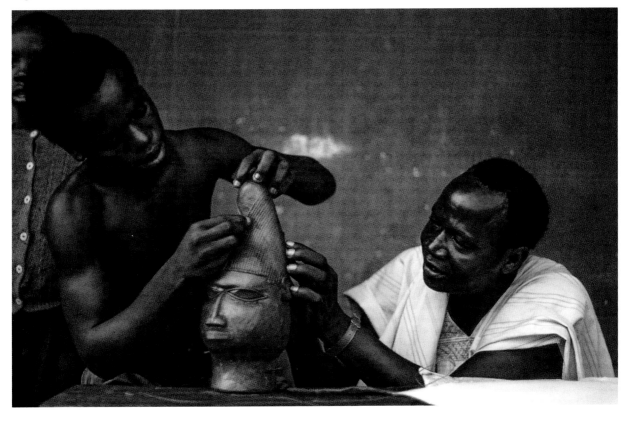

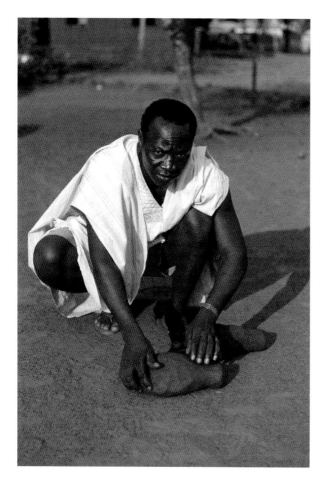

Left: Before firing in the "lost wax process"

Right: Juju Man made by "lost wax process"

Our next stop en route was Ife, to see the museum that houses samples of the famous bronze statues made by the "lost wax" process, and less-well-known terra-cotta works done in this region in the past. This town, as I mentioned earlier, is also known and looked to as the center of Yoruba culture, where the first Oba or Alafin or leader was born.

The museum, as is true of all art collections in Nigeria, is quite new. Its exhibits are expanded each year, as so much comes from excavations in process. Appreciation for, and thus collection of, Nigerian and other African art forms has arisen only recently. The 6d stamp that appears on all the air letters that I send you, and some of the regular mail stamps, have pictures of an Ife bronze head.

As we walked around, pausing to study each exhibit, and then moving on, a growing crowd of Nigerians walked around, paused to study *each of us*, and then moved on—as we moved on. I'm not sure which "exhibit" was more carefully scrutinized, but at times <u>this</u> individual exhibit was appreciative of the glass protection enjoyed by the bronze heads, which preserved them from black hands, always anxious to touch.

We bought a bronze Juju man made by the lost-wax process, complete with skirt, beads, walking stick, and packet on his torso to carry herbs.

We ate lunch in a quiet schoolyard surrounded by a cocoa, bamboo,

Fulani Cattle

and mango forest. Columbus had made us a mound of egg salad sandwiches. He roasted a stuffed chicken, which he had disjointed, and then he wrapped a tasty, moist dressing separately. Ummmmmmm.

A sight that is very common along the roadside as one travels from North to South, or vice versa, is herds of Fulani cattle being driven 700 to 1,000 miles from the North to Lagos and its vicinity by tall, slender Fulani herdsmen. These "cowboys" are clad in their usual white robes and the caps of their Muslim religion. The other day, I was struck by the similarity between these very tall, unusually skinny white cows and their masters. The great dignity shared by both master and beast, however, is not only in their height, but in the cattle. Their startlingly large horns rise almost straight into the air, three to four feet from their heads. They also have a gross hump that extends forward from the downward slope of their neck. Another hump rises on the top of the beast on its back above its forelegs. These muscular animals are the beef we eat: a long cry from the square-shaped, pampered animal that reaches the American stockyards, courtesy of someone else's locomotion.

Another sight that we saw on the road, this one not so common, was that of a man, either practicing Juju—a representative of the soul of some village elder—or he was a joker dressed up in a green-white and brown grassy, hairy costume that covered his entire body and head with the proper exaggerated apertures for eyes and mouth. As we approached him, head-on in the car, he fairly well succeeded in speeding our continued passage down the road with his menacing, breath-stopping leaps and gestures that were only further exaggerated by the mound of flying grass and hair that were his costume.

We arrived in Lokoja just prior to sundown, had cocktails at the home of one of the hydrologists for the Inland Waterways Department (IWD) and then had dinner at the government-run "catering rest house" (as they are all referred to here). These are the only commercial accommodations available for the traveler or visitor. There we stayed during our four days. The food was good, typically British: steak and kidney pie, Yorkshire pudding, bread custards, tarts, our morning eggs always served on top of the toast with fried tomatoes on the side and tea at our bedside in the morning when we woke up. Tea was also available midafternoon. Like all the rest of this isolated bush-town, there was no electricity. We used kerosene lanterns and candles. A steward had set up a canvas cot in our unit, on which I slept. They also brought down a mosquito net, which was quickly hung on the wires that run across the ceiling of every such room in Nigeria for that purpose.

Monday breakfast we had fish cakes and beans. Peter and Lyle left for the beginning of four days of very hard, intensive work with the IWD while I and my entourage of boys (Anthony, the "small boy," is an Ibo of about 18) were off to the market. I can't very well call it the "local" market, since *Confluence of the Niger and Benue rivers at Lokoja* it is *the* market of the town, there being only one or two stores (which have the appearance of being barns) that carry "European" goods.

Lokoja Market

We immediately fell in love with this picturesque Nigerian village/town that is situated on a hillside right next to the wide Niger. Its people are cosmopolitan, located right in the center of the country: the Hausa predominating, but with a large admixture of Yorubas, Ibos, Ibibios, and Nupe, all living peacefully together.

The market carried all the usual products.

<u>General food section</u>:

- red and green varieties of peppers, a staple in the African's hot diet
- all the forms of cassava and yam: pounded, ground, fried, etc.
- rice, beans, and seeds of all types
- bowls of salt and various types of flour
- vegetables, some familiar, some very odd and different
- a wide variety of green leaves and brown roots
- many dried, condensed stringy or powdery or mushy-looking substances used for flavoring soups and stews
- heavy, thick red palm oil used as a base for many stews, for all frying and much boiling (Nigerian groundnut oil, what we would call peanut oil, which we use, is too expensive for the average Nigerian)
- fruits
- pulverized and nonpulverized stones, one that comes from the

sea and is rubbed into meat as a tenderizer, one that is used as "snuff"; another soft black one is used (I've forgotten how it is prepared) to blacken the eyes—an attractive form of make-up.

There is even a red stone that the individual uses on her lips, though more traditionally it is dropped in powdered form into the long, thin tube of a calabash into which the woman can just slide her arm or foot, depending on its shape. There she rubs it around, giving a red color to her entire appendage.

The "meat" section was a long, open-roofed rectangle just wide enough for customers to amble down an aisle between two long chopping-block counters. On these counters, "butchers" not only display their bloody cuts of meat, but this is where visitors, attempting to avoid the butchers' cajoling greetings, could not possibly avoid being greeted, also, by the glassy stares of rams, goats, or pigs whose heads belonged to the meat one had come to buy. To add to the gaiety, lined up on top of the roof, like bald cronies at a long bar, sat a row of several dozen vultures, whose more energetic brothers were scavenging on the ground.

There are many other sections of an African market such as this:
<u>The long, open sheds,</u> where:

- tailors pedal away madly on their foot-treadle machines, making everything from hats to wedding dresses
- a textile and dry-goods area
- Juju stalls with their indescribable contents
- furniture-makers' quarters
- Hausa craftsmen, decorating calabashes [shown above], making ebony carved heads, doing leatherwork for purses or "poufs" (hassocks), carving ivory objects—all to sell at outrageous prices, if possible, to the enchanted "tourist," if there is such a thing in this part of the continent
- fish market: dried, smoked, or fresh
- rug, mat, and basket-weaving section
- pottery and calabash containers of all sizes and shapes that are made locally
- imported goods, such as enamel or plastic pails, bowls, dishes, etc., that are very widely used.

My many visits to and transactions in and around the Lagos local markets with Columbus's careful tutoring in products and their uses has put me in a certain command of the "market" situation. (However, I did

Tailor and basket weaver

find it more difficult in Lokoja, as I cannot use my Yoruba with these Hausa people.)

As we wound our way through this labyrinth of commercial activity, stepping over black bodies in their long robes and around the confusing variety of goods displayed on the ground, I noticed Lyle's sons (David, 8, Mark, 10) sticking closer and closer to my side. This was their first experience in African crowd, and I suppose they were as confused and frightened as an African would be at a noon hour shopping at Woolworth's. To add to their malaise, like the Pied Piper, we were attracting what became a very long parade of tiny black followers who peered, giggled, touched, stared, and in general made the boys feel like original Martians. By the time we got to the water's edge, where I negotiated with a local fisher boy to take us out in his canoe and up the Niger a bit, I am sure that every child in Lokoja was standing there on the muddy bank calling and cheering and waving to us as we, to the boys' relief, pushed out onto the water.

The canoe, a hollowed log with branch thwarts, was skillfully guided along the riverbank by a singing black 8-year-old who paddled furiously in the stern under the directions of his idle 12-year-old superior, who sat facing us in the bow. Passing the large fleet of river boats (again constructed of enormous hollow logs) that were pulled up along the bank, we had glimpses of their compact interiors. At the same time, the boats'

Upper Lokoja is a riverside town on the Niger.

LETTERS FROM NIGERIA

Laundering in the Niger River

inhabitants poked their heads from all sorts of apertures to get a glimpse of us, as strange and new a sight to them as they were to us. We found great amusement in what I would call the "bowsprits" of these river craft. Most had very fancy, wooden white gates there, as the portal to their home. One had a large animal's head. And the best of all was the radiator grill from some lorry (truck) boldly attached at the foremost part of the bow of the boat.

The town, with its large, mud-structured residential section there on the hillside, was a postcard sight as we ventured out into the middle of the river to round an island. Then, from somewhere in the middle of town came a large parade of drumming, singing, and dancing people moving slowly down the road toward where our car was parked.

On the other side of the island, just as we were about to remark on the bright red flowers blooming on top of the rushes growing there, the "flowers" all rose, *ensemble*, and resettled on a new set of reeds. It is hard to believe the intensity of the color of African birds.

We returned to the riverbank downstream at the very spot where, little more than 60 to 70 years ago, the first Western traders landed to develop this town into one of the major inland trading centers of Nigeria. Now the bank, from water's edge to the top of a long rise, is firmly held in place by a wall of cement steps. At the top, as 70 years ago, sit the long, white storehouses of the United Africa Company (UAC), with its flag flying overhead.

The only activity on the great, wide steps as we approached them from the island was that of a half-dozen Hausa men, some of them totally naked, doing their laundry in the river water, scrubbing it on the rocks and cement steps.

The only time our 12-year-old friend in the bow lifted a finger was now, as we headed upstream whence we had come. To help his little assistant, he poled with a long stick against the current. By this time, I was bailing furiously with the broken calabash bowl that I found floating around my feet, hoping that we would make it to shore before there was more water inside than out.

By the time we scrambled up the bank to our car, we found it buried by the hindmost part of the parade, which had reached its destination. It was a large, whitewashed house wherein some important chief of the town or province was located. After proceeding through town and then up to his house, the crowd stood outside chanting, as the drummers got wilder in their rhythms and the dancers more and more frenetic. This performance continued until, at great length, the Big Man emerged, joined the crowd in his very ornate, long white robes and headdress, and, en masse, they proceeded, carried forward by throbbing drums, back into town.

As timing would have it, just as we reached the top of the bank, the Big Man came out of the house. The crowd turned, engulfing me, and before I knew it, there were drummers on all sides. I was being greeted in very ceremonial fashion: arm extended, elbow stiff, and fist clenched high in salute by all the tall, white-robed elders of the procession. We had been swept up and were on our way back into town before we could disentangle ourselves from this gay crowd. One man got carried away, and in his excitement and desire to greet us in as many ways as possible, including great bows and scraping, he shook my hand, Western style, much to the great amusement of the crowd.

Returning to the rest house, the boys gloated over their purchases of the morning. Each had a handful of slingshots, obviously the most interesting objects to them in the market that morning. I also bought each of us a stringy, crunchy fried groundnut ring, which they happily munched on until we saw a Pepsi stand—large picture out front of Satchmo advertising it. There they bought warm Pepsi-Cola. Aarrghhh.

We also had another stop on the way home: a World War I memorial to the Africans and British who had fought and lost their lives in the Bight of Benin. While I marveled over Nigeria's role in that war, the boys had scrambled to the top of the monument to find big cannons there. Immediately they became part of their own imaginary battles, menacing the peaceful African valley that lay below.

That afternoon, I took the boys to a swimming pool, built by a handful of Europeans in the area for their recreation and to escape from the heat. We had dinner that evening with the Nashes of IWD. Mrs. Nash wore mosquito boots made of long, thin, white leather that extended up to the knee. Interesting, but hideous. Conversation kept getting back to the number of snakes they had been finding in their yard and house. Just before bed, the boys announced that they would like to climb the mountain that rises directly behind Lokoja.

Thus, the following morning, up the mountain we went, much to the amazement of the local British and to the delight of the Africans. There is a road, one not navigable by our car. The road is maintained for the sole purpose of being able to operate the Marconi repeater station that sits on top. (I doubt that the "mountain" is more than 1,000 feet.) Up the road we hiked, marveling all the way over the endless variety of fruits offered by the forest trees, Anthony, Lyle's "small boy," showing us which ones we could eat, which we could not and how to eat them. Dad would have loved the different, strange, beautiful, exotic trees, plants, bushes, grasses, lichens, and vines that grow in such profusion in this tropical forest. It was everything I had imagined it to be, including 10-story long, thick, strong vines hanging and swinging from the tall trees down over precipices, some with smaller-stemmed, broad-leafed vines winding around them. All we needed was a Tarzan to swing down on one! We came close to that, too, for we did see a monkey swinging through the forest and taking great leaps from branch to vine. It may have been a baboon. We weren't sure.

As we got higher, the occasional views became more spectacular. At the very top, we were able to look out over a large section of the river valley and see very clearly where the Niger and Benue Rivers come together. Sounds of the town activity rose in distant clarity to our perch. Mingled with the pounding of construction, if this is what it was, was a drum tattoo of some idle person whiling away the time. It was getting near noon when we reached the hilltop. The descent was easy, and we were back at the rest house in time to have the 2:00 hot lunch with Peter and Lyle. ("Lunch" is really a full-course dinner the way the British have trained the Nigerians to serve it.)

Theoretically, this should mark the end of the government worker's day, as you know from my reports of our life in Lagos. But with time limited and much ground to cover, Lyle and Peter had the IWD people continue into afternoon and even evening sessions! I went back with them that afternoon to do some of my own typing while PBC and Lyle went through the files in their library, gathering data and statistics with the specialists that evening. The boys rested and played war games with the assortment of toy soldiers they had brought with them from home.

At 5:00 p.m., we all drove down to the river, this time to have an extensive trip up and down the Niger River with the IWD people.[29] While they were pointing out the changes in shoals and the diversion of the Niger's course, as compared with diagrams of the river of five years ago, we were looking at the small villages situated on an island here or a main bank over there. Best of all were the huge river canoes loaded with 20 to 40 passengers, who were probably making their monthly trip into the big town from their self-contained, self-sufficient villages. We were rewarded with wonderful salutes by the paddlers. Several of the gaily clad passengers nearly fell overboard with their enthusiastic waves and greetings.

". . . Lyle and Peter had the IWD (Inland Waterways Dept.) people continue into . . . evening sessions."

The next morning, Peter and I were up early, mainly because of the incredible bird sounds that filled our room at that hour. I shan't try to reproduce them for you here. If only I could give you an idea of the tones, phrases, chuckles, wheezes, hollow hoots, twitterings, and melancholy sounds that make the African morning what it is when one is in the bush! Yet, no matter how hard we tried, we could not catch sight of the birds producing those wonderful sounds.

With Peter and Lyle off to work, we headed back to the market so I could get some pictures and so the boys could get more slingshots. (They were intrigued when they discovered that if they could get two for a penny, they could have 480 for £1, just the way I used to figure out how many ice cream cones I could get for one dollar.) When the pictures are developed,

Plateau near Lokoja

LETTERS FROM NIGERIA

I will send them to you and let them tell the story of that morning. Most interesting was our long walk beyond the market area along the river past the "residential section" of Lokoja, where we found great variety in architecture and building materials. We even saw the remains of the original mission that had been built there in 1861 by the first white men to come to the area.

That afternoon, the boys stayed home and swam while Peter and Lyle and I were taken by a Dutch member of the IWD to a plateau where there are iron deposits. It is several miles long and wide. We talked of the tribes and villages in the area—which were very few, indeed. We marveled at the expanse of unpopulated forest, savanna, and bush. We were surprised to find only one village in the entire area on the plateau high above the village's garden and water supply, which lay in the valley several hundred feet below. Why?

Where were all the inhabitants one would expect to find? Like the paintings of Cezanne I went to see in Aix-en-Provence—and found none—those paintings (in this case, those inhabitants' descendants) were in the United States and the Caribbean. It was a sharp reminder of the intensity with which slaving was carried out in this particular part of Africa. There is hardly a soul left to tell of it. The people in that village high on the plateau could only say that they had remained there, all these years, instead of going down to the valley where their food and water came from, because they did it out of habit, a habit originally formed for the sake of safety and security.

The end of the road took us to the village's schoolyard. We got out and were greeted by the schoolmaster, about my age, who spoke with great pride of his primary school. It has four standards (grades) of approximately 28 in a class. A placid spot: a man actually reading a paper; a half-naked woman on a stool sitting behind her hut having her hair plaited by another; children playing with sticks and what-not, the way all children play; the chief's residence; and so on, as we passed back through the village. What will happen to this village if the projected iron mine should be started, an airstrip put on the plateau, and white men and trained Africans come to live and work for short periods or long periods of time? 'Twould be an "interesting study" for an anthropologist—this tranquil village now and 5 to 10 years hence.

Before supper that evening, Peter and Lyle had their final meeting with the IWD. Then at 7:30, we were invited to have cocktails with the Resident—what we might call a Provincial Governor. It is to him that all the District Officers report, and then he reports to the Regional Premier in Kaduna. The District Officer (or D.O.) was traditionally a young British, new-to-the-service colonial servant who was sent out into the uncivilized bush. He, in effect, would become the mayor, the local police force, doctor, judge, and God. The Resident's home, as in all provinces, we were told, is a sumptuous structure. It's built in the old Lugard style[30] on a hill overlooking the river valley and mountains beyond. It is fully staffed with enough servants for a dozen D.O.'s.

This particular Resident is representative of a type of men who came here to Nigeria twenty or more years ago. He has lived in all sorts of conditions, always isolated from not only the world but also the rest of Nigeria. Yet he, and all the others we have seen like him, maintains his immaculate appearance in dress and bath, his interest in the outside world, and his touch with the indigenous people. This, year after year, without going nuts!

We sat sipping cool drinks on his golf course of a lawn, while black servants dressed in white padded around silently on bare feet. The moon, a large white circle around it, was bright enough to light the countryside and make a silver path of the winding river. We discussed the policy of "Northernization" in this, the Northern Region, whereby it is almost impossible to get a job unless one is a Hausa, Fulani, or Nupe. Even being a Northern-born Yoruba or Ibo with every intention to remain in the North would do one no good as far as securing a government job. An interesting sidelight, however, is the fact that the Northern Regional Government still leans heavily on a large number of British administrators/civil servants and plans to do so for a long time to come. Due to the British policy of indirect rule in the North, feelings toward the British are quite different in this region, compared with attitudes toward those who serve in the civil service in the southern regions.

That night we slept well, sorry that we would have to leave Lokoja in the morning. The trip home, which took the whole day, was interesting, since it was a special Muslim holiday: the celebration of Muhammad's birthday, and evidently a special day for children. We came upon many parades with the ubiquitous drum and hundreds of children dressed up in matching costumes. As we approached Lagos, I found myself none too excited to see the teeming mass of people, shops, cars, activities, noise, and clutter. I'll never make a very good city girl. But it was nice to see Columbus and the kittens again.

"The weekend was the . . . Long Distance Race . . . 50 miles to Badagry."

The weekend was the occasion of the Long-Distance Race to Badagry, some 50 miles up Badagry Creek almost to the Dahomey border. Columbus and I spent all Saturday morning preparing hot thermoses of coffee and homemade soup, two wide-mouthed thermoses of chicken curry and rice in one and macaroni and cheese in the other—both piping hot. We also prepared two dozen sandwiches and stuck in the same number of bananas and chocolate bars. Yes, food for two for just two days, not two weeks. At 12:30 p.m., the fleet was off on the 90-mile race, which is more a test of endurance and luck than skill, I am convinced. The tide was in very strong ebb, so Peter and his crew, Laith Page, sailed up the creek a way and then dropped anchor for one and a half hours to wait for the tide to turn. (The rule is that you can subtract your stopped time provided you stay at anchor in the same place for over an hour.) By 10:00 in the evening, they still hadn't reached Badagry: One must tack back and forth all the way up, because one is going into the wind; and then one can "run" with the wind from behind—a straight shot, all the way back. So they dropped anchor next to André, who, they thought, had anchored there for the night. They discovered later that André and his crew had simply gone aground and had been struggling to free themselves for 10 minutes. When they saw Peter and Laith approaching, they could not bear for them to know they had run aground; so they anchored.

At any rate, Peter and Laith had their supper there and spent the night under a full, warm moon. Aside from the numerous fishnets and occasional sandbars that lay across the estuary, they had no trouble, and arrived home much less tired than I had expected. They were the first to cross the finish line at 5:05 Sunday afternoon, but with the handicap time added on (something like 22 hours), Peter placed third from last out of two dozen yachts! The other Cat, André's, was last with handicap time added.

A dozen or more of the Crossroads Africa groups from all over the continent were gathered here in Lagos for a few days last week prior to their return to the U.S. Art Hyde's group was one of them, so we saw him again and got caught up on their adventures. Mimi Winter's group, led by Dr. Ferwerda, was another one of them. She is so cute. She and two of her fellow Crossroaders walked over here one morning and we hashed over the summer. (Sorry to say this, Mom, but evidently Vernon Ferwerda is a pill. He obviously was barely tolerated by his group, which I thought a darling bunch of Americans.) We ran into Vernon in front of the House of Representatives when I went to pick PBC up from work, and then again that night when we went to King's College to see their skit night. I had meant to give you our impressions, the latest ones that is, of the Crossroaders with whom we talked, this past week—and to share their own impressions and reactions to the summer. But that shall have to wait, for I know you are tired of my gabble at this point.

I do want to tell you about Grace's baby, though. She finally had it a week ago Saturday, having walked the three miles to and from the maternity clinic each of the three or four days preceding her delivery. Each time they told her to stay, but each time she returned, barefooted, since it would cost them money for her to stay there and then not deliver. She also had her children, all four, to take care of. Friday night, Columbus woke us up at 12:30 to say that they were now sure that Grace would be having her baby within 24 hours. So Peter took her to the clinic in the car,

Sample of some of the clothes I designed and made for myself while in Nigeria

and at 1:05 p.m. Saturday she had a little (*white* baby—their color at birth) boy. Columbus was so excited he could hardly contain himself. By Sunday, she was back here in the same old routine! We had set up the crib, which, by the way, you smarties, is several feet wide, not just one foot, as I mis-stated it. Columbus has started Grace on his village diet, a rigid one of no fresh meat or fish but just hot-pepper soup and roots and herbs—"to pull her womb together," he says, for the first week. Then he will allow her to have some dried fish and green leaves to add to the diet for the remainder of the month.

Peter and I have been having some dental work done by a Nigerian dentist and his nurses at the Federal Dental Clinic. I can't resist quoting you the sign that appears on the door of the waiting room: **"Patients or their children in this waiting room found making a mess will be requested to leave."**

Peter has been working every afternoon this week and many evenings, too. I'm pleased, however, to see him get excited about the work he has been doing lately. Evidently Lyle has been giving him much more extensive assignments where he is not only collecting the data and making calculations, but he is writing up reports and making policy suggestions.

Meanwhile, all this week I have been either pulling together some thesis material, or visiting the summer program for teaching that is being given by a group of imported U.K. teachers for a month. This is one of the projects recommended by the Ashby Commission as a means to improve the teaching quality and the ability to teach in English. There are similar groups running the same program in each of the regions. From everything I have been able to see, it is a tremendous success. It has also been a wonderful opportunity for me to meet a great many Nigerian teachers, talk to them, and find out not only about their teaching abilities but also to know what makes them tick, what their attitudes and aspirations might be. What a friendly lot they are!

September 2 [my 25th birthday]: Thank you for all your silly cards and the money for presents. Columbus and I have all kinds of clandestine plans for the 6th (Peter's 27th birthday).

It is race time and I must go help Peter rig the boat.

Much love to you all,

G

[Somewhere the news that I was 4+ months pregnant reached Peter's family, because the following was handwritten at the bottom of the copy of this letter sent to Peter's parents.]

Yes, we're pretty excited about this "first" of the new Clark generation, too. So far I can report that, in utero, it has been a very good baby—and so considerate to come just when we desire it!! Mom will probably tell you that we can get what we need here, and that sending things would be just too expensive. The only chore is designing and making an entire new wardrobe with a hand-crank sewing machine. But that's good practice for me, too, since I do enjoy sewing, and material of all types and varieties is available, even though it is not very cheap.

Top: Northern Region market
Bottom: Selling men's clothes in the Kano market

LETTERS FROM NIGERIA

— Letter Twenty-Nine —

September 9, 1961

Dear Aunt Jan and Uncle Archer,

Despite all the efforts that go into the communal family "DEF" letter, I know you don't care a whit about economic or educational developments in Nigeria when it comes to hearing just a personal word about the physical developments in our family (my tummy, to be specific . . . which is very active these days!).

We are terribly pleased and grateful, too—not only that at last, what to us appears a good time to start our family has come (as you know, Aunt Jan, from our conversations last year), but also that it is coming to us so naturally and easily.

Having babies, we realize, is old hat to the world. But when one gives life, or participates in the mysterious creation of one, this very natural thing becomes highly significant, its revelations touching every aspect of our own lives. Even now we begin to have an inkling of the extent to which this will deepen our own relationship as husband and wife, broaden our own experiences henceforth, and enrich those nonmaterial ingredients that are really the woof and warp of existence.

Expectation, I guess, is half the fun. We are glad to have had our initial years together, alone, full of the adventure and, to a certain extent, the irresponsibility that they afforded us. We have changed a lot, both individually and collectively. Now we are in a transition state, on that bridge between being a "couple" and becoming parents. It is tantalizing, but, thank goodness, no longer than three-fourths of a year. We are anxious to start playing our new role.

We know that you have been anxious for us to begin. But now, dear grandparents, that the gate is down—watch out for the Clark tribe! We have only begun. [Indeed, within four years and four months, we would have four children.]

Much, much love to you both,

Gretel

— Letter Thirty —

September 14, 1961

DEF,

    Well, the rains have returned, but this time not in such profusion or with such intensity as in the past. July through to the beginning of September is looked upon as the time of clear, cool, windy weather that marks a respite in the rainy season. I must say that this whole summer has been the pleasantest of weather. We certainly have not suffered from any heat, and the rains have not been nearly as bad as I had thought they would be. In fact, we were told that this rainy season was a rather mild one.

    The consistent good sailing weather has returned (i.e., no rained-out races) and we seem to have returned to some good, consistent sailing, too. Yesterday PBC had an afternoon session with the River Transport man at John Holt,[31] so I had a stranger-crew (who had been in a Cat only twice before), and I must say we sailed a good race with lots of luffing matches, close maneuvering at the mark, and windward beats that took skill in calculation against the other Cats. Although I didn't get as good a start as I should have, being something like fifth or sixth around the first mark, we had passed them all by the time we crossed the finish.

    Saturday was an excellent race, a long and hard one in a rather heavy wind. I skippered and Peter crewed. We had a good start and were ahead all the way until, at the second-to-last mark—way out at the mouth of the harbor, sailing against a very heavy flood tide—I tacked too soon coming around the mark and came "into irons," and the flood tide crashed us right down onto the buoy. A terrifying experience, with two boats right behind us. No damage done, though, thanks to our steel-strong coat of polyurethane paint. Nonetheless, it was disappointing to be disqualified after we had done so well. It was a wonderful, windy day. We had some good competition and we did enjoy the race, up to that point.

    A week ago Wednesday, Peter sailed the new boat and I sailed *Miss Tibbs* (the old one). It was fun competing against each other. And who should I find calling to me for water at the first mark, but *mein Herr*. He did quite well, too, considering it was the first time he sailed the boat. I had a good crew, and even with a large handicap, we beat the entire fleet of about 25 that day.

    The new boat from Ghana needs a bit of tuning up, but basically we feel that, with some good sailing, she should prove herself reasonable in the fleet. She is registered in my name, since Peter is not allowed to own two boats. I have had to pay £10 in berthing fees and to become a full member of the Yacht Club (instead of holding a wife's membership). We'll go on sailing it and racing it until the right person offers the right price.

Last week, we had such fun making fusses over each other, what with two birthdays in the same week. (It will be so much more fun when our family is larger.) Your many cards added to the gaiety. And my goodness! Such an indulgent family you are!! We don't know whether to spend all the checks together on one thing or to dole them out separately.

Again, Peter has been keeping very late hours, not only in the afternoon but in the evening, writing reports for the preliminary "Plan" for the Federal Territory. According to the latest deadline, it should be finished by October 15th. Wolf has been up in the Northern Region getting information from the Northern Regional Government and from agencies up there. He also spent a good week gallivanting around on various safaris. The Nigerian part of the staff here in Lagos has no concept of what real work is, so that leaves Lyle and PBC to carry the main burden of the load.

Within the past two weeks, Peter has really assumed vastly expanded responsibilities, not only supervising the junior Nigerian economists but also taking over some of the major research and writing of chapters for the Five-Year Plan in such fields as inland waterways and aviation. Originally, Lyle and Wolf were going to write those chapters. Lyle has been so impressed with the caliber of Peter's drafts that he has been encouraging Peter to use them as the focal point of his thesis. Wolfgang, who vociferates about being Peter's professor and having taken this little protégé under his wing, etc., etc., hasn't, in fact, done so. He is a brilliant economist, but too much of a "lone wolf" and too harassed by the volume of work. He is unable to delegate much of it, as a good administrator should do. Therefore, Lyle (Dr. Hansen to most) has stepped into his place and has really taken Peter in tow; given him important, interesting work to do; tutored him in the process; and, *en somme*, has given Peter a great deal of encouragement.

Things are really looking up these days. We have even embarked on a French tutoring arrangement whereby I am drilling Peter about 15 minutes a day and he seems to be making some progress. Meanwhile, I have started German on my own and plan to enroll, also, in a class that is starting the first of October.

In the past month or so, we have had two interesting visitors. The first was a visit, over a month ago, by John and Ann Culver (acquaintances of Steve and Laurie Ells)[32] from Harvard Law School), who were doing *le grand tour* of Africa with some money that John happened to have recently inherited. We showed them around Lagos on Saturday and had them over to watch the race, and then Sunday we took them down to Badagry (the village I have spoken of that is some 40 to 50 miles down the coast near Dahomey), where we saw a Juju house with all its ornamental trimmings. We were taken to a section of the town where a large trunk containing slave chains and shackles is proudly guarded by the inhabitants, who will let you see the objects if you "dash" them a few "bob" [see photo]. We also took them through the local market there, teeming with business activity, even though it was a Sunday. (The inhabitants might be pagan.) There we saw them smoking alligator meat, caught right there in the creek, for stew; and we bought some Juju beads after much haggling.

Most interesting, however, was the Culvers' "enlightened" attitude about the white settler situation in East Africa: much more sympathetic toward the settlers' view and toward colonialism in general. Will have to save details till a later date.

The other visitor was a Japanese boy, whom we took east to some local villages. He was interested in problems of economic development. We had a marvelous time stopping and talking to local civil servants about related issues.

[Written on the margins of the air letter.] 'Scuse the squeeze. I always seem to run over on these letters. Again, many thanks for the B'day money. We are contemplating its use . . . maybe for a trip North.
    Love, G

[Peter wrote on the other margin.] Thank you, Mom and Dad, for the birthday money and card. I'll write soon, but I do a great deal of writing all day, every day and half the night. I do, however, look forward to writing you.
    Love, Pete

Peter being shown slave chains and shackles in Badagary

— Letter Thirty-One —

DEF,

The rains really have returned. Last night we were wakened by a full-scale line squall á *la* two and a half months ago. Very heavy rains!! But this time, in between the squall and showers, we are having just enough very pleasant weather of cool breezes and warm sunshine.

The parcel with Nan's clothing arrived two weeks ago. It is wonderful to be able to augment my wardrobe, but, as I had suspected, we paid close to $7 on import duties and customs charges, plus one entire morning of red tape out at the airport. This prompts me to make my plea again: Please, please do NOT send us a thing through the mail other than simple printed matter or something that can come in a letter. The cost to you in sending it and to us in receiving it just isn't worth it.

Big excitement, though, when Tante's envelope ($1 air postage, as though it were a letter—the best way you could have sent it, Tante) arrived with the very first item we have acquired for our child-to-be, all wrapped in special paper: a pair of nylon pants. Probably sounds silly, but such firsts (and reminders) are really exciting. We got a tremendous kick out of it.

A tragedy is taking place on our front lawn. All the trees are being torn down (giving us a lovely view) and then the entire point is being dug up so that a new seawall can be put in. This is done every 30 years, taking four to six months, and we happen to have hit it right on the nose. No more serenity, what with all the activity: a pile driver banging up and down and a derrick in operation. I dread to think of when the Harmattan comes and we have the addition of all the sand that will be flying around down there. Guess the main reason I'm upset is that things won't be up to snuff when Mother is here.

The Yacht Club continues to operate. Last Saturday we had a stunt race, which included, while sailing the course: (1) dumping your crew overboard, sailing on for 10 seconds, and then jibing around alone and going back to pick crew up; (2) dropping a buoyed anchor and then taking an 18-inch reef in the mainsail, under which we had to sail two legs of the course and return to pick up the anchor; (3) then second-to-last leg of the course had to be sailed *sans* rudder, with the use only of a paddle and one's sails. This was quite a feat, since the day was one with a very heavy wind. During the course of the race, one had to splice a rope (three splices on one end and tie a bowline on the other). I skippered and let Peter do much of the dirty work (mainly jump overboard). We placed second. Now, had we had more time to practice. . . .

Wednesday, as usual, Peter had to work very late, so I took one of the gals from the club as crew. We trounced the entire fleet, with handicap added on, by over four minutes. Incidentally, while I am bragging, we now have five trophies—each must be returned when the race is sailed next, in half a year or a year, but we also have five accompanying pewter mugs, which we get to keep. We also get to keep a sugar bowl.

The news of Dag Hammarskjöld's death[33] has come as a great shock to us all. The reaction that it sparked in the Nigerian press, however, has been rather surprising. In fact, the entire African attitude has been interesting. When the UN forces went into the Congo originally and supported anti-Lumumba forces, they were soundly condemned by African nationals on general principle as supporting the "colonial" imperialist interests. Now that the UN has taken action against Tshombe, the arguments have been neatly reversed, yet they still manage somehow to condemn "the colonialist powers." There was an editorial in Zik's strongly leftist *West African Pilot* in which they actually blame the U.S. and the UN for Dag's death. The following is an excerpt from it:

> The British principally, and the Americans, cannot however escape blame for his [Hammarskjöld's] untimely demise. The UN took swift police action last Wednesday to end Katanga's secession; but the British and the Americans went out of their way to stiffen Katangese resistance and fan the embers of civil war by their all out support for the traitor, Tshombe, against the legitimate Government of Aboula, which had already won recognition by the UN. It was this treachery that took Dag to the Congo and Ndola—and his death—to talk Tshombe down and repair the damage done by the colonialists. They will shed crocodile tears at the UN—but they killed Dag—the man of peace!

And then later they reiterate:

> Britain and America, when the crucial hour struck[,] were found wanting. They did not give the total backing O'Brian [diplomat Conor Cruise O'Brien] needed to crush Tshombe's revolt at one fell blow. We say this is treachery to the UN cause in the Congo . . . the neo-colonialists are responsible for the death of dear Dag. They know themselves. Nigerian editors—all of them—are agreed on that. We stand with them.

I must add, this type of writing is not an isolated case. Illogical reasoning appealing to biased emotionalism, just using certain adjectives, a disregard for anything that resembles calm objectivity (i.e., responsible press) are, unfortunately the rule, not the exception. What is even more disturbing is that the readers of this kind of irresponsible writing in the press have, for the most part, only a simple education. They are not equipped to read this glop with some degree of discernment, discretion, and discrimination.

They must know, though, from listening to the radio, that attempts are being continually made to keep information from them. During the weeks following the USSR's break-off of the nuclear test ban and the accumulation of Russian detonations, we tried to get the Voice of America broadcasts in order to hear American reaction and comments. VOA was taking advantage of the marvelous propaganda offensive that Russia's behavior afforded the U.S. during those few days, before the U.S. was stupid enough to announce that it, too, was going to resume testing. If it was so necessary to do so, we (the U.S.) could at least have kept quiet about it during the weeks of the prior preparation required for implementation of such policy. Then the U.S. could have let the world know, de facto, when the first explosion took place—as the Russians did—having meanwhile had the inestimable propaganda advantage that the interval would have given the U.S.

Each time the VOA turned to the subject of Russian testing, the Voice was quite effectively, and obviously, jammed with static sounds or an

Peter and friend in Juju market eyeing monkey skulls

unpleasant hum. During those two weeks, Radio Moscow, which broadcasts on many more frequencies than VOA's one frequency in West Africa, stepped up its jamming activities by at least 300 percent. When that rarely heard American accent—in its painfully factual manner—begins to tell of an important world event, and its diction becomes an indistinguishable accompaniment to a variety of weird tones and crackles, it is a very real reminder that sends chills down my spine that we, in West Africa, are right in the heart of the Cold War with its ubiquitous assaults on the minds of people. Our efforts—mine toward instituting a sound education for all, and Peter's toward the growth of a healthy, broad-based economy—will be, we are convinced, much more valuable weapons of defense for Nigeria than 16 dozen anti-missile missiles.

Love to all,

Gretel

P.S. Speaking of the Cold War, I ran into the first arrivals to Nigeria of the Peace Corps. Will write about it next week.

Mud bricks are baked in the sun, before being used for construction of this village.

— Letter Thirty-Two —

October 13, 1961

Dearest Mamá,

This is the first morning I shall be here at home and can finally tend to your questions. I have been visiting teacher training colleges and primary and secondary schools until early afternoon, and then reading through material I got from the various institutions, much of it to be returned the next day. Guess I'm really getting somewhere, at last, and will have a good acquaintance with the system and problems. This should give focus to my field research, which I hope to do with you in Ibadan. But more about that later.

I went to see Dr. Elsie Austin at USIA yesterday. I had met her previously. A most pleasant woman. When I told her about your coming and asked if they might be interested in having you do a workshop for the Council of Woman's Societies, she was delighted. Without knowing of your special abilities, she said that the biggest thing that the women's organizations need training in is programming, organizational procedure, etc. She asked me all about the activities of the Women's Service Bureau and what you might be able to offer. I tried to answer as best I could. I think you would really enjoy meeting with some of the women's groups here. It certainly would give you a perspective on American women's activities, to see your Nigerian counterpart.

Could you find out my blood type? It will save me one guinea (about $3). I should know before I have the baby. . . .

Much love,
Gretel

— Letter Thirty-Three —

October 14, 1961

DEF,

We just got our latest batch of pictures from Lokoja and Badagry and other miscellaneous events. (It only took seven weeks for them to be developed.) I will sort them out tonight, write little scribbles on them (they are color slides), and send them home so you can see them in time for Mother to bring them back with her when she comes.

Latest events in our neighboring English-speaking country [Ghana] have been disturbing, to put it mildly. Up until this past month, though there was a certain reservation in the minds of our African friends, including all ranges of the political spectrum, for what Kwame [Nkrumah] was doing. Generally their feeling was: "We're in this together as emergent, former British colonial territories. We are both striving to prove ourselves as strong 'neutral' forces in our battle to wipe out the last vestiges of colonialism and neo-colonialism (*such hackneyed phrases around here*), and build up our economies and educational systems (*thanks mostly to those colonial powers, though most of them wouldn't admit it*), etc., etc."

Now Nkrumah has seen to the total abolition of any opposition-party members. Moreover, the judicial system has been completely destroyed. It was a system whose democratic foundations were skillfully laid by the British—based on the cultural setting present when they first came to the Gold Coast (Ghana). So despite their different ways of doing these things, Nkrumah (who took over from the British) still had the support of many. But NOW, one is very hard-put to find even one voice among the most radical here in Nigeria that will support the man any longer. Where the papers in their editorials were expressing dismay a short time ago, they now, even the extremist *West African Pilot*, have outrightly condemned

"Stories of the dictatorship of Nkrumah"

the latest developments in Ghana. Our friend André got back from several days in Accra last week, and the stories he tells gave us goose bumps: arrests in the night, the numb expressions on the faces of all on the streets wondering what will happen next, the common man almost embracing "Europeans" and begging them to help them to return Ghana to the "Gold Coast" days. They would rather live under the freedom of British colonial rule than the dictatorship of Nkrumah!! André says that the streets are literally jammed with Russians and Chinese, and that when one has a conversation in public, one looks around carefully to see who is nearby before one says anything.

André knows Erica Powell, Nkrumah's private British secretary and biographer. From her stories of Nkrumah's latest actions, it sounds like the man is desperate, in the sense that his determination to keep control, absolute control, is coupled with a strong fear of not only losing it, but of losing his life. From what we hear, it looks like the Russians are supporting him as long as they think necessary before assisting in bumping him off. Then they will step in, with great grief and indignation at his death, but also play on the hatred that is rapidly growing for the man, and take over the country. André tells of a friend of his, a prominent Ghanaian, member of parliament, who, on his way to his farm on the other side of the Volta, but still in the country, was arrested as he reached the river and was brought back to be confined to his home with guards around his house, because Kwame was afraid he would leave the country . . . this so-called friend of his!

Nkrumah declared high customs duties to be placed on many imports; forced 10 percent savings of all government and other employees' income, to go into government bonds; required that all ministers state their outside financial interests and give

"How to make a nation's economy grow. . ."

up, in many cases, stocks and positions of company control "when they might be in conflict with the public interest" and "encourage corruption." He demanded that everyone state all the details of their monetary activities, declaring that inaccuracies and omissions could bring on the penalty of imprisonment, etc. Actually, we wish that all these things could be enforced in a moderate way here in Nigeria. PBC's concern is unavoidably centered on this major problem of a developing economy: the importance of holding back the tendency toward immediate consumption of all that is produced before any of the GNP can be siphoned off into savings in the form of investment for future growth—i.e., cutting immediate consumption in order to make possible *growth* that will allow an increase of consumption in the future. Eventually, the theory goes, the economy, if it is able to store up enough reserves, which in turn will stimulate growth, the time will come when there will no longer be the need to undergo hardship in order to bring about future growth. This is what Walt Rostow calls the stage of "take-off" in his *Stages of Economic Growth*.[34] At this point, a country will have achieved self-sustained, continued growth.

To put it simply, it is extremely difficult to force a poor man to save . . . to force him to put off consumption if he is already near starvation. But somehow you have to get him to "tighten his belt" and "invest" whatever small surplus there might be so that agricultural and industrial growth can take place and so that there will eventually be an increase in production to permit his future consumption.[35] But how does one make a man, or a nation, "tighten its belt"—i.e., save—when its "belt" is already in the last notch? Well, Nigeria's (and Ghana's) people are not living on quite such a subsistence level. In fact, their belts are already out many notches. Nigeria has a 4 percent annual growth in GNP. Nonetheless, it is still difficult to tighten or induce the tightening of belts. Nkrumah has done this, though, the easy way—force it. The Russians and Chinese have or are doing it. In fact, the British did it, too. How else could they have had the Industrial Revolution without the "forced" low wages of factory and mine workers? This enabled the owners to have enough surplus left over so that they could reinvest in their operations, bringing about phenomenal growth that created that revolution.

Fine, fine, so you raise the level of capital savings. But in what is Nkrumah "investing"??

- a mammoth Black Star Square—counterpart of Moscow's Red Square—quite a thing to see with its great Romanesque triumphal arch in the center
- a large armed force
- a "prestige" fleet of Russian Ilyushin jets that are putting the Ghanaian government £3,000,000 in the hole each year
- big public shrines, à la Mussolini

and so on and on. None of these things are contributing to the further growth of the nation's economy, except in the form of higher wages and employment for a few. This, in turn, will have the effect of raising prices, and thus the cost of living, bringing about an ill-afforded inflation to the already very unstable Ghanaian pound. What's more, European businesses are leaving the country in droves and prospective investors from abroad have been scared away. In order to prevent their own businessmen from sending their capital to other parts of the world where their money is safer, the Ghanaian government has forbidden the departure of *any* capital from the country. André's boss just sold his house in Accra (the one we stayed in while we were there), to the West German ambassador; and the government has required that the proceeds be paid in the form of Ghanaian bonds, which can be realized only gradually over a period of, say, 20 years!

Just one other note on this subject: It has been interesting to watch Columbus's reactions. He says that in town, among his laborer (illiterate) steward friends, when they gather to drink palm wine, everyone is talking about Nkrumah and the latest developments, with great indignity and growing mistrust and apprehension for what used to be considered their "sister" nation. Many of their relatives are living in Ghana. They are anxious that they should return to "free" Nigeria, which surely it is. Peter talks of "dashing up there" so we can see for ourselves the changes that have taken place since we were there only a few months ago.

Yes, you're right, Janell, the "warm" weather is returning, when "only the mad dogs and Englishmen go out in the noonday sun." It has made afternoon sailing most pleasant, though, since we still have the "rainy season" breeze when we get wet. And this is inevitable in a Cat, being so low on the water, and passing through it so rapidly. We don't have to shiver and freeze. We rather enjoy the water on our bodies.

Two Sundays ago, we sailed out to Tarkwa Bay, where we had a picnic lunch and then walked over to the deep-surf ocean side where, behind the protection of a sand dune from the wind, we inflated two air mattresses (the British call them "lie-lows"), basked in the sun, and read aloud a chapter from Ladder of Bones,[36] a most interestingly written history of Nigeria. The easy solitude one finds out on those miles of soft sand beaches is heaven after the banging of the pile driver, the noisy engine of the crane, and all the Africans (always twice as many as are really needed to do a job) that are here on this "rip-em-up-and-lay-a-new-seawall" project that is going on right in our front yard. When I am here during the day, going through documents and studies, gathering material for the thesis and preparing questions for the colleges and schools that I plan to visit the next day, I just lock myself in the bedroom with the air conditioner on. It cuts out some of the noise and the smell, plus the humidity. Then I emerge only when I have to.

Back to Tarkwa Bay: Before sailing back home, we decided to sail out into the ocean a way. It was a wonderful, easy rolling sea of waves the size of mountains. The sea and the wind were in concord that day, going

Extending the Lagos mole entrance to the harbor. Note men fishing in protection of the mole.

in the same direction, so we didn't have to smash through the chop that one finds out there so often. Just up and down, rollercoaster-like on the giant undulations. We sailed out on the sparkling water, not quite a mile, and then decided to turn and sail back on a "reach" to the mouth of the harbor. Just as we came about, or were in the process of tacking, there was a great CRACK, and the front port paneling of the cockpit sprang forward, revealing a great fissure down the center of the wing that holds the two sides of our boat together. In that split second, we held our collective breaths, waiting for the mast to come down and render our sail and us vulnerable to the prevailing currents of the Bight of Benin. In that moment of suspense, we were lifted and dropped; our anxious glances toward distant land caught only a momentary glimpse of the West Mole, that arm of rocks whose inner side would mean safety. We swallowed hard, completed the tack, and set the sails (which were miraculously still standing), so they would permit us an easy "run" back home. We literally skidded toward the West Mole. Despite our pounding hearts, it was exhilarating the way we were able to plane like a skier schussing down a mountainside, on top of one giant wave, then to be picked up by the next and carried along again, building up such momentum that at times we must have exceeded the actual speed of the wind. We remained on the same tack all the way home.

For the past two weeks, with the skillful but slow help of a Muslim Nigerian carpenter, we have ripped out the crosspiece of the foredeck and reinforced the entire area. Now all we have to do is to paint it over and we'll have a yacht that is not only as good as new, but better than new. We'll soon be out menacing the Cat fleet on the race course again. (The good sailors have mostly come back from various leave "tours," so there have been almost a dozen Cats out in the past month for the races. It's great fun. I'll have to start sailing our second Cat more often, too. Just wondering when they will start disqualifying me and my crew for having three of us on board. In fact, the way that "third member" thumps away, I wonder if there aren't four of us!

Did you know that we have a fall season here, too? This season, as far as most outward signs indicate, marks the end of the rainy season and the return of hot weather, as I remarked earlier, but, believe-it-er-not, the leaves are turning! Yup: yellow, orange, and red on all the mango, almond, orange, avocado, mahogany, teak, and acacia trees . . . most anything that had green leaves is changing color. Palms are the exception. Moreover, the leaves of these other trees are falling to the ground. This is so out of context!

While I've been busy visiting schools and interviewing teachers, Peter's pace of work has continued to increase. I feel lucky if I get to see him other than at the breakfast and dinner table. He not only works all afternoon until 6 or 7 p.m., when everyone else knocks off at 2 p.m. In the evening, he frequently works either here or at the office until midnight. Oftentimes I go over to the Secretariat in the evening with him so we can at least be together. Lyle and, to a certain extent, Wolf have been driving themselves at the same pace; but the Nigerian Assistant Secretaries—who now are working *under* Peter and his direction instead of *with* him and under Lyle—don't put forth more than a bare modicum of effort. It's been disillusioning.

Meanwhile, as I have implied in other letters, Peter has grown tremendously in stature in Lyle's eyes. This is indicated by the kinds of work Lyle is giving him, and doing with him. Now, when Lyle goes to a ministry or business, he not only takes Peter along, but Peter asks as many, if not more questions than Lyle. They approach the research projects and evaluation papers that have to be done and written as equals. Peter has been interviewing and reviewing development plans of certain ministries completely on his own and writing up his own reports. These are now becoming a part of The Plan.[37]

Right now, he and Lyle are deeply involved with negotiations with several foreign firms bidding for the construction of a steel mill here in Nigeria. This not only involves economic evaluation but also being able to see through the arguments and presentations of each separate interest, in addition to weeding out the political implications, connections, and undertones. I wish I could get Peter to write to you something of his work, because I can't begin to do it justice nor convey to you the excitement of being involved at such a high level. He has been able to learn so very much through dealing with the problems involved in economic planning, and in the very pulse of a nation's growing pains. As it is, however, he hardly has time to read the paper; and I can't bear to sacrifice him to you to write letters during those few hours we may have to relax together on the weekend. I must say, however, I am pleased to see him so involved, feeling that what he is doing is not only worthwhile but also is needed— and that it has the potential of wide-reaching ramifications.

Love,

G

[A note on the bottom of the letter to my mother] "The enclosed are two malaria pills called Daraprim. I am hereby issuing orders to Mrs. Pauline B. Tyler for her to take one exactly two weeks before she expects to arrive in Africa, and to take the other exactly one week prior to her arrival here. She will then take one a week while she is here, and one each week for two weeks after her departure. . . ."

Yes, we do have yams here, though they are a tuber quite different from the delicate ones you eat there. It is a large, white "root" of much coarser texture than a potato, most often eaten in these parts in a pounded form called fufu. It is made from the boiled yam or yam flour boiled up, then pounded with a mortar into a glutinous mass. When it is the right consistency, one squishes it into one's cupped fingers in the shape of a spoon and thus scoops up the groundnut stew/soup to one's mouth.

[The following came in a letter from Mother. She had taken a group from Connecticut to NYC to visit the United Nations for a series of lectures, and meetings with UN delegates. etc. While there, she escaped during lunchtime to go to the U.S. Department of Health, Education, and Welfare, where she could get her required inoculation for yellow fever, "which Nigeria sez I must have."

Among her comments: "They were very cool and casual at the Nigerian Mission. I don't think they really CARE that I'm making this momentous trip. I don't think they even glimmered an iota of an idea of how MUCH I know about their country's present, past, and hopes for future. So I was cool and casual and oh-me-what-a-great-bother all this is . . . just for a silly little ole trip to Africa. TO AFRICA! (Butterflies leap around in my middle and I get all goose bumps.)"]

New fountain in downtown Lagos

Downtown Lagos

— Letter Thirty-Four —

October 22, 1961
Sunday

DEF,

I don't know quite where to start, or if I should start at all, since the rumors that have been flying around in the past week leave little doubt in my mind that outgoing mail is not safe from the scrutiny of Nigerian "security guards," etc.

Only a week ago, perhaps one of the biggest "stories," and subsequently furors, that the papers have gotten a hold of in the past year came out in headlines and has remained there every day. Even you have probably heard the details of the story of Margery Michelmore, one of the

Open sewerage canal behind market stalls dumps into Lagos Harbor

34 Peace Corps participants who is completing—or, rather, up until this week, *was* completing—her training for her two years in Nigeria at the University College, Ibadan (UCI). Well, she wrote a postcard home. It was much like what I wrote to you on first arriving here, quite innocent. The postcard somehow fell into the (malicious) hands of the very radical "youth leader." He is what I would call a "professional student," who has been at UCI for the past 5 years, and has been waiting for an opportunity to ruin the Peace Corps. Within 24 hours, he had the postcard published and duplicated (describing the "primitive" way people live here). On the whole, it was a very apt description of what does exist here in much of urban Nigeria. It was distributed to the entire campus so that the next day they could have a hate-America and vilify-the-Peace-Corps campus-wide rally.

In this they were successful; and with the publicity they have received in all the papers, I can assure you the entire country has been talking of little else. "The pride and dignity" of the Nigerian has been offended by this "little American upstart," they say with great tones of indignation, while the ungrateful foreign visitor, I suppose, should look the other way every time (which is all too often) s/he sees a Nigerian going to the bathroom in the street, and smile and say, "Of course, it doesn't exist." Most disturbing, however, has been the number and content of the letters that have been flooding the papers, none of them designed to make the Americans living in this community feel any too comfortable.

Expatriate reaction has been mixed. On the whole, it has been rather disdainful for all the silly nonsense blown up over such an innocent thing. And people you hardly know will part from you saying, "Now don't write any postcards home that you wouldn't want all of Nigeria to read," etc. I will send you some clippings that will give you the flavor of the affair much more powerfully than I could.

I think I mentioned in an earlier letter that I had run into this Peace Corps group at King's College (*the* boys' prep school here in Nigeria) just after they had arrived here. They had a day or so in Lagos and then were going to Ibadan: a very bright, fresh, young but realistic-looking group. My conversation with the half a dozen or so of them left me with a hopeful feeling of what they actually could do for Nigeria, though in a small way. Their biggest drawback is the fact that the project that they are on and everything they do is so much in the public gaze, and so easily in the line of fire of anti-U.S. people of any type hoping to stir up trouble.

I am sure that Peter and I have made much bigger blunders since we arrived here, but we are a bit safer since our mission hasn't been so widely publicized. As a member of the American advisory team engineering the Five-Year Plan, and also being connected in a remote fashion (paycheck, that's all) with the Ford Foundation, Peter, Lyle, and Wolf have come under fire at least three times in the Federal Parliament. Fortunately, publicity hounds haven't made much of it. They, for example, have been accused of passing on "secret" information to outside Americans. Ah me, I guess we should just learn to grin and bear it, to recognize that it will be a long time before these people get over their inferiority complexes, manifested in anything concerning "culture," a quickness to take offense to any kind of criticism, and a great desire to be soothed by the flatterers' words of praise.

This week has been another one of long work hours, usually late into the night for Peter B., with two evenings off for cocktail parties[36]—an extravagance at government expense, held far too often around here. Both were for the American economic mission, sent especially by Kennedy and headed again, as it was a few months ago, by Arnold Rivkin of MIT. One was given by the Ministry of Economic Development and the other, by the ICA [now AID]. We met an interesting crowd at the latter, since we have had little to no contact with official U.S. representatives, whether in the diplomatic corps, ICA, or USIA.

I have been busy visiting schools in the area, going through piles of government documents. I have spent some time over at the library of the Ministry of Education. People there evidently think that I am still working there. My connection and work there has been very useful. It unearthed for me lots of good information.

We had our Cat all repaired in time for the race yesterday, which we won, Peter skippering. We finished at about 5:45. We came in for some tea, as is the custom, and some race-talk on the lawn. Then we picked up our gear and sailed out, just as the sun was setting, to the mouth of the harbor and Tarkwa Bay, where we arrived after dark. We anchored and waded our things ashore to the Yacht Club hut. The hut had been built by members of the Lagos Yacht Club on a coastal gun emplacement about 15 years ago.

There we cooked our dinner, and as bright moonlight lit our scene, we watched breakers pound up on the distant seashore. Yet looking out across the bay, calm ruled the waters. There we could see an occasional fisherman wading, then tossing his large circular net over the water. We wrapped up for the night, each in a blanket on a canvas cot. With warm sea air blowing through the hut, what few mosquitoes were there didn't linger long.

Love,

G

Directing school traffic

— Letter Thirty-Five —

October 25, 1961

Dear Mom and Dad, [Handwritten from Peter to his parents]

. . . Here, in Lagos, the weather is turning hotter and more humid each day. I'm afraid I depend rather heavily on air conditioning to make working and sleeping tolerable. The problem is that the constant changes from extreme humidity (outside) to 15 to 20 percent (inside) have reactivated my sinus trouble reminiscent of my childhood struggles.

On the other hand, we are eminently happy. First, it is exciting and fortunately no discomfort to Gretel to wait around and prepare for the child. Second, we live in a lovely location; our view (aside from the pile driver now working on the seawall at the Yacht Club) is always uplifting to our

> *. . . we are eminently happy.*"

spirits. Third, we have not become disenchanted by Nigeria, as so many others have. We are growing, learning, and modifying our view as regards the people and their hopes and possibilities. Finally, Gretel has had a wide and varied encounter with the prospects for education in Nigeria. Her field is as basic to the development of the country as is mine. Which brings me to the final point and probably the most important: I am *now* highly stimulated by my work, exceedingly fortunate to be working with Lyle Hansen and, indirectly, Wolf Stolper; and gaining a fantastic variety of experiences. My main disappointment is that I have not yet succeeded in communicating and teaching my Nigerian colleagues what it is to work, what their possibilities are: i.e., to be thoughtful and creative.

In our day-to-day work, I deal with a vast variety of possible investments, etc. For example, I have recently been trying to sell the Lagos Executive Development Board on a vast program of land and house development for the next five years. I have set them a target of 16,500 low-income housing shells, 10,500 developed plots for medium-income housing, and 3,000 upper-income (one-acre) lots. The real problem is finding the land, working out the financing and credit facilities, and pushing architects to work up designs, etc. Simultaneously, I've been doing the analysis for a proposed iron and steel industry. Two feasibility reports are in, a consortium of Westinghouse/Koppers/Chase International. Studies were also received from a German group, and reports are expected from General Electric. We've done a lot of study of transport investment, roads, airways, inland waterways, rails, etc., water supply, agricultural development (cocoa, rubber, groundnuts, palm oil, cotton, etc.), sewerage, monorail development, negotiations for radio and TV.

Would you pay the enclosed three bills for me? Some have taken as long as four months to get to me. Thank you. Gretel sent you our Weathers tone-arm needle. I hope you can replace it.

Love from us both,

Pete

We've done a lot of study of transport investment . . . inland waterways . . . see footnote 29. The choice was between investing in a new railroad vs. dredging sand from the Niger River to allow cement to be barged up river to build a dam at Kaingi. [In fact the dam was constructed between 1964–1968.]

— Letter Thirty-Six —

Well, Happy scary day, people. I s'pose you are all munching on corn candy and licorice goblins and ghosts. Imagine Halloween without ghosts, and in the evening a ringing doorbell. Well, we couldn't, so we're gathering up as many urchins as we can and giving them a real apple-dunkin, hot-dog, cider-and-doughnut party with a room full of scary experiences and noises at the Hansens' house tonight.

When Columbus went to the market this morning, I asked him to see if he could find a very large melon so we can go equipped with a jack-o'-lantern. Despite all my explanations as to what we were trying to do, he was a bit mystified, but he came home a short while ago with a medium, oblong green thing that he says they call a pumpkin!! He is all excited with the scheme now, since he ran into the Hansens' cook in the market, who asked him what in the world he was going to do with a whole melon (as did many other people as he was cycling home). So he put on a great air of mysteriousness—anxious to see what the reaction of his friend Anthony (the Hansens' cook) will be when he sees our finished product. I guess the selling point was Mother's card that came yesterday, which was sitting here on the desk when he just came in. It *is* a jack-o'-lantern with the face and all! So now he understands.

On the pleasant side, the hot weather is really beginning to come back in full. And with it, the pile driver in our "front yard" has increased its hours of work and volume of sound. We can't hear ourselves think if we try to sit in the living room during the day, to say nothing of being able to breathe the oil-laden air. Columbus says he is sure Mother will be able to tolerate it because she will understand it as a part of Nigeria growing. (Sometimes his observations really startle me.)

You should hear him these days. Every morning he comes in muttering about how the Russians have done it again. If they keep on their bomb testing, none of us will be left. Editorials in the papers are also becoming less tolerant. Up until now, they have not really condemned Russia as they did France, for example, because Russia is doing its testing on Russian soil, whereas France did it in Africa.

Meanwhile, the atmosphere has settled a bit with the departure of Margery Michelmore—though some people are still trying to verbally beat the girl to death. Promises for another eruption in about two weeks are in the air. The Eastern Region holds its elections for the Eastern Regional Parliament. There are sure to be all sorts of accusations back and forth between the Action Group (Western Regional Party) and the NCNC (of the East). They are major parties in the respective regions and really make life hard for each other, appealing for support mostly on the basis of tribal allegiance, which is very strong (Yoruba vs. Ibo). It will be interesting to see what crops up. Recently in the Western Region, the NCNC (of the East) was accusing the Action Group of there being a "break-down of law and order" in the West, and that the Action Group was unlawfully throwing members of the NCNC (or simply Ibo tribespeople) into jail, even killing them. Much of it was hot air, but I suspect that there was an element of truth. The same thing has been going on in the Northern Region during the last elections—when the dominant party of the North (NPC) was jailing wholesale, anyone who dared to run as opposition—especially opposition to the desires of the Sardauna of Sokoto (Ahmadu Bello). More often than not, they were Action Group people. So, I guess the AG was trying to get back by giving the same treatment to opponents in their own (Western) region.

Last Saturday we had an exciting race. This was a "points" race, and there were seven other Cats out to win. It was one of the windiest days we have had in the past month. The course was a wild series of zigzags down the harbor, with our class encountering, passing, and crossing over and beside the other classes of boats. There were probably more than 30 yachts out for the class races.

I was skippering and got us off to a bad start, not coming over the starting line until something like 45 seconds late. This put us at the rear of the fleet. But there was Peter leaping around; hauling the centerboard up and down (with the frequent change of "legs" in the course); holding down our thrusting and heaving bows against the choppy waves; occasionally helping me haul in the mainsheet; coaching as to tactics, since the traffic coming and going in all directions was really thick and heavy (the course crisscrossed in a restricted area). And there I was with one foot on the tiller bar, leaning out with all one and three-fourths of "us" to help hold the flying hull down, both hands clutching the mainsheet. A little over midway through the race, we came out ahead, passing the four Cats that had been leading us, luffing or blanketing us for all they were worth to keep us from passing them to windward or leeward, as the case may have been. 'Twas great fun, and we crossed the finish line with more than a four-minute lead ahead of the next Cat. Needless to say, we went to bed early and slept hard that night.

> *"And there I was with one foot on the tiller bar, leaning out with all one and three-fourths of 'us' . . . "*

We have been reading articles in the *C.S. Monitor* and the *N.Y. Times* about Nigeria and Prime Minister Balewa. It certainly is interesting to observe the "Western" opinion of our PM. The *Monitor* recognizes the fact that most Westerners look on old Tafawa Balewa in very favorable terms because of his moderate approach to problems. At the same time, it recognizes the fact that he is not loved by all at home. However, the U.S. press tends to minimize the size of this "group of young intellectuals," and to minimize the intensity of their feelings—which, unfortunately, are fanned to even hotter degrees whenever they hear a "Westerner" (or should I say colonialist) praise Balewa. I would venture to say that on the whole, basically, this really large body of non-Northerners, not just young intellectuals, agree with his policies. But they are impatient to see some "dynamism," forceful leadership, outspokenness on such subjects as pan-African-ism, anti-colonialism, rapid socialization of the economy, etc. More about this later.

Mobile restaurant

Love,

G

[P.S.] Great excitement when the phonograph needle came yesterday! Many, many thanks! We have been starving for some good music, so we played records all yesterday afternoon and evening.

— Letter Thirty-Seven —

November 3, 1961

Mom,

You must shudder each time a letter from Africa arrives for fear of what else I will ask you to bring. But these are such small things (famous last words). I'm sure you can fit them in.

I would like three Simplicity patterns in size 12. Two are sportswear that I'll make sometime early next year: #3916, #3937, #2663=an old pattern that may be hard to find in stock. It is a (maternity) pattern that Nancy sent me. I laid it out on the material I had bought on Tuesday afternoon and didn't finish in time before the Halloween party. So I left it on the dining room table to cut out when we returned that night. During our absence, the cats had a hilarious time with a lizard that they brought up and proceeded to chase around and mangle amidst the crinkly pattern paper. Material (spotted and smelly), shredded paper, and lizard (dead) were all scattered about on the floor when we returned. So, in order to return the borrowed pattern, do you 'spose you could find one?

Ships anchored off of Appapa docks

Stationery: I need several packs of 3x5 blank file cards, a set of 3x5 card dividers (the ones you can put headings and titles on, that rise above

the regular ones), and, if possible, two 8x5 blank pads of scratch paper. The latter is not absolutely necessary. I can improvise.

How go the final preparations? Do you have your visa? Did you take your pill this week? Be sure to bring sunglasses and comfortable "open" shoes. Of course, if you'd like, we could get you some lovely Italian sandals (really dressy, but comfortable), here in the local market. I have a pair that I wear all the time.

If you would like, and if they fit, you are most welcome to wear any of my clothes while here—since I can't wear them. I have a box of Wash'n Dris, so bring only what you'll need traveling. In fact, there should be plenty supplied you on the plane in the toilet compartment. These are indispensable in the bush. Not sold in Nigeria!

Tell Grandma that we have spent $5 of her B'day money on two new LP records. Handel's Water Music and Ravel's Daphnis et Chloé ballet. Our first record purchase since we've been married! How we enjoy them! Thank you, Grandma.

Just two weeks. Can hardly wait! I can't tell you how much we've been looking forward to your visit.

Love,

G

Millet from the Northern Region Marketing Board might be exported through Appapa (Lagos Harbor).

— Letter Thirty-Eight —

Dearest Grandma,

I wish you could have been a fly on the wall to hear the hilarious time I had trying to explain to Columbus about what the ghosts were on your Halloween card. Imagine how hard it would be just to explain to a Nigerian the meaning Halloween has for an American "as the night when all the ghosts and goblins, witches and devils come out and roam the land," when he has his own Juju man and secret societies that perform magical rites with regularity (and with real power) throughout the year.

You must have the latest word about what happened to part of your B'day money: two new LP records that have already received a year's worth of playing since we got them last week. When the fixed needle for the phonograph came back, we decided right then—we'll take Grandma's money and go get a real treat for our ears, which we did that very day!

Are you going to hold the fort for Papa while Mother is here? It is wonderful to have you there to make Mother's leaving that much easier. And the felines . . . they need someone, too! I just hope it isn't too hard on you. You must keep us informed about Knob Hill, etc., during that month. When do Hans and Janell come home for Xmas? That will be hardest for us—our first Christmas away from home in 98-degree weather. It will be hard to realize it is winter. But from what Columbus says, everyone here in Southern Nigeria (not the Muslim North) makes a big fuss over the Xmas holidays.

Well, back to thesis writing. Thanks so much for the Halloween money!

Much love,

G

— Letter Thirty-Nine —

November 8, 1961

DEF,

It is hard to make me sit down and type you a letter when I am already sitting down and typing away at the composition of the first chapter of my thesis: "Development of an Education System in Nigeria and Its Impact on Traditional Culture." It's fun, but, arrgh, as you can tell from these letters, writing does not come easily to me. (You may put your prepublication orders in for reduced-rate copies now.) And in case you're interested, the title is: "The Role of Education in a Developing Society—with Specific Reference to Teacher Training."

Did I ever tell you about the 1,000 Grenadier Guards who arrived in Lagos the first week of last month? Their troop ship stopped here on its way from the Southern Cameroons, which until the first of October had been a part of the former British Trusteeship territory, administered as a part of Southern Nigeria. (The Northern Cameroons, about five months ago, voted to become a part of Northern Nigeria; the Southern Cameroons chose to leave the Nigerian fold to reunite with the French Cameroons. Years ago, this used to be a German colony, but then after the First World War, I believe, it was divided between the British and the French.) The arrival of the famous Grenadier Guards en masse the day after the proclamation of Cameroonian (the French and British spell that word differently) independence was a very tangible reminder to us of the new political entity that has just been formed; but not without strife.

Reports in the papers indicate that there is a reasonably well-organized string of outpost stations in the mountains along the borders of the former British Southern Cameroons—that are receiving strong Communist assistance and direction—whose main purpose is to stir up trouble. It will be interesting to see what steps the new coalition government takes to bring them under control. The old problems of splitting tribal groups (in this case, it is the Ibibio and Tiv and "other" tribes) with national boundary lines that make border skirmishes at this time of new political orientation a commonplace. The Cameroons, we are told, is a beautiful mountainous country along its coast, dominated by Mt. Cameroon, which is 13,350 feet high. Her main resource is the banana, but she also has timber, rubber, oil-palm products, cocoa, and tea—all of which will need a great deal of overseas investment to be adequately developed.

This comes in cycles. We happen to be on the upswing of one in which the papers are full, every day, of notices about people "missing," numerous court cases on slave dealing, and reports from, this time, the Sudan, of numerous Nigerians who have been captured by slave dealers as they were on their way in a pilgrimage to Mecca across the great Sahara Desert. What amazes me are the ages of many of the subjects who are being sold by their fellow countrymen: 28, 34, 35, both men and women.

Well, while our African neighbors in Accra are in a frenzy over the materialization or nonmaterialization of the Queen's visit, we are having our own minor crisis—much of it trumped up by the papers—over the jockeying of different political forces for a favorable position in the elections to the Houses of and Parliament in the Eastern Region. There has been an uproar from the Action Group Chiefs. The NCNC campaigners are appealing to the voters (nearly all of whom adore Azikiwe) to give him a nice birthday present by returning an all-NCNC representative body to the Eastern Region capital, Enugu. Being Governor-General, Zik should be in a position that is all about "politicizing."

In the Western Region, Chief Obafemi Awolowo, opposition leader to the federal government, gave a speech to the National Press Club on "Twelve Months of Independence," in which he had the courage to proclaim that "the most outstanding feature of the past year is the dangerous decline in moral values among the entire populace of Nigeria. Honesty is at a discount; and there is a high premium on corruption and mediocrity. . . . The wealth of the nation is being pillaged by some unscrupulous foreign . . . entrepreneurs, notorious financial crooks," etc. The reaction? He has been soundly condemned by the government and NCNC as having given a "reckless and un-guarded address" designed to ruin the image of Nigeria abroad and discourage foreign investment. So really, no matter who it is that is criticizing, Margery Michelmore or Nigeria, there is much fear that "bad impressions" will be projected on the world screen. There is enough basic insecurity in this new country as to the national image, both at home and abroad, that Nigerians are touchy and quick to take offense at criticism.

A month ago, when all the streets were gaily decorated and parties, banquets, parades, exhibitions, and national festivities of all kinds were going on to mark the end of the first year of independence, attention was turned to the numerous new institutions and remarkable progress that has been made here in all fields. Huge changes have taken place, with the exodus of more than a thousand British civil administrators and their replacement by Nigerians, to a growing awareness of the complex problems involved in managing one's own house, with the concurrent opportunity for maturation and at the same time for irresponsible opportunism. These things, and many more, cannot help but pass through the mind of those of us who have witnessed the better part of the first year of this country's independent growth.

Unfortunately, things that Chief Awolowo pointed out are all too true, too predominant, and widespread. At times we have become very discouraged with this rampant "corruption" and lack of any sense of responsibility, to say nothing of moral obligation on the part of the public civil servant or private businessman. It seems as though everyone is out to get the biggest "dash" with no regard to whose expense. But when we think of the opportunists, the cutthroat practices, and the amoral administrators who were very much a part of our own country's early history, we can take heart. As the electorate has greater opportunity for better and more education, competition for all positions will become keener, and tolerance for amorality will be at a much lower level.

Other short new items: Missed the German Embassy cocktail party last night because we were giving sailing instruction to novices on the harbor yesterday. Gretel won the Coleman Trophy for Cats on Saturday. We took Columbus out sailing on Monday. The PLAN for the Federal Territory has finally taken shape and comes before the National Economic Council soon.

Love, Gretel

[P.S.] I haven't written about where I am going to have the baby because I haven't decided. I've seen a private GP four times now, but am quite sure I will have it in the Government Maternity Hospital. New and close-by. Will cost $25. They have a good man, too, I am told.

Back of the Lagos Island Maternity Hospital where expectant moms wait on benches

Top: Lagos Cathedral; Bottom: Shagamu, NW of Lagos during Ramadan - Christians and Muslims coexisting happily

— Letter Forty —

November 19, 1961
Monday
[Letter from Mother in Nigeria to the DEF]

Hi!

I have three air-o-grams in the machine, one for the Clarks, one for Knob Hill, and one for the Chicago contingent, assuming JET [Janell] will be with Tante at Thanksgiving. This is my first encounter with an electric typewriter, so if this epistle is a bit odd, don't blame it on Africa, but on this machine.

First of all, I know you all want to know how the children look. I can just say "wonderful!" Gretel looks so lovely, it is odd to say anyone seven months pregnant looks slim, but she does. Where the baby is there is, quite properly, a good-sized bulge, but the rest of her is long and lean (but not skinny! She is rounded) and so golden brown! Her hair is streaked taffy and the rest of her is a soft suntan, not leathery or dried-up at all. Of course you must take into account this is a slightly doting maternal ancestor speaking. But she truly is so radiant and serenely happy, she is a delight. And Peter looks very well. He has gained back most of the weight he lost when they first came to Africa. Except for occasional sinus trouble, he says he feels very healthy. I do think living here on this beautiful harbor and having the marvelous fun of competitive sailing is a beneficial factor.

Columbus is just as we have seen him in the pictures and imagined him from Gretel's descriptions. He came to the airport with them to meet me. They all shrieked with laughter when I involuntarily gasped at cars driving down the wrong (to me) side of the road. Columbus is obviously fond of the young Clarks. And Gretel was pleased I had remembered to bring him a present (a box of chocolate turkeys for his children). I met Grace, his smiling little wife, and their four children, and they are darling! And the two cats are very nice cats, one ebony black and the other a tawny gold, like Gretel. She has talked to them so much, they have real personalities.

The apartment and the location of the apartment are wonderful. From their enormous living room, which has three walls of windows, you look right out onto the harbor, the entrance of the harbor; and tho' I expected to see the freighters come right into the living room as they headed for us, I still was astonished at how close they come: great huge freighters from all over the world. This morning at breakfast we saw one from Japan, one from the Netherlands, one from Israel, and one from England. The kids know the meanings of all the signal flags, and that is fun: like having an introduction to each ship as she steams slowly past us. The high-ceilinged bedroom is about 28 feet by 28 feet. They have a desk and bookshelves in here and it is air conditioned. There is a small alcove off the bedroom that they have cleverly half-screened off. This is where I sleep. There are no closets, just great wooden wardrobes: two of them. A nice bath is off the bedroom.

One thing that is strange to me is the way everything is locked up. At night we close all the windows in the living room. There are no screens at all—and NO bugs! The friendly little lizards that live mostly on the ceilings take care of the bugs. Then we go into the bedroom and lock the bedroom! The horror tales they tell of thieves here make my blood curdle.

Saturday evening we talked and talked. They had an elegant meal. A delicious roast of beef, string beans, baked potatoes, tossed green salad, and a very special dessert Columbus had concocted for the special occasion. Something fluffy and cakey and creamy and good.

Sunday we were leisurely, me getting used to the change in time with no trouble at all. We went for about a hundred-mile drive, through the bustling city, tho' not as busy as Saturday. Still plenty of activity. I shan't describe it. Gretel did such a good job, why should I repeat? One thing she didn't mention was the assault on the olfactory senses—the undertone of kerosene, and overtones of, well, I guess you would just call it Africa, wood smoke and spicy things cooking and then a queer musky odor.

Western Region. Socializing at a well.

The clothes are as varied and colorful, the contrasts as startling. And I still turn and look at Nigerian women walking down the metropolitan streets in their colorful clothes, balancing enormous loads on their heads, with babies slung into their clothes, balancing another enormous load on their lower backs. Their gait is so interesting.

We drove out of the city and into the bush, through many little villages. Clay houses, thatch roofs, swarms of people around open fires, naked children, past little streams where women were washing clothes that they spread on the ground to dry; trays of peppers drying; the wooded land on either side of the road with palm trees, orange and lemon and kola and banana and cocoa trees. Some little clearings with tall midwestern corn tasseling; and when we stopped to eat bananas and drink iced tea, the sound of the birds was enchanting. One thing definitely surprised me and that was the number of two-story houses we saw in some of the villages. Peter explained that these were built by wealthy cocoa farmers who would start such a house after a good crop, and add to it whenever they had repeated success. They have windows cut into them and then boarded up and panes painted on the boards! Some are terribly fancy and utterly incongruous because they obviously have mud floors and no conveniences at all.

Today we went shopping at the Kingsway store, the big British department store. We bought things for the layette. Some of the prices horrified me. But the sight of so many familiar trade names was fun. Cosmetics: Coty, Cutex, Yardley's, even counters of Metrecal! And in the big supermarket they have Campbell's soups, Heinz products, even frozen foods of every kind. And ridiculous prices: fresh eggs are about $1.50 a dozen, frozen asparagus was 66 cents a package. I can't remember any other specific prices, but I was interested in my feeling about the store. When I left, I had the impression that we were in a summer resort town where you saw things you had at home, but everything costs more and doesn't look as tasty. Probably people added to this impression of resort-y-ness. All the black ones are barefoot and the white ones were in sleeveless low-necked dresses with toeless shoes and no stockings.

In a little while we are going to see Dr. Elsie at the USIA offices and find out what she has planned for me to do. If these first days are a forecast of my month here, I am utterly enchanted. Even with the weather. It is in the 90s, but there is a delightful breeze off the water. Peter and Gretel are wonderfully thoughtful, comfortable hosts, and, as you all know, perfectly charming, interesting people to be with. I just wish you could all be here with us.

Love,

Pauline

— Letter Forty-One —

December 7, 1961

Dear Aunt Jan and Uncle Archer,

Mother is at the hairdresser's, so I have a few moments to get a quick note off to you and let you know that all is well. I didn't write earlier since Mom sent you a communication last week on the latest developments.

We arrived back from our 11-day tour of the three regions last night, but I think it will be days before we get all the orange-red dust and sand out of our hair, clothes, and car. It was highly successful: We are all in good health, and I am especially pleased that it was as easy for me as it was. Had no discomfort at all despite the fact that three of our days we traveled on dirt roads. We took rolls and rolls of film, extras for you—enough so that we can throw away half the slides and still have too many! You will be getting details of the trip, so I won't go into them now.

[Here they are in pictures.]

Kano Mosque. Note Peter (far right of photo) surrounded by school boys

Top: Mother and I, the only uncovered heads, being observed in Kano market

Bottom: Bargaining for "manila" (bronze bracelet form of currency) with a Hausa trader

Top: Cosmetics shop - see page 154 for explanation; Bottom: Kano textile market

Top: Poultry market, Kano
Bottom: Meat market. Note vultures on roof.

Top: Note how male dominant this market is. Complete contrast to Yoruba markets
Bottom: Camel and Fulani cattle market, Kano

Top: Tuaregs arriving off Sahara and heading into the Kano market
Bottom: Tuaregs with camel whip. Note, even the goats are running.

One of the most dramatic events was witnessing the Tuaregs' arrival. They are a nomadic tribe that controls the trade routes of the Sahara. Clothed in their dark blue robes, they came roaring off the desert, leapt from their camels, and dashed through town toward the market, some still carrying their camel whips and sweeping all aside as they passed.

Interesting meals could be had from meat that was cut up, slapped on a wall to "cure," and then put on a skewer.

Top: Making kabobs
Bottom: Dye vats in Kaduna Market

Giant dye vats in the Kaduna market—here, in background

LETTERS FROM NIGERIA

As ever, there were the urchins taking care of younger siblings, often with interesting jewelry and all manner of clothing. Some fabulous textiles. I imagine the boy is asking, "Dash me two shilling, master."

From elegant robes to nearly naked

Kaduna, capital of the Northern Region, had government buildings set apart from the city looking ever so much like they had been dropped out of the sky from Europe onto African soil.

Top: Kaduna government buildings; Bottom: Gretel pictured here in a black checked maternity dress nicely matching the architecture

Different means of transportation

Women of a lower-caste tribe. They had large lumps on their shoulders from the many miles of carrying heavy loads.

Help loading chickens

More ways to carry loads

Millet

We have a theory about the hats these Hausa men wear (in the noonday sun). There must be a large additional cloth, perhaps moist, wrapped around the top of the head under the hat, that provides a nice cooling effect as it evaporates in that space up there.

We always laugh when we see this picture because it was taken just minutes after we took the one of the Hausa man (above) — relaxing in the sun!

Passage across most of Nigeria's rivers was by ferry.

I think this is the only picture of the two of us together, during our whole time in Nigeria. Mom took it when we had stopped for our lunch by the roadside on our trip north. We discovered that when we opened our thermoses to pour out the hot meal into tin cups, the moisture evaporated so fast into the crackling dry air that our hands stuck to the tin. This, in fact, is why the Tuaregs and many Hausas wear cloth around their noses and mouths—to keep the natural moisture in and prevent them from spontaneously bleeding.

Haggling over the price of a pot

The Baubab, looking like it was upside down—with its roots in the air, always fascinated us. Now, tall, slim Hausa Men about to pass, one far more substantial than the beast carrying him.

Top: Northern compound in urban setting. Bottom: Northern (Muslim) compound in the country

Top: Muslim women are rarely seen outside their compounds.
Bottom: Outdoor classroom in Jebba. We loved this picturesque town by the Niger River.

Top: Jebba where the railroad crosses the Niger River
Bottom: Women in the Northern Region around a well. Friendly greeting with a raised fist.

Two different school houses. Soccer being played at one.

Tomorrow I will go to the maternity clinic and perhaps find out when the doctor thinks the baby is due. My guess is around the 30th of January, but Peter insists that it will be much earlier, maybe because he thinks I am too enormous already!

Mother and I have shopped around, and from the very minimal choices in the department stores here in Lagos, and even one in Kano(!), I think we shall be fairly well prepared. I just have to cut up the sheeting and flannel material to make the sheets, flannel squares, and receiving blankets and cotton pads for the mattress. Diapers, which are coarse, cost in the vicinity of $5.00/dozen!! I got one dozen and then wrote to Grandma to send two dozen as rags at no value. What do you want to bet, customs will charge more than enough to make up for what we might have otherwise saved. Oh, well, they will be softer.

Will write in more detail later. This is just to let you know that all goes well, and that it is such fun to share some of our part of Africa with real, live family.

Much love,

G

This young man has a "talking drum." He skillfully changes the tone it produces with the pressure of his left arm. The drum is hourglass-shaped with strings drawn over its pinched waist from end to end, which allows the drummer to create a near-human tone of inflection. Here he is drumming for a "dash" from us, to go into his bowl.

— Letter Forty-Two —

January 3, 1962

DEF,

Yup, we're celebrating our third wedding anniversary today . . . three whole years! It is nice to have this occasion to celebrate now. The other two that just passed last week (Xmas and New Year's) were really just exercises. We need only two to make the occasion of January 3rd complete; but December 25th and 31st aren't the real thing without family, snow (or at least cool weather), carols, and so on.

We missed you, I am sure, much more than you missed us. It was interesting, however, to experience a tropical Christmas and see how the British and Nigerians go about celebrating it. I must say that, aside from the presents (there was the Xmas shopping rush here, too), the main feature that dominated the celebration for both holidays was the firecracker and the fancy hats. On Christmas Eve we went to the Olmsteads' for a cocktail gathering and on our way home drove around the streets and side alleys (which is what most of the streets are, anyway) of Lagos to see what people were doing. If they were not throwing firecrackers, they were having them thrown at themselves. Everyone was dressed in his or her best clothes, whether native or Western, and everyone, but everyone was wearing a bizarre colored and styled papier-mâché hat. Some people had on masks, and a few, full costumes! The raucous noise and crowds of people that filled the hot, muggy night streets were a far cry from snow-hushed towns and heavily wrapped carolers. If you worry about the Christ missing from our Christmas, try and find it when you are dodging cherry bombs and run into a Juju sacrifice!

Christmas Day, Lyle, whose family was in the U.S., took us out to Tarkwa Bay in his motor boat, as there wasn't enough wind or even breeze for us to sail out. There we spent much of the day spearfishing off the edge of one of the training moles that keeps the ocean swells out of the harbor. We are really becoming quite the addicts of underwater fishing, what with our flippers, goggles, snorkels, and spearguns. These next few months are the months for fishing, too. The flood tide waters are so clear, and for some reason there are many more fish in the harbor during this time of year. Almost every day, now, we spend about an hour fishing when the clear flood waters are coming in or off the end of the point. Disgustingly convenient. A few days ago, Peter caught a gray snapper with his speargun; it was some 20 inches long and nearly a foot high. We gave half of if to Columbus and his family and served the other half last night to Lyle and Dr. Henry Bretton, well-known political scientist from the U. of Michigan. It was delicious.

The day after Christmas is Boxing Day, which the British, and thus the Nigerians, have as a holiday for opening their boxes; though I don't know of anyone who waits until that day to open their boxes since they are theoretically in church all day on Christmas. On that day I took the Mini Minolta (tiny, cigarette-lighter–size camera, made by the Japanese, which Lyle, the extravagant soul, gave to us for Xmas) to Bar Beach. Peter lugged our dainty 4x4 camera bag with two-ton camera and lenses (Mother can testify to this). There the merrymakers go,—not only to make merry, but a few brave souls actually swim. (Very few Nigerians know how to swim.) The rest, crowds and crowds, stand on the beach and simply stare at the waves and surf coming in, everyone fully dressed in not only their best, but usually their most cumbersome agbadas, lapas, and headgear. Still 'tis a strange sight to us "Westerners," who get our bodily covering down to the bare minimum when going to the beach, especially in this climate.

Back to the photography: I had a marvelous time sneaking around to get pictures of a chief's lower molar cavities while he would never know it. Meanwhile, Peter was getting good arm-strengthening exercise carrying

Boxing Day holiday on Bar Beach

our other high-powered equipment, but he never got a picture. In case he reads this, I had better quickly add that all of our "Northern trip" pictures have come back except for one box, taken with our Topcon and various cumbersome lenses. [These photos are in Letter Forty-One.] We are quite satisfied with their performance. So many of the images we couldn't have captured without the telephoto or wide-angle lenses, nor would the image have been as satisfactory without the single-lens reflex camera. But then there are many that we did *not* get for fear of risking our skins by snapping a photo of some irate African. Some Nigerians believe a camera will steal their soul. We had enough trouble as it was, every time a Nigerian, especially the children, saw our camera equipment. Now, with this "cigarette lighter" camera, we will be able to get away with murder, or at least get pictures in the marketplaces and crowds without drawing attention to ourselves.

Mother has probably told you of her experience walking down the street taking pictures right behind our house. A man followed her and tried to take her camera away. She had recorded the open sewers (which line every street) of the middle–upper-class housing, that only a picture can describe. She had also recorded a woman taking snuff. Mother hadn't even noticed her, as she was taking a picture of the colorful red peppers and tomatoes that the woman was selling. I must add that now I can get my picture of a man urinating in the street; but frankly, I doubt that he would care or budge if I should stop right in front of him and focus our monster camera on him. Talk about children being nonchalant and indiscriminate in the performance of such functions: The other day I had to walk around a "functioning" man in order to get out of my own compound on the way to the Lagos Museum.

The pressure is really on now, and some days Peter and Lyle work nearly around the clock. I am not exaggerating when I say that these two alone are, during the past three or four weeks and the coming two to three weeks, pulling together and writing the first draft of the Five- (now Six-, thanks to an impulsive decision by some irresponsible ministers) Year Plan. Wolfgang is off on what is amounting to a month and a half Christmas holiday with his family in Europe and a conference of African economists at Addis Ababa. It is just as well, though, as he is more trouble than help when he has to work under the pressure that Lyle and Peter are under right now. If only the Assistant Secretaries, civil service economists, who are working under Lyle and Peter in the Planning Unit, would buckle down and do their part of the real work. Evidently they don't know what work is. It's a struggle to get them to come in after hours. In addition, so much of their work is of such poor quality that Peter spends valuable time doing over what they have drafted in order to make it usable. Peter and Lyle have been crying for the assistance of well-trained (or even not so well-trained) Nigerian economists whom they can take into the Planning Unit. Then, with special tutelage, they could groom them for their jobs so that when they leave the country there will be Nigerians to carry on where the Americans left off. As it is now, should Lyle, Peter, and Wolf pull out, the entire Plan would collapse.

I really don't mean to spout off like this, but I was upset by an editorial in one of the more moderate newspapers this morning. Comment is not needed to explain why. These excerpts will explain themselves.

> We have accused the Federal Government of plan-lessness in regard to our economic progress. . . . We acknowledge the help which foreign economists may be giving. But we believe that Nigerian economists (and there are many of them in our universities) should be given the opportunity to contribute their own quota just as Nigerian politicians are contributing to the country's political development. What can shatter the hopes we cherish for peace is the economic crisis which looms ahead now. And apart from the unscientific system being adopted by the Governments of the Federation to find money hurriedly, we cannot see any real attempt to grapple with the problems. . . .

@#$%^&*+#?!! (quote from me)

I am no longer surprised to find a monkey going hand-over-hand (brachiating) down the clothesline in the bathroom or helping herself to bananas from my fruit box in the kitchen. In fact, day before yesterday, I went out into the living room (can't hear anything when in this air-conditioned bedroom) to find the hairy monster lounging on the dining room table. She's really cute. She is actually not a monkey but a gibbon from Malaya. She belongs to our next-door neighbor, Lord Head, the British High Commissioner. You should see her tease Columbus. She is extremely graceful, with very long arms and legs, delicate "hands," and a small body, all of which she manipulates so she can move from branch to branch and tree to tree almost as though she were flying. The other day we were standing in the back compound talking under the avocado tree when she came swinging down off the roof, dove through the air to the near pawpaw tree, and bounced down onto the clothesline to swing out just far enough so she could reach out and bop Columbus on the head with one long arm and dangle there from the other arm, chuckling at him. Columbus turned and she retreated to the tree to repeat the performance until they were chortling at each other, boxing and swiping at each other (one black arm reciprocating a hairy gray one) and chasing each other all around the compound. Evidently she likes females, because during a lull in the play, I held my arm out to her and, with a few delighted sounds, she perched on my waist with her arms around my neck and her head snuggled down on my chest. Eventually, after her visits, I take her back home and put her back in her cage, which never makes her very happy.

Love always,
G

Visit from my neighbor toward end of my pregnancy

— Letter Forty-Three —

[From Peter to his parents]
January 4, 1962

Dear Mom and Dad,

Thank you for such a very generous Christmas gift. It was overwhelmingly large and will take a long time to spend (I hope). We are dedicating it all to outfitting the "expected one."

Christmas here was rather sad! The tropics just don't emit the spirit of Christmas as we know it. It is celebrated here as a combination of New Year's, Fourth of July, and Halloween, with the Mardi Gras Festival thrown in. Christmas Eve, we suffered from shell shock and finally turned back in our effort to go to church because of the firecrackers and exploding bombs. Christmas Day, everyone is drunk, English and Nigerians alike, parading and masquerading all over town.

Anyway, my reason for writing is to tell you of our plans for next year, etc. I have just consented to staying on here until next summer. Lyle is putting strong pressure on me to stay longer, but I am convinced that what I need now are the theoretical and analytical tools that must be learned in graduate school. Therefore, I am going to return to graduate school next fall. The question is WHERE and at what PRICE?

"I am still very anxious to get my degree either from Harvard or MIT."

I am still very anxious to get my degree either from Harvard or MIT. It will be far more negotiable than a University of Michigan doctorate. I have seen this repeatedly here. I would like to shoot for the very top. Why take second best? People here seem to think I can do it, and Lyle has been encouraging me indirectly. Another reason is that I am pretty well committed to doing my thesis for Wolf if I return to Michigan, and I don't really want to. He is too vague and romantic to be *my* thesis director. His type of intellectual wandering might have me struggling to complete my thesis for years. Also, I'm not overly impressed with the manner in which the economics department at the University of Michigan approaches economic development.

I am therefore presently in the throes of making applications again. I am hoping to get scholarship aid. The tuition is higher and I would have to give up my National Defense Education Act Fellowship, but I think we can get other aid, somewhere. Most important to us is that we will be able to live for several years on the East Coast close to our families and friends before we start a series of overseas jobs. We would like to do this, especially while our family is beginning. Then, too, Cambridge is far better from which to make contacts for future work.

So this is to let you know we are holding our fingers crossed, hoping a break will come along so we won't have to go back west to the University of Michigan.

Love,

Pete

Jebba, a village beside the Niger River

— Letter Forty-Four —

January 19, 1962

DEF,

    I shall simply preface this communication with a "yes, I am waiting, too." According to the doctor's calculations, our production (or shall I say reproduction) should have taken place around the 16th, but according to my calculations, based on the thermometer, it will take place around the 24th. From the dates above, you can see I am walking a weeklong tightrope between those two dates. Peter keeps reassuring me we could take another tour of the North for three weeks, since, as idle talk has it, most birth days, at least for the "white man," come much later than expected. Impatient? No. Very sore ribs.

    I get the impression that the entire Yacht Club is waiting with me, too. Ever since it happened last week, I have been told this story at least a dozen times. The NBC (Nigerian Broadcasting Company) arranged to do a live broadcast of one of the One-Design races on Saturday, with the Commodore commentating. Since the Catamaran class is the fastest and thus most spectacular, arrangements were made for us to start 25 minutes later than usual, so that the broadcast, which comes on at 4:30, could have a 10-minute introduction to the proceedings in addition to the countdown of the last five minutes before the "gun" that starts our race.

    Unfortunately, there wasn't much of a breeze, and there was a strong ebb tide. I skippered, since this requires less physical activity. The first mark was down the harbor, and thus down the tide. Since we had 15 minutes, we decided we would sail down to it in order to determine which of the various ebb currents was strongest, thus deciding which end—windward or leeward—of the line we would want to shoot for at the start. Well, when we turned to head back for the area of the start, we realized that we had come downwind too far and would probably not even make it to the right side of the line for the start.

    Meanwhile, we had brought our portable radio on board with us and were listening to the Commodore giving a rundown of those participating in the race. Then we heard his astonished exclamation: "What in the world is wrong with *Miss Tibbs*?!! She is the red Cat down there on the wrong side of the line! Looks like she won't even make it to the start what with two and a half minutes left! This should be interesting since *Miss Tibbs* has been the most successful boat of late; winning most of the races." (He never mentioned our name, since, being the stodgy, British conservative that he is, he is mildly shocked at, and a bit resentful of, a woman helming in the big races.) Well, to make a long race short, we *were* late, even last over the starting line. But by the second-to-last leg of the course, we were leading, and when we tuned in again to the broadcast, the Commodore was saying to the Master of Ceremonies: "Yes, it looks like *Miss Tibbs* is in the lead over there across the harbor, with Ron Jones not far behind." "Do you think *Miss Tibbs* will win, Mr. Commodore?" "Yes, it looks like she has a commanding lead. She is being helmed by Mrs. Gretel Clark, and if nothing happens to *her* before the end of the race, she will probably hold it." For the next 45 seconds, one could hear the roars of laughter from a large group of lawn-sitters and sailors from the earlier races who were obviously listening to the broadcast. They have been predicting that "one of these races you will have to be disqualified for returning with one more crew member on board than when you started."

It is incredible how little time Peter has at home. His hours have been roughly 8:00 a.m. to midnight. But more about his work later. What little time he has had at home, he has spent recently on his Harvard and MIT applications, sailing an occasional race with me, or an odd job such as the workshelf, to double as both darkroom for our new Minolta enlarger and infant processing center. He installed it so that it is at a nice, high working level with a shelf underneath. It fits into a small, three-cornered alcove in our toilet room.

Lyle has been promising me every month since we went to Lokoja in August, that: "This is the last month that we shall have to work on Sundays or maybe even Saturday afternoons. Not long now and you can get to know your husband again." Lately he has transferred that time span to "this is the last week. . . ." I don't know whether to take heart in the fact that The Plan (which you now know has been extended to a Six-Year Plan for the Federation) is fairly well finished: the writing, that is. This Peter and Lyle have done singlehanded, pulling together and chapter-writing a few days prior to Mother's departure. The only chapter they have had trouble with is the one Wolf wrote, on the Balance of Payments, which he started before he went on his month and a half "vacation." Peter and Lyle spent nearly two weeks trying to figure out where Wolf had gotten his figures and then what model he had used to determine his annual projections of expected GDP (Gross Domestic Product). On top of that, Peter said that today, in the meeting of the Joint Planning Commission, for which Lyle and Peter have been feverishly pulling together the document for preliminary discussion (before it comes before the National Economic Council on Monday and then the Prime Minister of the Council of Ministers on Thursday), there was much greater general approval of the Plan as they went over it chapter by chapter. There was an exception, however, which was for Wolf's chapter, which they just couldn't understand, because it was written in such technical terms.[39]

On Tuesday, Columbus left with his eldest daughter, Victoria, age

School boys in Lagos

eight, to take her via lorry transport to her grandmother's home in the Eastern Region. It is not uncommon for a youngster to be shipped off to live with a grandmother in the bush. There are two very strong reasons for doing so: It is cheaper, and in many cases, including that of Columbus, it is the only way to give the child any formal education. No matter how hard he tried, he, with my help, was unable to get Victoria in school here in Lagos—where Nigerians boast about a free, universal primary education. Ha! Thousands of children right here in Lagos will not be able to attend school this year, which commences in another week, because there simply isn't room nor enough teachers for them. So, too, in the regions, though perhaps less limited to those who desire to send their children to primary school. Any position above that level is under strong competition. It is becoming an expensive proposition. Annual school fees in the East, for instance, will amount to something like £4 for Victoria in Standard 1 or 2, roughly equivalent to grade 1 or 2. For Standard 6, it is £8, expensive for most people who are likely to have several children in school at once. Consider what this means in a country where the average per capita annual income is a mere £30.

This little incident serves to illustrate a number of cultural practices. Originally, Columbus had made arrangements with one of Grace's nephews, who lives over on the mainland in Mushin, to take Victoria home to the Eastern Region. Columbus would pay all the fare and any expenses the boy might incur.

This trip is not an easy one. The traveler must sit on a wooden bench in a lorry driven by a maniac over very rough, uneven roads that are 12 feet wide. Thus, every time one meets an oncoming vehicle, another lorry packed to its splitting gills with wet, none-too-pleasant-smelling humanity, both vehicles must drive off into the unshouldered ditch, always at top speed, in order to pass each other. It takes two days of driving in one direction, with only one stop. There one has a long, hot delay at Asaba or Onitsha, where one must take a ferry to cross the Niger River.

Well, at the last minute, the boy refused to go. This came as quite a surprise, because members of the extended family system are expected to

help out when called upon to do so. This is true even if it means sacrificing two years' savings to help start a second cousin once removed in training for the photography business, as Columbus did about five years ago for this boy. One doesn't refuse, because the request for sacrifice goes both ways. In a way, bettering or helping to better a member of the family is an investment in one's future. Now, if need be, Columbus can call on this "cousin," who is now a money-earning photographer, to help him out.

All students dress in school uniforms

I don't mean to digress, but consider the problems the young Nigerian must face, whose extended family pitched in to help pay his secondary school fees. He may have won a scholarship to study at a university in the U.K. He then returns to Nigeria and gets a job in the civil service. No sooner is he established in his job, made the first down payment on a car (that he can't begin to afford, but which, for prestige, he feels he must have), taken out a loan (so that he can pay his electric bill in a flat that the government has allocated to him because of his position), than his relatives (of whom there always seem to be an infinite number when you consider how many wives his father had) descend on him. He is the boy who made good and they can ask all kinds of favors of him. Of course, he doesn't dare turn them down for fear of being ostracized by the clan. A fate worse than death!

Well, as an alternative, we got permission from the Hansens for Columbus to ask their small boy (not their cook) or their gardener if either would go for him, since they come from the same area and they attend the same Ibo Clan Union that Columbus attends here in the Federal Territory. (Clan ties are important.) But neither of them would go. Why? Because it would be so expensive for them. They would have to save for a few more years before they could go back to the hometown. But how could it be too expensive if Columbus were going to pay for food and transportation? Very simple: A relative comes back to the bush from the big city where he has been working, and everyone, but everyone expects to be "dashed." So you see, it is very much a part of their own system. They do it to each other, evidently as much as they do it to the "white man." "Dash me one shilling, Massah." "Dashi dashi!!"

There wasn't much else we could do but let Columbus, himself, take the youngster home. I can assure you he was equally as worried about having to dash the relatives. He got back about noon today and said that he had stayed safely apart at his wife's mother's home. He didn't even go to see his own people, who live in a neighboring village. He was there just long enough to have something to eat. This is the first time he has been back to his home village since October 1959.

Michael, our garden boy, commented on the fact that Columbus had gone the other day. I explained that it was in order to get his daughter in school, which opens January 22. Michael then complained to me about "this Nigeria"—where one has to put nearly all one's earnings into the education of a single child. Of course, one does so, since education is the one avenue to a decent earning capacity. A Nigerian is still proud of the fact that he tried, though failed his School Leaving Certificate (which marks successful completion of primary school). And, Michael, still grumbling, notes that one must know the education authorities or a minister or some other Big Man in order to get one's child in school in Lagos. I must hear this at least twice a week: "We poor people must suffer because of this Nigeria here. Our ministers may have been poor like us at one time, but once they become Big Men, they forget what they had known, and only vote themselves higher salaries." (Unfortunately, this is true.) "Now," continues Michael, "if only I lived in Russia. . . ." "Why Russia?" I ask. "In Russia there are no poor people. The government got the money to give everything to the people. They just print it when they need it," he says. "Where do you hear such things, Michael?!" "Ooohhh, I have many friends that tell me about Russia."

Lagos is really getting spiffed up for the big [African] Summit meetings that are going to take place here next week. I have forgotten what the latest count is, but it is going to be an impressive array of African heads of state. While the common laborers, the PWD (Public Works Department), and the LTC (Lagos Town Council) are bustling around clearing the streets of refuse and beggars, cleaning the open sewers (which, although they don't smell as bad as one would think, never look too pretty), and decorating the light poles, trees, and gates around town with colorful banners.

The political and intellectual leaders are talking in rather idealistic terms of forging the first links toward a Pan-African Federation. The predominant view seems to be that there must be a reorganization of African states on a regional basis through the establishment of practical bonds, such as better road and telecommunication networks. To telephone someone in next-door neighbor Dahomey (just 40 or more miles distant), one must place the call though London! And nearly all the roads in West African countries go from south to north rather than east to west. Thus, there are only two roads that cross the Nigeria–Dahomey border of 400 miles. They also want interterritorial schools and universities, possibly even a common market and common currency. The latter two possibilities are viewed with great skepticism by Nigerians, and even more so by the Ghanaians, who consider most of the French-speaking African countries as only halfway independent, being ruled by French "neo-colonialists." There is no doubt that an economic federation of West African countries would be very complicated to forge, since the former French colonial territories still depend very heavily on France to run their administrations, balance their budgets, and provision their armies.

Aside from this basic difference between the French- and English-speaking African countries, the more outwardly explosive difference has been expressed in the growing rivalry between the Casablanca and Monrovia Blocs.[40] The five powers that met at Casablanca in the beginning of 1961 (Ghana, Guinea, Mali, the UAR, and Morocco) have, as you know, taken a more radical approach to African unity. Nkrumah, who appears to have appointed himself as their spokesman, states their position in his usual strong anticolonialist terms, that political

"The leaders are talking in terms of forging the first links toward a Pan-African Federation."

unity must come first. The Monrovia group holds that political boundaries must be respected. I think they have been intimidated by the expansionist tendencies of Nkrumah toward Togo, of Morocco toward Mauritania, of Ethiopia toward Somalia, and Nasser (Egypt) in general, though lately, he less so. The Monrovia group feels that economic and cultural links must be forged before political unity can be brought about.

Within this group, however, there is a more conservative approach, just as there is within the body of Nigerian leaders, vis-à-vis the eventual possibility of real union. Balewa, who has done a commendable job making the first overtures toward bringing the two rival African blocs together, thinks that economic and cultural ties on a regional basis are worth aiming for. But he is doubtful as to whether this will actually lead to political unity. As for Nigeria's political leaders, Azikiwe [Eastern Region] and Jaja

(Wachuku) [Western Region] "seem to think that a more unified Africa is inevitable in the long run," as *The Economist* put it recently. This more extreme view strikes me as the view to take if one wishes to be popular with the intellectuals. Balewa [Prime Minister and from the Northern Region] is the more practical politician, more realistic, and not given to the grandstanding style of ranting and raving of the leaders from the other two regions (Azikiwe and Wachuku).

Headlines have been leaning to the spectacular, and many of the political and intellectual leaders of the country have been called on to write on the subject: "Background to African Unity," etc. Yesterday, an article in the government paper with the headline "This Summit May Write Off Blocs in Africa" starts out:

> This is[,] indeed, Africa's Decade of destiny: It is a decade in which the continent will not only be free from the shackles of colonialism and imperialism, but even more important, will realize its dream of African unity and Pan-Africanism. A proof of this will once again be in evidence when the forthcoming Lagos Summit Conference would have achieved, to a large extent, what it has set out to do—to close the gap which had hitherto existed between the Monrovia and the Casablanca groups of independent African States. . . .

An editorial in the same paper takes usual advantage of playing the old anti-imperialist and how-we-have-suffered tune:

> Years of foreign domination did at least two things to Africa—it deepened the gorge of social differences; and cut, at the roots, all thought of political union. It is not that the continent itself by its size, does not contain the seed of social and political incompatibilities; but since it suits colonialists each to keep his sheep within his own pen, years of European rule were devoted to keeping those who lied (*not my language*) under different flags strictly apart. . . . But so long had slavery lasted that even in trying to put down the heavy yoke our people could not tread the same path to freedom . . . .

It then goes on to say that "the path to political union" must be brought about by first instituting a lingua franca, economic ties, and cultural exchanges, and furthermore suggests that a Central Fund be established from which to finance interterritorial institutions. This is definitely the conservative approach to "intimate union." I wish I had the editorial from a recent Ghanaian newspaper (all of which are government controlled, now) to show you the contrast.

I don't mean to go on about this, but I just happened to turn the page to read the headline "Keep Out Imperialist Influence (Lagos Summit)." An excerpt reads:

> That all African States recognize the necessity for Unity is no longer in doubt. Recent speeches made by Heads of State show that willingness for unity is increasing with time. After all, we are all interested in solving the problems which imperialism has left behind. . . . Delegates must be careful about imperialist tactics . . . (*and must not*) pay attention to unpleasant comments from propaganda sources . . . . We must have by now realized that those who have extorted us for so long will be very uncomfortable when we all unite.

Much love always, *Gretel*

Prison bars (in distance) framed by prayer

— Letter Forty-Five —

[Written about a week after Bryn's birth, which was January 24, 1962]
Dear Mom,

I will address this to you, though in the long run I know I am speaking to the Extended Family, because I am thinking of you when I relive the past few days. You are right; no amount of description could make me understand what it is to give birth, to become a mother. And, I am discovering, when experienced, it brings this daughter—the new parent—much closer to her mother. Will this be an increasing appreciation as our offspring matures?

Right now I am thinking of birth itself. I thought I had it all so well rehearsed, but I must confess I never anticipated what actually took place. That was merciful, for the terror that remained with me for nights afterward would have incapacitated me had I known what was to unfold beforehand. Is the uncontrollable demon that seized my body God's way of showing that this step in the creation of another human being (in addition to all the other "steps" before and afterward) not my (or human) doing, but rather the unfolding of an unstoppable sequence of developments that are beyond my control? What has struck both Peter and me since January 24th is the relentless progress of physical events that developed with methodical precision since we took the initial step toward the creation of our child . . . and that such unbelievable results could accrue from our mutual desire, and single simple act, for an offspring. Anne Ridler expressed it very well in her poem "For a Child Expected":

> . . . the birth of a child is an uncontrollable glory;
> Cat's cradle of hopes will hold no living baby,
> Long though it lay quietly.
> And when our baby stirs and struggles to be born
> It compels humility; what we began
> Is now its own.

I used the words "uncontrollable demon," but it *is* a glory, too, which does compel humility in addition to terror, exhilaration, and wonder—in just that order as birth takes place!

Let me go back to where I left off in my last letter. As you know, from the note I squeezed into the air letter just before mailing it, the whole morning that I was writing to you on the hall bench waiting for the doctor to see me, I was in labor. This doctor, by the way, I had never seen before, being the fifth different doctor I saw in my total of eight prenatal consultations. How long I had been in labor we will never know. And you know from what I wrote to you during those four hours of waiting that my thinking at the time was it might be another week. I never suspected what was going on inside me. The doctor was Dr. Nwapa, a large forceful woman, sparkling though intense, strongly self-assured as a professional, though self-effacing socially, educated in the U.K. She announced with a great expletive that I was well into "labour," as it would be spelled here, and that I should come in to the hospital that afternoon.

I went home, packed my bag, and then sat down to type out the addresses on our announcements, and to wait until I could feel something. I felt nothing. Peter came home. We had our usual cereal bowls of fruit and talked about what had gone on at the Planning Unit during the morning. Read the mail and then Peter went back to do some extra work at the office (as usual), and I was to call him if anything developed. Nothing developed. Columbus brought home the biweekly ton of fruit, a lovely black-and-red cock, some prawns, vegetables, and rice from the market. He killed and dressed the chicken but prepared a light meal of prawn salad (in deference to my very expectant state), accompanied by delicious cheese-potato cakes. We had large slices of pineapple for dessert.

Wolfgang came by in the evening to entertain Peter and was surprised (and disappointed, I think) to find me still at home. By then, my back was a bit tight, and I could feel slight tummy cramps. Wolf went home shortly after nine.

Sometime that evening, I've forgotten just when, Lagos shot off a 21-gun salute, which reverberated clearly across the harbor and rumbled back through the narrow barefooted streets, where most of the 400,000 inhabitants were preparing their evening meal over open fires or perhaps kerosene burners. Maybe the meal was already being eaten communally from a large container, a pottery or enamel bowl, which undoubtedly held palm oil, Stockfish, ground egusi seed, a green leaf, and always lots and lots of hot pepper, "stewed" together with other ingredients in one form or another, accompanied by glutinous fufu or gari.

I wonder if the Lagosians were wondering, while they were molding a glob of fufu in their fingers and dipping it through the soup, just as we were wondering: For whom was that cannon salute? "Why, de born of a king, Mastah," Columbus remarked to Peter the next morning. We averred that we, too, had thought it was very nice of Nigeria to greet the arrival of our child into this world in such a grand way. However, we also conjectured that it might be His Highness (Nkrumah) arriving to attend the conference of African and Malagasy States, even though he and his Casablanca Bloc buddies tried to ruin the conference (which Balewa and Co. had for so long been working to bring about) by refusing to come at the last minute under the pretext of a complaint that the Algerian (rebel) government had not been invited. I think that all of us (in Nigeria) didn't believe that they [the Casablanca Bloc countries] were really not going to come. Being the optimists that we are, we thought—even hoped—that after the conference had commenced, Ghana, Guinea, Mali, Morocco, etc., would come down off their high radical horses and attend in order to keep this gathering from solidifying even more the differences that exist between the so-called Casablanca and Monrovia Blocs.

But it wasn't the "Osagyefo [Redeemer]" from Accra arriving after all. The majestic, sleek yacht that cruised silently by our windows up the shipping channel toward the gaily lit and decorated marina was that of President William Tubman of Liberia. Standing on the water's edge, we watched the craft return the salute as it passed the Governor-General's house (which is right next door). For a moment, we had forgotten about our own expectations as we considered the expectations of African leaders from all over the continent who were gathering here for the conference. We spoke of the wide-ranging benefits that could come from economic and social ties, from political respect for one another instead of rivalry and covetousness. I think I shall always associate the excitement and birth of our first child with the excitement of this impressive gathering of African statesmen.

After a sleepless night, with the evidence of something starting at about 4 a.m., Peter stayed home from work, exhausted partly from anticipation and also from the heavy work schedule he has been keeping. Then nothing happened. All morning, nothing. By midmorning, I called Dr. Nwapa, who told me to come see her at 1 p.m. I finished addressing the announcements. We had lunch which we munched, Peter sitting on the back steps and I perched on the edge of the open gutter that runs back through the servants' quarters; put my suitcase in the trunk ("boot," they call it here) just in case; and then we drove the few blocks over to the hospital.

Again, we waited in the hall on a bench for an hour while the doctor completed a cesarean section. We watched what seemed like hundreds of barefoot Yoruba ladies in all stages of pregnancy pad by—hiking up their multi-patterned blue lapas, occasionally carrying purse on head as they did so. When Dr. Nwapa checked me again, she said that I was now "three fingers dilated." I stayed. Peter and I decided that January 24th would be as good as the 25th or 26th for a birthday. Then I was given the works.

First came an "OEB" (oil, enema, and bath), which is the usual medical induction. I remember being mildly amused by the large, golden bug with long feelers that crawled between the cup of castor oil and orange juice on the stark white plate that the midwife held out to me. "This is to remind me that I am in Africa," I thought to myself.

Then began the surgical induction. The midwife took me to the "theatre," where Dr. Nwapa intended to break my "bag of waters," but evidently she did only a "membrane sweep." I was to take Trilene, the only anesthetic I would allow during the entire delivery. The idea of anesthetics frightens me. I scribbled on a paper I had on the "table" with me for recording contractions after returning from the operating room:

> It is strange, this business of child bearing! Dr. Nwapa has just broken my bag of waters, and for the first time in my life I have been given a drug. A terrifying experience! Just like in the movies. There is a mass inoculation center outside my window. A telephone booth-sized structure covered with woven straw mats. People passing by, many look like civil servants, others stop to raise a shirt sleeve or pull up an agbada tunic sleeve for a few seconds' "shot." Looks like a silent movie.

Then, a little later, I wrote:

> Mrs. Adequeba caring for me. Has four children. An Acting Assistant Mid-Wife. Very soft spoken. Deep liquid voice. Moves slowly, deliberately. Short hair, but not "plaited." Eyes blacker than her skin. Compassionate, though must experience people like me every day. . . . Need to hold her hand.

Intermittently I was trying to keep track of the time and duration of contractions, though they never seemed to have any regularity or pattern of any type. So all my "book readin'" did me no good.

I was given an intravenous drip. Counted them going in: one every other second for 45 minutes. Later we discovered that the hose had a leak. A little after that, my blood was clotting the needle. This, in addition to the castor oil, Mrs. Adequeba explained, was to make the pains really "grip hard."

5:00 p.m., contractions really "gripped" in earnest. At last!

7:00 p.m., the midwife left to send Peter home, telling him not to return until 8:00. He came in to see me for a few minutes and then spent the rest of the time sitting on a lone chair that had been provided for him right outside my room in the hall.

From 8:30 to 10:00, it was a real struggle. What strong women these midwives are! What work "labor" is! I'm not sure when Dr. Nwapa came in, but I remember worrying that she might have to leave me to do another cesarean section. They had expected me to deliver by 9:30, but Bryn, as you know, was big for a first baby, with a head circumference of 14 inches. This head, by the way, came out posterior position (facing up instead of down), which made his entry into the world even more difficult. The last half hour, sympathetic reassurances turned into stern commands: "Push!

This time you've <u>got</u> to give him to me. Your baby mustn't stay there any longer. Now GIVE him to me!"

Nine months spun before me as I thought of failing my baby in the last hour. Yet, I couldn't push hard enough. Four times the knife seared into me, eventually making an aperture that required 13 stitches to sew up. (Peter, hearing all this from his perch, said later that he forgot all about the baby and just hoped that I would survive.)

And then . . . how is it that a moment of excruciating pain and terror can in an instant turn into one of unbelievable exhilaration and wonder . . . with a boisterous cry, another human being was in the same room with us!

"Look," Dr. Nwapa shouted as she held up an enormous child. "You have a baby boy! Isn't he beautiful!"

My cries turned to those of such relief and joy. "Are you sure? Are you sure?"

And then there was Peter, his hand shaking, holding mine. "We have a son." Dear Peter. I didn't give him a very good performance. Those two hours must have been equally as painful for him.

When it was over, the midwives were amazed that he was unconcerned that his first-born should be a son: that his concern was for his wife; that I had survived.

I slept for an hour, I guess, while Dr. Nwapa performed the operation. She had to dash off before suturing me up. "Can you wait?" she asked. "The life of this other woman's child depends on it."

Then back to the theatre for an hour where we had an interesting, amusing conversation (the two student nurses tittering outside the ring of light) while the doctor sutured me up with catgut. At midnight, the job was done. Drowsy barefoot boys, their masks askew, pushed my stretcher down the hall and along the long, open corridor that connects the two wings of the hospital.

The city was still in the warm night lull. All I could see was the black sky, the Harmattan dust blanket from the Sahara obscuring all but the brightest star; the black head of the "porter" in front of me, swaying back and forth as he shuffled down the hall; the porter pushing my table stretcher from behind set the pace with snatches of a Yoruba song. The short syllables of the Yoruba language set both rhythm and tone. He sang almost in a whisper, placidly to himself. We passed two, then three nurses-in-training who, perhaps because of a momentary midnight lull in duties, were sitting out in the quiet tropical night. Exchanges in Yoruba went back and forth as we passed. The midwife on night duty in my lying-in ward was a wonderfully warm, rotund, Yoruba mammy type who usually had a mischievous glint in her eye and a slow, liquid laugh that always lingered just under the surface. She greeted me and said that they had expected me the night before.

I was awake in my room just long enough to try and re-see that son. Oh! A son! Born to Peter and me. But since he was upside down and very wet and red at the time, I couldn't visualize him very accurately. What had made a strong impression, however, was the large body and lusty cry, the cry that said, "Here is a new life!" Thrill and wonder subsided into a sense of well-being, satisfaction, and gratitude just before sleep closed what had been a long and very unique chapter in my life, a chapter that had begun nearly a year ago.

Early next morning, as every morning at 6:00, the baby was wheeled in to me in his cradle. It remains at my bedside until 10 or 11 at night. As I was peering into the cradle to see him closely for the first time (how remarkably complete babies are!), the nurse warned me that I had a big feeder. She said he must have been born hungry, for she had to feed him four hours after his birth. Not surprising, since he arrived at 10 p.m., and I had not had my supper. She was right, too. He has been nursing every two hours or more since.

We have both been cared for so well. I have an air conditioner in my private room, share a bath with the only other "amenity" patient (which means that we pay a £25 fee for the whole process, plus £15 a day while we are here, instead of the 15 shilling fee paid (approx. $2) by the others in this ward. Peter can come and go any time he pleases. His offices are just around the other side of the Race Course, so at 8 a.m., he usually comes in for a few minutes on his way to work. He brings fresh flowers from the garden, the four local daily papers we subscribe to, a pail full of washed diapers ("nappies") and clean clothes, wrappers for the baby, plus a thermos of milk (the powdered stuff we make, since there is no such thing as fresh milk here) and greetings from Columbus.

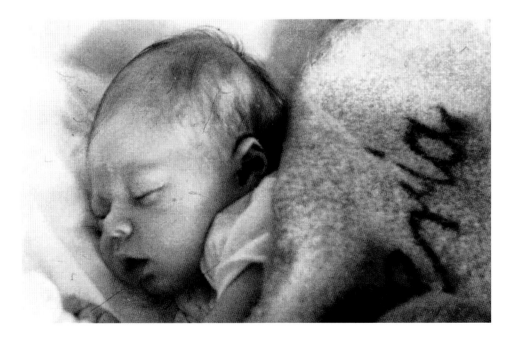

Baby Bryn

Post birth, in the hospital

Then he comes in at 4 p.m. bringing the mail, which arrives at his office, including <u>the</u> *C.S. Monitor* and the *N.Y. Times*, a huge container of fresh mixed fruit—our ritual, prepared by Columbus—and news of the latest crises over the National Plan. Taking a pail of dirty diapers, he leaves to be home for his supper, since Columbus has it ready at 7 p.m. The second day, he came in with one of those marvelous "mammy pails," such as the ones we saw in Kaduna. They are big, clunky enamelware jobs with bright designs painted on them: "MY HUSBAND LOVES ME" in big letters around the side. On the lid: "A HAPPY DAY FOR MY HUSBAND." How appropriate!

This we alternate with the blue plastic pail you saw me bargain for in the market, which makes our home diaper service quite efficient. Then he returns in the evening to read aloud to me *The White Nile* by Alan Moorehead.

I have a magnificent view of the harbor from my window (as if we don't have one at home), which I enjoy because it is a different perspective than what I get every day. It is fun to still be seeing the same ships, only I see them docking from here. At night the lights and occasional noise from the Apapa shipping yards are very clear across the harbor.

Top: Indispensible diaper pail
Bottom: Harbor view from my window in the hospital

I never tire of watching the passersby. Nigerians in their many modes and styles of dress are so colorful. Except for early in the morning and at 2 p.m. during the shift when all the clerical and professional workers are going and coming, I would say that the majority of the people are barefoot, about half of them have babies on their backs, and if I had the time and patience, I would count the number of bicycles to automobiles (foot is still

Street poster celebrating Conference of African and Malagasy States

the major mode of transport); but I can guess without counting, bicycles outnumber autos by more than 25 to 1.

From his perch on a lamppost just under the map of Africa (like the hundreds of other posters depicting African heads of state around the city), His Highness Haile Selassie looks right up into my window on the 4th floor. I feel as though he has been watching over us. I can't look out of the window without first looking at him. Too bad he had to leave the Lagos Conference so precipitously yesterday, because of his wife's ill health. He has been made much of while here. His speech the opening day of the conference was printed in its entirety in two of the local papers.

Another thing that has amazed and touched me is the stream of visitors who have come to see us. I had not realized how many friends we have out here. Columbus got all dressed up and came in with Peter the other day. Even our gardener, Michael, has come!

A very welcome guest was a friend from Wales, who left us a list of Welsh names from which, after much debate between the two of us, and threats from the hospital that our baby would not be allowed to leave until he had a name, we found our baby boy's name: Bryn. (It means "hill" in Welsh.) His full name is Brynmor Forman Clark. "Mor" means "sea." Thus: "hill by the sea," with a nod to Dad's Welsh ancestry.

One more word about the hospital: I hope that I can have all our children where "rooming-in" facilities are available. It has been just wonderful having Bryn here with me all day. I change him and dress him. The first few times I watched the nurses bathe him and now do that myself, if I wish. They have taught me a great deal. And the food is very good, as English food goes.

I think I had my biggest laugh the first morning when my breakfast was brought in. It was a concrete example of what the rest of the meals would be like: kippers and baked tomatoes. Of course there is always the 5:45 a.m. and 4:00 p.m. tea. Most of the desserts are custards, rice or bread pudding; all the vegetables, and sometimes the meat, are boiled. I get boiled cabbage every second or third meal; liver and bacon, steak and kidney pie, both about twice a week; and so on. But then you, Mom, are very recently familiar with this. It's reminiscent of what we had in the rest houses all over Nigeria. I'm not complaining, mind you. The food is

<u>always</u> good, and very well prepared, except the rice. You can't blame them. It is impossible to get *all* the worms, gnats, and bugs out of large quantities of rice. We don't even manage to do so here at home before cooking it.

* * *

The above was written at the end of my first week in the hospital, when I was expecting to go home. But then, the catgut didn't hold, which meant starting the whole process over again: having the remainder of the old stitches removed and new ones—nylon this time—put in their place. That second week in the hospital was not much fun. But all is well now. I hardly feel a thing.

Top: Courtyard of Maternity Hospital

Bottom: Ben, the "night watch"

Leaving the hospital was quite an experience. It was about 5:30 in the afternoon. When we walked out of the building, it was like walking into a totally new world. It was like coming to Nigeria all over again for the first time: the novelty of the colorful dress; the awareness that the majority looked at *us* as an oddity; the thrill of having others see our own son (as many in the street were anxious to do, for they don't very often see a white baby, especially coming from that hospital); the desire to run and show him to everyone, to shout to the world: "Look what we have!"

But there was another reason why the world looked very different to me. It *was* different!

The Harmattan had come! It had come with such force down across the Sahara and all of Nigeria that, with the winds prevailing from the north for the first time since we have been here, the sun set very high in the sky, at about 4:30, behind a very dark curtain of dust and sand. Not only was the air very dry, it was hard to breathe—just as we had found it in Kano, Mother, heavy with tiny particles of sand. The entire atmosphere had a tannish tinge to it. Could things have changed so since I had gone into the hospital? Even our house looked strange to me. Everything was dreamlike. There was Columbus rushing out to the car. There was tall, gangly Ben, the night watch (as he calls himself)—his spare-toothed grin—running

Baby Bryn

toward us. Before we could get into the house, Grace had come around from the servants' compound in back with all her and Columbus's children, and some of the other servants' wives and children: "Madam is home! Madam is home! How is de baby?" It was like plunging into a black sea of warmth.

Weeks seem to have gone by since I started this letter.

At four weeks, I took Bryn to have Dr. Nwapa circumcise him. I was upset at having to wait so long, but she insisted that she could do a much neater job on a bigger baby. At one month, Bryn weighs 11 pounds. Can you believe it is impossible to buy a set of baby scales in Lagos? The only one known to exist is in a store, at Kingsway, which is put out on the baby goods counter so that mothers can bring in their babies and weigh them. Sneaky way to get business. Peter came across some scales with a little wicker basket on a stand in which we put our mite of humanity.

They were being sold for a mere 10 bob by a man who had had them for his youngster, and needed them no longer. He was going back to the U.K. Such people, of whom there are many, leaving Nigeria after many years in the Colonial Service, stick up notices along with the blizzard of others on a bulletin board at the Ikoyi Rest House.

It is hard to see him resembling anyone in the extended family. But if I had to make a choice, I would say he looks most like his Uncle Hans. I'll enclose some pictures that we took of Bryn when he was three weeks old. They were developed over a week ago. Then you can decide for yourselves whom he resembles. I think he looks like Bryn Forman Clark.

The winds have been wonderfully strong this month; almost gale force today, so Peter and I went out for a most exciting and very wet half hour. We must have been going about 20 mph on the reaches. When we came in, I dashed up to the house, where Columbus was doing the ironing out on the back step with an ear out for Bryn. I asked him if he would like to go out for a jet-propelled harbor ride. He dashed back to his quarters and returned with shorts on. Then I went out on the front lawn of the Yacht Club to take pictures of our *Miss Tibs* as she came screaming by, great sheets of water spraying up over the sides (good thing Cats are self-bailing), with one hull flying high in the air. Only three other yachts out today and one of those capsized.

Bryn has even been out for a sail. We took him out a week ago Sunday. He enjoyed it almost as much as we enjoyed him enjoying the sail. Incidentally, club race for a pennant last Saturday: mass start with all classes competing against each other for the prize; Peter skippered us to a decisive victory!

So much more to tell: some interesting people we have met of late; Nigeria's reaction to Capt. John Glenn and his heavenly ride (circum-navigating our globe three times!); the meeting of the National Economic Council in Ibadan last week to deliberate over the Six-Year Plan; plans for the future—i.e., PBC's professional and academic thoughts of late. Ford Foundation really wants him to stay, with a great increase in status and position in addition to salary and possible guarantees for financing of PhD and thesis research, etc., etc. But I'll let that stew a while longer until things are more definite. Just let me say in my objective, unbiased manner that they think he is pretty valuable; that he has done some significant work; that he is being given the opportunity—as he has this past year—to further, not only influence but determine what general direction the entire economy of Nigeria will go during these, her formative years of development. Now, if they could offer him some snow, I'm sure he would stay without hesitation.

Much love to all,

G

Peter and Columbus out for a windy sail.

— Letter Forty-Six —

February 12, 1962
[Letter to Peter's and Gretel's mothers]

Dear Grandmothers,

I have written the better part of a "DEF letter," giving details of Bryn's arrival, which I wrote during the first week in the hospital. I expected to type an air letter as soon as I got home. Then, as Peter wrote you, on the day I was to leave the hospital the doctor checked me to discover my stitches (13) had come out and that I would have to have the remains removed and then be completely resutured. This meant starting all over again. I was there another week, and this time with a slight relapse. I felt wonderful during the first week, probably running on nervous energy and the sheer excitement of our first-born. I even managed to get out all the announcements and write to you, which you will receive eventually.

Anyway, this first week at home has been much more hectic and tiring than I could have imagined. The nice feeding schedule we had managed to establish (Bryn and I) went out the window on coming home. Nights have been up-and-down affairs with not half enough sleep. He wants to eat/nurse every two to three hours. Consequently, I have spent the days trying to catch up on sleep when I haven't been bathing or changing or nursing Bryn.

Wheeeeu, I'm still exhausted. But as we start to get things down to a system and intervals between feedings lengthen out, I am beginning to regain some strength. Meanwhile, all I can say is, thank you so much for your patience waiting for word from me. That is the best gift you could have given us!

I promise details, some of which may be repeated, soon. I'm not typing now because I don't want to wake Bryn.

Despite all the trauma of readjustment, Bryn is such a joy, and much cuter than I ever expected! As the doctor said, "He looks like a three month old baby!" No wrinkles, splotches, etc. Beautiful skin, long dark (!) hair, big blue eyes, and so BIG! He is about nine and a half pounds now. Today I started feeding him cereal from a spoon, which he gobbled up. And he drinks gallons of water, in addition to nursing all the time. Of course, his father and I are sure there was never such a remarkable child born before this one.

Much love,
Gretel

— Letter Forty-Seven —

March 12, 1962

Dear Folks,

Gretel has had some trouble this last week with an infection in her breast, but we have solved that now and I hope we can bring her back to full health. We have been amazed at how much energy the birth and care of a child demands from the mother. We may have a steward, but the climate and crudeness of life still make daily living more arduous than it would be at home.

I have finally found time to finish the renovation of the Catamaran that I bought in Ghana. I've raced it twice now, winning both times.

I have heard very promising things (unofficially) from MIT and Harvard. The full choice should be before me in the next month. I have heard no comment from you folks as yet. I wrote you a letter three months ago, spelling out my thoughts. What are yours? I've also been promised a very large research grant from the Ford Foundation. They want to keep me!!

Love,

Pete

Our Gibbon neighbor, admiring Bryn in his crib. She swung in through the second story window.

— Letter Forty-Eight —

March 31, 1962

Dear Extended Family,

I must start out by telling you about our son, who is now two months old, and gets more engaging with each passing day. It is still hard to believe he is ours. At exactly two months, he weighed 14 pounds 1 ounce, and was 24.5 inches long. His blue eyes, shaped like almonds, are so alert; he seems to see everything, following objects and people as they move about.

The Hansens, when they were in the States for Christmas, bought Bryn a toy that only could have come from the U.S. He adores it—a bird mobile, seven different species and colors, hanging at different levels from four wires that are suspended from a yellow birdhouse. The bird house revolves as a music box inside plays "Rock-a-Bye-Baby," and a little bluebird just outside the house rocks back and forth. Positively fascinating! His parents spend almost as much time watching it as he does.

Bryn has a healthy appetite. He is getting bananas, fresh orange juice, as well as cereal. He nurses at 6, 10, 2, 6, and again anywhere between 9:30 and midnight. He is such an easy baby, never cries except when he is put to bed and then only for a few minutes. Sleeps straight through the night. I have let him determine his own schedule of eating and sleeping, since there is no doctor out here to advise us on such details. So between him and me and Dr. Spock's book, we are doing fine. The one thing I do miss is being able to buy inexpensive attractive baby clothes, and panties. The ones Tante sent have been a godsend. He wore that pair until the shipment came in from Switzerland last week, costing as much as $1.40 each! Of course, when he is not in the air-conditioned bedrooms, which is for an hour or two each day, he doesn't wear much of anything but a diaper.

One thing I have to remember when I have him out with me in the car is to keep a close eye on him. Baby stealing (for Juju sacrificial purposes) and slave trade still run rampant right here in Lagos. I imagine a white baby would pull down a handsome price. Then again, some find their babies expendable. Twice in the last week, recently born babies have come floating by the "hard" here at the Yacht Club. Week before last, a set of twins and one of triplets were killed (up in the bush) for tribal reasons.

The Nigerian reaction to Bryn, and some of the comments (especially Columbus's) have been priceless. For example, during the first week after his birth, when both Columbus and Peter were visiting me in the hospital, Columbus asked, looking at Bryn's typical baby pug nose: "When you start to tape his nose, Master?" It took us a moment to figure out—why the question? Then we realized: Our baby's nose looks like an African's, lots of cartilage on either side. And his hair . . . it has positively amazed Columbus and the attendants in the hospital (to say nothing of me!). Bryn had long, dark hair when he was born (until I cut it all off). Columbus had thought all white babies were born bald. All African babies (who, incidentally, are born white) are born with full heads of thick, kinky hair. Then, too, I have noted that when Nigerians look at Bryn, invariably they will remark that he looks like his father, which, no matter what his father looks like, is supposed to be a compliment; whereas, when Europeans look at him, they say he looks like his mother. I think *my* mother is right—he looks most like Bryn Forman.

Incubating and then having a child has been a boon to our social relationship with almost any Nigerian acquaintance, since having babies is such a frequent and important occasion in their lives. Here everybody loves a mother or mother-to-be. All our servants seem to have newborn babies. Our cook-steward's wife, Grace, had a boy five months before Bryn. Our tailor's wife had a baby ten days afterward; our gardener's wife, a fortnight later. Olu, the tailor, stopped in this morning for a short chat and to see if I had any business for him. He was surprised to "witness de big boy!" He says that his boy only grows "small, small," so they are giving him native medicine: chopped, boiled pawpaw leaves. He told me, "Na European babies be cared for different." His "pickin only grow small small."

When Olu left, I took Bryn in to "bath" him, as the British would say. I was thinking about all these babies at the same time when Heziah, the cook-steward next door (whose wife has a seven-month-old baby) distracted me. He was singing an African tune with great abandon. Most Africans we know sing in the strangest manner, in a high falsetto . . . a song that has no melodic line whatsoever, but rather wanders aimlessly in both rhythm and pitch.

"Good morning, Heziah. You sing a gay song today!" I said.

"Good morning, Madam. How is baby?"

"Oh, he is fine. He is about to have a bath. How is your baby?"

"Thank you, he is fine, Madam. I am very happy this morning. I get letter from my sister. She has successfully delivered a boy, and it was a man-child!"

I congratulated him, and shared his happiness for a moment, and then turned to "bath" my own wriggling man-child.

The rainy season has come much earlier this year. Last year it didn't start until the end of May. We have been having regular storms all March, with blustery line squalls arriving in force almost every night this past

week. Many of the days now are overcast; though, as usual, always hot and muggy with some relief from a harbor breeze. On the whole, however, the weather during these months has been much cooler than it was a year ago.

With the exception of one flat day, racing afternoons have been blessed by some good strong winds. We have been sailing both of our Cats. I helm *Miss Tibbs*, usually with King Lowe as my crew. (He is Harvard '58, now Assistant Director of Chase Manhattan Bank in Lagos.) Peter helms *Kitty*, which we have given a new coat of yellow hulls and varnished deck. Marci Lowe (Skidmore '58) is his crew. It's been fun to compete against each other. The other day we were both about five minutes late for the start, because Peter was negotiating for some American foreign aid for the Six-Year Plan. So, instead, we raced each other out to Tarkwa Bay and back.

It has been most interesting to see the months of February and March come around again. We find ourselves thinking, "Yes, last year this time . . ." This is our fifth home and the first time we have lived in the same place for more than nine months. As the annual festivals, tribal ceremonies, religious holidays, and seasons return, we now have a much better frame of reference to appreciate them. Now the climate, as related to the months of the year, doesn't seem quite so unreal and ridiculous. . . . (February: 90 degree heat, open sandals and sleeveless shirts . . . a long cry from the February we have always known!)

With the return of Ramadan, the Muslim monthlong fast, and its termination in the *Eid al-Fitr* celebrations (nationally observed, since Nigeria is predominantly Muslim), we were reminded of our drive home from the Eastern Region last year. You may remember from my writing at that time how fascinated we were by the native dress, the color and style, how excited we were by the intricate and impelling rhythms of the drums we heard everywhere. A year and more here has only slightly altered our views. Should we remain the rest of our lives, I doubt that we would ever tire of looking at the endless variety in color and style—bizarre, grandiloquent, ragged, strange, beautiful, pathetic, familiar, amusing Nigerians. Nor will we ever cease to be amazed by the natural rhythmic ingenuity of the African and his inclination to create a beat that becomes a virtual musical composition in itself, on any available hard surface: a child on his books as he walks to school; the boy on his enamel food bowl in a moment of idleness; the laborer on his pail or head pan; a gang of men with their voices while they do any form of communal work—with caller and chanting chorus that make their black, shiny-wet bodies perform difficult tasks with rhythmic ease. Rhythms that are so intricate and complex that neither you nor I could ever duplicate, the Nigerian creates as easily as he breathes. And when he brings his body to it, it is hard to separate body from rhythm itself!

This year we have seen great strides taken from "backwardness" and underdeveloped status toward growth in both the physical and emotional stature of the country. Economically, good progress has come with the establishment of numerous new indigenous industries and the expansion of government services, such as transport facilities, education, utilities, the improvement of local produce (cocoa, palm oil, cotton, groundnuts). Greater progress yet will come with the implementation of the new Six-Year Plan. With the first year of independence complete, the new leaders of the nation, flush with their past successes, are realizing that "peaches and cream" cannot be the bill-of-fare for the citizens of this country if they wish to move ahead. Every speech now is not a speech unless it calls on the people to make sacrifices for the "austerity" measures that lie ahead. And it hasn't been all talk, either. All of the regions and the Federal Capital, too, have decreed great "slashes in pay" for both ministers and civil servants, cuts in car and housing allowances, and shortened annual leave periods from three months to 1.5 months. (These incredibly high fringe benefits were inherited from the British administration: a necessity, in order to attract Englishmen to come to this part of the world.)

"This year we have seen great strides from . . . underdeveloped status toward growth . . ."

With the reconvening of Parliament for its annual Budget Session this past month, the greatest changes of all have been enacted. They hit the country in the form of a mass rush on all the markets, both local and European, which is threatening a serious inflation. This came after the Minister of Finance, Chief Festus Okotie-Eboh, during his budget speech in Parliament, outlined an overall change in the national tax and tariff structure *upward* on nearly all imported goods (from present 10 to 25 percent to 33 to 75 percent). There would also be taxes on many local products and government services in order to "find money to promote the national programme" (i.e., Peter, Lyle, and Wolf's Development Plan). To us, it means that our cost of living will probably go up about 50 percent. It was already 25 to 50 percent higher than it is at home in the U.S. For Columbus and his family, theoretically it should mean a very slight rise in their cost of living, because the tax increases are designed to hit the upper classes, those who live in European-style houses and depend on a Western style of living. But when Columbus came home from the market the day after Okotie-Eboh's announcement, his eyes were as big as baseballs. "Everyone is crazy in de market today, Madam. Everyone rushing, rushing . . . crying out for de taxes Festus announced. Everything cost more." The newspapers are calling on the government to institute price controls.

Most exciting for me, however, was the day before, in Parliament, when the Minister of Economic Development presented the outlines of the Six-Year Plan. It was received by everyone with great acclaim. The press was most enthusiastic. One paper said:

> The Plan, in brief, is a formula for creating new sources of wealth through the full utilization of the country's natural resources. It also envisages the provision of improved social services, the strengthening of the nation's defense forces, and the discharge of our international commitments. Every Nigerian and all others interested in the progress of this country should read the Paper carefully. We believe it is food for thought for everyone; and that everyone, whatever his or her station in life, can make a useful contribution towards its successful implementation. In this new series of editorials which begins today the Daily Times proposes to lead public discussion on the Sessional Paper with an examination of its highlights.

Other newspapers are similarly enthusiastic.

Dean Brooks, of Williams College,[41] and his wife were here the week Parliament convened. He is recruiting and interviewing [Nigerian] government employees for the Williams–Ford master's program in development economics. We were their hosts while they were here, so we took them to the opening session of Parliament.

Again, I was reminded of a year's passing. It was thrilling to see the Royal Nigerian Army troops in their crisp green and tan shorts and shirts, black wool kneesox, and heavy boots, march up in formation before the Parliament building. The brisk marching band added official gaiety to the bright sunshine, the impressively tall robed and turbaned emirs and MPs from the Northern Region, the Oba of Lagos and his large palace entourage, plus the arrival of other personalities such as rotund Chief Festus Okotie-Eboh in his shirt and straw hat with feather; Leader of the Opposition Chief Obafemi Awolowo, who is always greeted by cheers of "Awo! Awo!" from the predominantly Yoruba crowd of Lagosians who gathered by the hundreds to line the streets to watch and cheer (or jeer) the national dignitaries. This year brought the added color of about 200 Surulere market women, who arrived packed in a dozen or more mammy wagons, clapping and singing like camp children. Soon they were marching in a long snake file, carrying signs that announced their grievances against the increased taxes on their market stalls.

Then came Zik's arrival.

Last year he shocked all the ardent nationalists by appearing in the military uniform of the Governor-General, as worn by the British administrator, so this year everyone was curious to see what he would wear. I doubt that he would have dared to appear in anything but the white silk robes of the national costume (agbada), which he did wear. After inspection of the troops outside, the national anthem was played, the gold mace was carried into Parliament, and everyone rose for the opening prayer, much of which had to do with the Queen! Then down the center aisle, which separates the Government coalition parties' benches from the Opposition, came the procession of Supreme Court Justices in their flowing bright red or black capes, high white-lace collars, and braided white wigs. It was interesting to note that while last year half of the twelve faces were white, this year there are only three white faces in this group. As soon as everyone was reseated, Prime Minister Alhaji Sir Abubakar Tafawa Balewa rose from his rather obscure seat at the end of the Cabinet Bench, climbed the steps, and handed Zik the Government's "message." This, he presently delivered to the Joint Session of the House of Representatives and Senate. It was this speech that gave "top priority" to the Six-Year Development Plan.

Ever since our arrival, we have anticipated this session of Parliament as marking the culmination of Peter's work. Now the time has come. Sometime within the next few weeks, the debates will be over and we shall see if the Plan comes through reasonably intact. So far, there have been no attacks on the planners themselves, as there were in other sessions of Parliament. I doubt if many know who wrote the Plan.

It is now April 4. Peter said this morning there is word afoot that a motion will be made for Parliament to unanimously accept the Plan exactly as it is written to show that the country is wholeheartedly behind it! Things are looking up. Meanwhile, the Planners are tiptoeing around in hopes they don't jar this delicate balance of national pride, willingness to sacrifice in order to bring about the developments that have been outlined to them, *and* high hopes for the future.

I must stop jabbering now. Just one exciting bit of news:
WE ARE GOING TO BE IN CAMBRIDGE THIS FALL!!

We are so happy and excited about it, we can talk of nothing but what we'll do when we are *home*. MIT sent the "yes" we've been looking for.

Dear Extended Family, in case I haven't written it individually, thank you for all your wonderful "welcome to baby" cards and greetings. They came flocking in from the Formans, Sullivans, Granny, Auntie Sybil, Tante, Rands, Grandma, McBrides, Nana, Clarks, Phelpses, Wilsons (Cousin Bernice), and Cousin Eleanor Martin. Next time we want mail, we'll just have to produce another baby!

You lucky dogs! We are green, green, GREEN with envy when you tell of stops at Friendly's Ice Cream stores. I dream about eating ice cream, especially Friendly's. The first thing we want to do when we get home is to go and stuff on some ice cream creation, after we have had a cheeseburger and milk shake . . . and LOBSTER . . . and good movies and oh, oh, oh, there are so many things we are really beginning to miss, aside from our beloved families. Besides, I can hardly wait to see Daddy with Bryn.

We've done some fishing. Caught a 14-pound barracuda right off the "hard." I came in to feed Bryn, and 45 minutes later Peter and Lyle came back, this time with a nine-pounder. The next night, we had a feast on the front lawn of the Yacht Club. Five of the Hansen tribe and Peter and I stuffed on baked barracuda. A large portion of the fish we had already given to Columbus and his family and to old, toothless Ben, the Yacht Club night "watch." While we murmured between mouthfuls, we could look down the black mouth of the harbor, back to the bright lights of Lagos and Apapa or straight up into the close, warm tropical night.

We think of you so often and send all our love,

Gretel

Statue on front of Lagos Island Museum

Afterword

Not long afterward we departed for home, via South and East Africa, Greece, and then a month in Germany, where Peter could work on the foreign language that he needed for his doctorate. For both of us, this was probably the last tranquil time in our lives, as Peter and I launched into the production of three more children over the next four years, completed our graduate studies, and taught in various locations (from Massachusetts to UCLA), acquiring doctorate and master's degrees at MIT and the University of Michigan, respectively. Then we left the country to live for almost three years in Chile, where Peter was again "seconded" by the Ford Foundation to the Oficina de Planificación Nacional. I took a job teaching on the secondary level at the Nido de Aguilas International School, where three of our four children were enrolled on the elementary level.

By then, many other young Americans like us were also serving as technical assistants, and members of the Peace Corps, volunteering all over the world.

The contrast between the two countries where we lived and worked could not have been more dramatic. While in Chile, we and our children learned Spanish and interacted with the Chileans in their own language, since we and our Chilean hosts had both come from European cultures. Thus, we were less "observers" of the experience and more an integral part of it. We loved the charm and challenge of becoming part of a Hispanic culture. But none of our Chilean experiences could compare with the exotic revelations that were continually assaulting our senses and assumptions while we lived and worked in Nigeria.

In the end, both our host countries spawned insurrections not long after our departure: Nigeria's around ethnic and tribal differences, eventually throwing the country into six years of civil conflict, and Chile, falling prey to a dictatorship brought on by class differences.

Some of what occurred in Nigeria after our departure did not surprise us, but it took place on a far greater scale than we could have imagined. We knew there was graft and corruption that oiled the workings of the political and social scene, but we were stunned by the report of a *Time* magazine article, April 27, 2007, that estimated $400 billion was stolen from the treasury by Nigeria's leaders between 1960 and 1999.

We also knew the country was an unnatural amalgamation of 300 to 500 ethnic groups and languages (sources differ on this subject). But we didn't foresee the extent to which these differences would lead to nearly half a century of coups, countercoups, and a two-and-a-half-year civil war. Nigeria emerged after 60 years of British colonial rule with three regions (and a fourth being proposed) when we left in 1962. Now there are 36 states with a new national capital located in Abuja, having been moved from the coast to roughly the middle of the country.

We left Nigeria with a healthy respect for what the British had done to bring together such a disparate group of tribal cultures, making it possible for us and commerce to travel from region to region without fear of being attacked or killed—an ever-present possibility during the previous several centuries. The British had also brought an education system to the two southern regions, albeit a Euro-centered one, and was building representative democratic processes, including the beginnings of a true parliamentary system in the two southern regions. (Note: English was the lingua franca of the Eastern and Western Regions, while Hausa and traditional Islamic education in Arabic script were the norm in the Northern Region. More about that presently.)

Growing agricultural surpluses and newly imposed direct and indirect taxes that were transferred to regional governments brought accelerated public spending on services and development projects. With a new Six-Year National Plan and its implementation worked out between the regions and the Federal Government, the future for this newly independent country looked promising. National pride was palpable.

But there was a dark cloud looming on the horizon. It may not have seemed so at the time, but with the discovery of oil in the Niger Delta in 1956, and the beginning of its exportation in 1958, the country was doomed to an unnatural focus on this one resource. Political rivalries intensified, while support for the development of the other underexploited natural resources (tin, iron ore, bauxite, natural gas, gold, tantalite, limestone, niobium, lead, zinc, palm-oil products, cotton, groundnuts, cocoa, citrus fruits, maize, pearl millet, cassava, yams, and sugar cane!) was transformed into greedy maneuvering for a part of this single economic bonanza. To this day, oil accounts for 80 percent of Nigeria's government income and 40 percent of the nation's GDP.

There was another factor that didn't occur to us. At the time, we had great admiration for the British administrators' choice to deal with the Muslim North by working indirectly through the emirs, who, deriving their authority from a semifeudal Islamic hierarchy, had absolute control over their subjects. In contrast, both the Yoruba and the Igbo (current spelling, with a "g") political systems, being less autocratic, were more amenable to adapting to the British political system, which not only allowed greater upward mobility but also encouraged commoners to participate in the political system: a political process unthinkable in the North.

With the reinforcement of these differing cultural and value systems, the British had unwittingly set the country up for its eventual disintegration along regional and tribal lines. More tragically, it allowed the continued teaching and reinforcement of conservative Islamic values in the

North—seen today in the devastating pogroms of Boko Haram coming from the Northern Region, and the splintering of the country into multiple states (36) along tribal lines.

Today, we look back on our path and the common thread that makes sense of our lives. Three years in Washington, DC, allowed us to continue on our "help the Third World" trajectory. Peter served as Deputy Director of the World Bank's Research Division, and I became involved with the National League of Women Voters' Overseas Education Fund, training women from Latin America (in Spanish) how to organize effective social units using nonviolent means to promote change toward more democratic processes.

After three years, we felt we needed to move our children away from what we saw as the too-sophisticated, drug-prone adolescent culture of the greater Washington, DC, environment. We also wanted to live in a town small enough so that each of our children would know what it was like to be able, as a citizen, to have an impact on the destiny of one's town. So we moved back to Massachusetts in the middle of the 1970s energy crunch.

Peter found a position as Director of the New England Energy Policy Council, aimed at turning our country's preoccupation with oil consumption to renewable energy resource development. Eventually he discovered a niche as a hydroelectric developer, taking his experience to Costa Rica and founding Energía Globál Internationál, with the goal of teaching his Latin American hosts how to harness their own water power to produce energy. I, meanwhile, continued my work with Third World populations, working 15 years in the Massachusetts State Department of Education as a bilingual specialist implementing Massachusetts's enlightened Bilingual Education law. My job was to protect immigrant children's right to learn how to read and write in their own language while they were acquiring enough English so that they could learn their academic subjects *in English*.

Since then, Peter and I have focused on environmental and social issues closer to home. Peter came to concentrate his renewable-resource efforts in Massachusetts on the renovation of 15 century-old hydroelectric installations on New England rivers. He also has served on our small town's Planning Board for more than 40 years, trying to preserve a healthy balance between the pressures of development and preservation of natural resources and the environment through open-space conservation. Some of my energies turned to the horses I and our children trained and rode in regional competitions and (in Bryn's case) national and international competition.

Coming back to New England and landing on a large colonial estate, I found myself surrounded by a dozen or more gardens to tend. My experience as president of the Potomac Conservation Foundation when we lived in the Washington, DC, area led us to place our own extensive open space under a permanent conservation restriction.

One other major project that consumed the energies of our family and friends over a decade (the mid-'70s and '80s) was to hand-build a house in the New Hampshire mountains with views across the great expanse of the White Mountain National Forest: half stone (from granite quarries nearby) and half old barn boards (from disassembled Connecticut Valley tobacco barns) plus a massive, five-flue Russian fireplace and chimney that took a year to build. The house is a testament to one family's ability to create a magical retreat in the winderness. We commuted 110 miles every weekend from our home in Hamilton, north of Boston. I cooked over a wood fire and we slept in a nearby tent that first year. By the time we were done, our children had navigated through high school and college, periodically joining us with school friends and cousins to help complete the construction of our Shangri-La in the North.

Two more passions caught my attention: (1) the keeping of bees, up to 42 colonies, and now mentor and lecturer on their importance to the health of our planet; and (2) trash! Al Gore's call in the 1990s to do something to help reduce greenhouse gases was the impetus for my work. I found that niche, becoming our region's leader (2010 Massachusetts Recycler of the Year) in convincing our town (and now neighboring towns) to find a way to reduce our methane footprint not only by maximizing each town's rate of recycling but also by starting the first town-wide weekly "curbside composting" program east of Michigan.

Perhaps our most important long-term contribution to the world has been our four children, who, now as adults, are true citizens of the world.

Bryn, our Nigeria-born child, rising to President of the NCCAOM (National Certification Commission for Acupuncture and Oriental Medicine), helped establish a world-recognized evaluation system whose credentials permit students of traditional Chinese acupuncture and Oriental medicine to practice their art anywhere across the globe.

Heidi, a year younger than Bryn, was comfortable roaming Europe to learn several languages, adding them to the two she already knew to become an opera singer. She is now sharing her art, teaching students from many backgrounds in a local college while raising three boys.

Joc, our third (born a year after Heidi), is practicing his art as a process consultant, specializing in leadership and organizational development training. He works with corporations, colleges, and universities, bringing together workers of diverse backgrounds to achieve the institutions' goals. He is currently working with Native American tribes in the Southwest and Northeast, helping them to collaborate in their efforts to recapture their lost languages. He was a founder of a pan–Latin American consortium of experiential educators, recently hosting their first conference in Medellin, Colombia.

Liesl, our youngest, has taken her skills as a film producer (for NOVA and National Geographic) to many parts of the world, most recently Everest and Nepal. She and her crew—her world-class climbing husband, Pete Athans (and their two young children)—have discovered, over the course of many expeditions in the high Himalaya, caves with pre-Buddhist texts, artifacts, and skeletons filling out a large chunk of pre-Buddhist Himalayan history.

Our focus currently is on our small town: the direction it is taking as it copes with the growing demands of a fast paced world. We wonder if it can do so while preserving the quiet charm that brought us here.

Heidi, Gretel, Liesl, Joc and Bryn in the south of Chile, 1968

Endnotes

Letter Two

1 "Aunt Jan" and "Uncle Archer" are names I used for my mother-in-law and father-in-law. Peter and I grew up at a time when the parents of one's close friends, and one's parents' friends, were referred to as "Aunt" and "Uncle." Peter and I had known each other since I was two and he was four, living in the same neighborhood until my family moved from West Hartford to a farm in South Coventry, Connecticut.

Letter Three

2 Standard parenthetical marks in the text were used in the original letters. When [brackets] are used, it is to indicate that the comments have been added, for clarity, when transcribing the letters 50+ years later.

Letter Five

3 The term *blacks* (when referring to African descendants) did not come into use until the late 1960s.

4 Although Nigeria has more than 371 distinct tribes, we tended to think of the country in terms of the major tribes inhabiting what were then the three regions of the country: (1) the Hausa, who dominated the Northern Region, which also included Fulani (non-negroid, Muslim), who often traversed the country tending their herds of cattle and bringing them to market in the other regions; (2) the Ibo, predominant tribe in the Eastern Region, and (3) the Yoruba, populating the Western Region, each with their own language and their own belief systems.

Letter Seven

5 Twenty-seven years later Gretel completed a second masters degree at Harvard's Graduate School of Education.

Letter Nine

6 Palm oil was the oil used by Nigerians (and most other West Africans) for cooking. Until 1934, Nigeria had been the world's largest producer of palm oil. It was one of the country's major exports, providing a basic ingredient for the manufacture of soap and cosmetics. It, along with olive oil, was the basis for the establishment of the Palmolive Company in 1898.

7 Palm-oil kernels are heated and pressed to produce palm oil.

8 Ramadan falls on the ninth month of the Muslim calendar and involves fasting from sunrise to sundown for the 29 or 30 days of the month. Then comes a holiday. The first day of the following month, Shawwal, is celebrated by observing *Eid al-Fitr*, or "Festival of Breaking Fast." This much-anticipated festival is celebrated with sweet dishes, wearing new clothes, gift-giving, and musical performances.

Letter Eleven

9 "Turning a collar" is what my mother taught me to do whenever a collar becomes frayed. Removing the collar and sewing it back onto a shirt, with the back side forward, doubles a shirt's life.

Letter Twelve, part 1

10 The land-tenure system in West Africa was quite different from that in East Africa. Europeans could own land in East Africa, and did so on a large scale. European ownership of land in West Africa was not possible.

Letter Twelve, part 2

11 For a full and fascinating account of Stolper's, Lyle's, and Peter's battles with Prasad over economic planning, see *Inside Independent Nigeria: Diaries of Wolfgang Stolper, 1960–1962*, ed. by Clive S. Gray (Farnham, Surrey, UK: Ashgate Publishing Ltd., 2003).

Letter Twelve, part 3

12 E. O. refers to E. O. Smith, a respected colleague of my mother's in the Connecticut legislature.

13 Kermit Gordon was on the faculty at Williams when Peter was there and then was brought to Washington, DC, by President Kennedy to be Director of the Budget (now the Office of Management and Budget). David Bell was an economics lecturer at Harvard, 1958, and then Kennedy's Budget Director. He interviewed us for our job with the Ford Foundation. We had come to know Walt Whitman Rostow the summer before, when Peter was assistant director at a summer camp for international graduate students in Lakeville, Connecticut (The Institute of World Affairs). Walt Rostow and his wife, Elspeth, spent a number of days there participating in the seminar discussions. See post script note bottom of letter twenty.

14 Stolper wrote in his diary about American government aid through Michigan State University to help build the university at Nsukka: "August 4, 1961. At dinner . . . I was scathing about MSU's effort at Nsukka. Joel [the head here of the ICA, predecessor of AID] said they were thinking of sending Edwards [of MSU] home. I said it was irresponsible of a university to accept an ICA contract unless they were willing to send their best people. . . . August 5, 1961. I worked first on the education ministry's program, trying to save money on capital by reducing building costs, and on recurrent expenses by raising student teacher ratios from 37 to 40. A poor country can't afford better ratios than rich countries. Besides, they won't get the teachers anyway. Also, building costs are higher than in England. There is no sense putting up American-type structures in the tropics, where there is no problem of snow and ice. Actually, this is a very tough program to evaluate, and when I am through I'll show it to Lyle for another go." From *Inside Independent Nigeria*, p. 162.

Letter Thirteen

15 Gari, derived from cassava tubers, is used in many dishes. We eat it in the U.S. as tapioca.

Letter Fourteen

16 The U-2 incident occurred on May 1, 1961, when an American U-2 spy plane was shot down over Soviet Union airspace. The U.S. government initially denied the plane's purpose and mission (to photograph Soviet military bases) but subsequently had to admit it was spying on the Soviet Union. (As a Naval Intelligence Officer, Peter was familiar with U-2 photographs, which he was trained to interpret.)

Letter Nineteen

17 In 1960 the nine member Ashby Commission produced what is known as the Ashby Report. It focused on Nigeria's needs for expanded teacher training and higher education over the coming 20 years.

Letter Twenty

18 Ben Lewis was a well-respected professor of economics, associated with Oberlin College. He trained many subsequently prominent economics professors, college and university administrators, and public servants, also working in those capacities. At the time, he was working for the Ford Foundation as a consultant for governments of developing countries.

19 Vernon Ferwerda was a leader of a Crossroads Africa group during the years when the organization was at its height.

20 The Harmattan is a dry and dusty West African trade wind. This northeasterly wind blows from the Sahara into the Gulf of Guinea between the end of November and the middle of March. As it passes over the Sahara, it picks up dust particles that, at times, block visibility and even the sun for several days.

Letter Twenty-One

21 Barbara Ward, who died in 1981, was a British economist and writer interested in the problems of developing countries. Her 1959 book,

Five Ideas That Change the World, had had a great impact on me. She did go on after the early 1960s to publish and speak not only on development issues in Third World countries but also on the importance of making development sustainable for the environment and humankind. In 1971, she founded the International Institute for the Environment and Development.

Letter Twenty-Two

22 Jaja Wachuku was the second Federal Minister of Economic Development.

23 Arnold Rivkin was at MIT's Center for International Studies.

24 Wolfgang Stolper refers to Peter's work in his diaries, as published in *Inside Independent Nigeria*, p. 74: "Peter has been doing yeoman's work at Statistics. I ask him to pave the way. Then he goes, digs up files, and brings them. Then I work on them, make my calculations and notes, and he takes them back. You would think that this is a routine chore but it is not. It takes a man with energy and economic knowledge to dig up the right file!"

25 The Berlin Crisis was triggered by the Soviet Union's attempts to block America's access to West Berlin, located 110 miles within Soviet-dominated East Germany. In an address to the nation on July 25, 1961, Kennedy announced that this had triggered the imminent threat of nuclear war, and thus there was a need to, among other precautions, call up increased military manpower. Subsequently, the United States broke the blockade by flying round-the-clock airlifts of supplies into Berlin.

Letter Twenty-Four

26 Due in four months, this would be my family's first grandchild.

Letter Twenty-Eight

27 *The Joy of Cooking*, by Irma S. Rombauer and Marion Rombauer Becker, now in its eighth edition and known as America's all-purpose cookbook, was and still is a kitchen bible for me.

28 Lokoja is located in central Nigeria, at the confluence of the Niger and Benue Rivers.

29 The Inland Waterways Department was charged with improving navigation on the Niger River so that all imported cement, for example, could be transported by barges to the site chosen for the Kainji Dam over the Niger River.

30 Lugard style refers to Sir Frederick Lugard, first Governor-General of Nigeria (1914–1919). As I recall, a "Lugard House" stood on the edge of the race course, not far behind our flat in Lagos. It was a large, square, one-story structure on stilts with a wraparound porch.

Letter Thirty

31 John Holt was a trade company with its own fleet of ocean and river craft. It had fortnightly service between Liverpool and Nigeria, carrying palm oil, palm kernels, rubber and cocoa from Nigeria to England, returning to Nigeria with textiles from Lancaster and bicycles from Birmingham.

32 Steve Ells was a lifelong friend whom Peter met during the Navy's Officers Training School in Newport, Rhode Island. They then served together in Naval Air Intelligence the following two years on Whidbey Island, Washington. Steve eventually became legal counsel to Massachusetts Governor Francis Sargent and then served the rest of his professional career on the senior staff at the EPA New England Regional Office.

Letter Thirty-One

33 Dag Hammarskjöld, a Swedish diplomat, was the second Secretary-General of the United Nations. He died in a plane crash while in office, in September 1961. He was en route to ceasefire negotiations between "noncombatant" UN forces and Katangese (Congo) troops.

Letter Thirty-Three

34 Walt W. Rostow, *The Stages of Economic Growth: A Non-Communist Manifesto* (Cambridge: Cambridge University Press, 1960).

35 For an interesting discussion of this issue, see Wolf Stolper's diary entry of September 28, 1961, on page 200 of *Inside Independent Nigeria*.

36 Ellen Thorp, *Ladder of Bones* (London: The Camelot Press Ltd., 1956).

37 Wolf Stolper's notes, from *Inside Independent Nigeria*, p. 285, say: "Peter had the task of evaluating the economics of the dam locks. It turns out there won't be enough water, even with the regulated flow over the dam, to provide a steady minimum draft of 5 feet everywhere below the dam. . . . So the water engineers were wrong. But how are we economists to know this? Peter was stuck on the facts and the theoretical approach. I could help with the latter, not the former. He also wanted me to read his application for Ford money to make a more thorough study of the Niger." The irony here is that Peter, years later, went on to form a company, Energia Global, which developed hydro sites in Central America, and then the Swift River Company, which created 15 hydro sites in New England, currently operating five hydro sites in Massachusetts.

Letter Thirty-Four

38 By now, after all the cocktail parties mentioned in these letters, one would think that Peter and I were happy alcoholics. In fact, neither of us drank alcohol: Peter because it gave him headaches, and I because I had no taste for it, having grown up in a nondrinking Christian Science family.

Letter Forty-Four

39 For Stolper's interesting account of the debates and tensions around the writing of The Plan, the many competing players involved pulling for or against an integrated plan vs. plans for four separate regions (North, East, West, and a Federal Territory), see *Inside Independent Nigeria*, chapter 12, pp. 237–52.

Letter Forty-Five

40 This was a nascent meeting of what would become the Organization of African Unity (OAU) in 1963, bringing together what was then the two blocs of newly independent African states: the Casablanca Bloc, consisting of Algeria, Egypt, Ghana, Guinea, Libya, Mali, and Morocco; and the Monrovia Bloc, consisting of Senegal, Nigeria, Liberia, Ethiopia, and most of the former French colonies. The Casablanca Bloc, comprising nations known as the "progressive states" and led by Kwame Nkrumah, wanted a federation of all African countries. The Monrovia Bloc, led by Senegal's President Léopold Senghor, felt that unity of the African states should be achieved first through economic and cultural cooperation; he didn't support the idea of a political federation. By the time the organization disbanded in 2002, 53 of 54 states had become members of the OAU, having more successfully achieved the original goals of the Monrovia Bloc rather than those of the Casablanca Bloc.

Letter Forty-Eight

41 Dean Robert Brooks' "rustic" home on a hill in Williamstown, Massachusetts, is where Peter and I spent the early summer, just two and a half years later. The Brooks were away on vacation, and we were taking leave from academic Cambridge, preparing for our third child's birth. That child, in fact, was born a bit prematurely, in the nearby North Adams Hospital while we were there: a second son, with a one-year-old sister between the boys. It wasn't until our fourth (a girl) was born, and we were then living in Los Angeles (Peter was teaching economics at UCLA), that I finished the master's thesis I started writing in Nigeria. My master's-degree deadline was nearing, and I remember sorting my bibliography cards on the delivery table. I knew that, once home, with four children under four and a half, there would not be time to finish those last pages of the thesis.

FEBRUARY - 12, 1961
MONDAY NOON

Ambassador Hotel

P. O. BOX 3044
ACCRA · GHANA

TELEPHONE No 4646 (10 LINES)
CABLE ADDRESS: AMBASSADOR, ACCRA.

Dear F. D's -

WE'RE HERE! AT LAST. It feels good to slow down a bit after our mad 2 days in Rome with brother Hans and Federico. They really gave us a tour of tours. of very large Rome on our very small feet. We arrived Thursday evening and went straight to bed. Next morning our phone rang and there was Hans — down in the lobby having taken a nite train from Milan, arrived at 7:00 & waited til after 8:30 so we could sleep!! He came up & waited while we dressed & washed and then ensued two fabulous days of seeing ancient Rome, St. Peters, the Vatican, the Pantheon, forum, many cathedrals, etc., etc. Each day we met Federico after work (1:00) in a building where he works on the ground of the Villa Borghese. You are right, Sandro, Federico is a peach. (Your letter arrived the day & ½ after we did!) One thing is for sure Rome would have been very dull (comparatively speaking) had there not been Hans + Federico! Took midnight plane from Rome Sat. to arrive Sunday a.m. in Nigeria. Kyle Hanson was there to meet us & bring us back to the V. I. P. Flats where we are staying til we move into our apartment over on the lagoon. These are really some quarters! 3 very large rooms + a kitchen very well furnished + supplied with a "boy" who cooks, cleans, washes and irons all clothes, polishes your shoes the moment they fall from your feet, makes your bed even if you nap on it, has your setting

+ children in their motor boat through channel ways that wind thru' the lush grass native dwelling to a sandy beach separating lagoon - swamp from the ocean the afternoon lolling in the sun, water skiing

---

Ambassador Hotel

P. O. BOX 3044
ACCRA · GHANA

TELEPHONE
CABLE ADDRESS

---

14 (12) when Peter
man I so
perhaps the we
posters clot
it is really n
ludicrous about
clothes (dirty
over a week he
in the U.S. Th
before the ste
scrubs it in t
ironed and in
turning to put
we could have
One more w
this seems to
terday Columbu
market to buy
into the nativ
alone, just to
what. I learn
to try to buy
"taken" in add
possible—bein
tunately speak
latter at leas
in front of th
(he took me to
known of, nor
point out the
and then he wo
within minutes
several dozen
mostly me, I
follow us like
the car. They
many with pork
allover the he
of the people
well dressed—
getting used t
very decided m
native market—
Evidently whit
Next letter I'
and more impor
Love